OEDIPUS

OEDIPUS
A Folklore Casebook

Edited by

Lowell Edmunds *and* Alan Dundes

The University of Wisconsin Press

The University of Wisconsin Press
114 North Murray Street
Madison, Wisconsin 53715

3 Henrietta Street
London WC2E 8LU, England

Originally published in 1983 by Garland Publishing, Inc.

Library of Congress Cataloging-in-Publication Data
Oedipus: a folklore casebook / edited by Lowell Edmunds
    and Alan Dundes.
        284 p.   cm.
        Originally published: New York: Garland, 1983.
        Includes bibliographical references.
        ISBN 0-299-14850-5 (cloth: alk. paper).
        ISBN 0-299-14854-8 (pbk.: alk. paper)
        1. Oedipus (Tale) I. Edmunds, Lowell. II. Dundes, Alan.
    GR75.0303   1995
    398'.352—dc20   95-31697

Contents

v

Introduction

The story of Oedipus is perhaps the most famous narrative in Western civilization. Its fame is due primarily to Sophocles' play *Oedipus the King*. The discussion of Oedipus both by classicists and by psychoanalysts tends to be restricted to the Sophoclean version. It is not widely known that there are oral tales which have the same story-line as the ancient Oedipus legend, and it is highly likely that the Greeks had oral tales which were cognate with the legend underlying the Sophoclean tragedy. We intend to present some of the evidence for the folkloristic tradition of Oedipus. Accordingly, we have chosen not to include studies focusing on the classical literary account, studies which are readily available in anthology form. Students of the play may wish to use the present casebook in conjunction with such literary anthologies (see under "Suggestions for Further Reading on Oedipus" for representative titles).

Even a cursory glance at our table of contents will reveal considerable variation in the genre terms applied to the Oedipus story. Some consider it to be a myth; others argue that it is a folktale, while other scholars call it a legend. The genre label seems to depend in part upon the disciplinary affiliation of the writer. For folklorists, if a myth is a sacred narrative explaining how the world or man came to be in their present form, Oedipus is clearly not the protagonist of a myth. For classicists, however, all stories concerning Greek gods and heroes can be called myths, although there are some who would maintain that stories of Greek heroes, believed to be historical by the Greeks themselves, would more properly be called legends. Oedipus falls in that category.

Oedipus is classified as a folktale in the standard Aarne-Thompson *Types of the Folktale*, where it is listed as tale type 931.

vii

The listing includes references to oral versions in such countries as Finland, Hungary, Ireland, Italy, Lithuania, Romania, Russia, Spain, and Turkey. The concept of tale type is based upon the assumption that the versions gathered under each rubric are cognate, that is, they are historically and genetically related. Most of the selections in this casebook are discussions of tales which belong to the Oedipus tale type.

The tale type references do not indicate that the story of Oedipus is universal. It is not found, for example, in aboriginal North and South America or in aboriginal Australia. We are speaking here strictly of the Aarne-Thompson tale type. But ever since Freud used the Oedipus story to illustrate what he called the Oedipus complex, there has been increasing interest in whether or not Oedipus stories are universal. If they were, this would support the contention that the Oedipus complex is universal. Here we must distinguish between versions of Aarne-Thompson tale type 931 and stories which, with reference to Freud, would appear to have an Oedipal theme. These latter stories, in our view, are not cognate with the tale type and presumably arose through independent invention. We have included a few of these "Oedipus" plots so that readers can judge for themselves as to the question of whether or not Freudian theory can be applied to non-western contexts. In this way, we hope also to make clear the differences between versions of tale type 931 and stories with an Oedipal theme.

We begin the casebook with reportings of texts. Some are versions of tale type 931, while others simply contain Oedipal themes. In a few instances, it is difficult to say with certainty to which category a given text belongs. After these representative texts, we have selected several essays which have a comparative orientation. These essays consider the range of variation within the tale type as well as the possible relationships between modern oral and both medieval and classical literary versions. Following the comparative treatments, we have included what is surely the major twentieth-century interpretation of the narrative by Freud, even though it deals exclusively with the Sophoclean version. The casebook concludes with interpretive essays clearly influenced by his concepts and methodology. The last two essays, however, break new ground by looking at the Oedipal plot from the perspective of the parents rather than the child.

One reason why few scholars have drawn upon the majority of the essays in this casebook is their inaccessibility. Some were originally printed in relatively obscure periodicals while others were not available in English translation. (We are presenting translations of articles written originally in French, German, Italian, Modern Greek, and Russian in this volume.) We have attempted to bring together what we consider to be the most interesting approaches to Oedipus folklore in the hope that this collection may encourage further research.

Lowell Edmunds and
Alan Dundes

OEDIPUS

Oedipus Rex in Albania

Margaret Hasluck

Although the Oedipus folktale appears to be fairly common in the Balkan region, this is the only Albanian version of which we are aware. The most unusual feature of the tale is the setting of the parricide in a carriage. While it strikingly resembles the corresponding episode in the Sophoclean account, the carriage element is extremely rare in oral tradition. In contrast, the occurrence of a riddle based upon incestuous kinship relations is widespread (and appears, for example, in one of the Indic texts cited in "The Indian Oedipus" printed in this volume). For additional discussion of incest riddles, see Paul G. Brewster, The Incest Theme in Folksong, *Folklore Fellows Communications 212 (Helsinki, 1972). Margaret Hasluck (1885-1948), a specialist in Balkan folklore, refers to F.J. Norton, "The Prisoner Who Saved His Neck with a Riddle,"* Folk-Lore, *53 (1942), 27-57, as having stimulated her to report the Albanian Oedipus text. For further consideration of what folklorists term "neck riddles," see Roger D. Abrahams,* Between the Living and the Dead, *Folklore Fellows Communications 225 (Helsinki, 1980) and B.H. Fussell, "The 'Neck Riddle' and Dramatic Form,"* New York Literary Forum, *5 (1980), 161-170.*

Reprinted from *Folk-Lore*, 60 (1949), 340-344, by permission of the Folklore Society. (The original article contained a fourth section, pp. 344-348, describing fairies in Albania, which has not been reprinted here.)

I. Introduction

Mr. F.J. Norton's interesting collection of incest-riddles in *Folk-Lore*, March 1942, pp. 27–57, recalls to my mind the following Albanian quatrain:

> *Nina nina bir!*
> *I biri i t' em bir!*
> *I biri i s'em re!*
> *S' ati vjehërr i ke le!*

> Hush thee, hush thee, son!
> Son of my son!
> Son of my daughter-in-law!
> Born to thy father-in-law!

In Albanian folktale this quatrain is sung to her child by a woman as they both die by the hand of her elder son, whom she has unwittingly married. It is in fact the conclusion of the Oedipus story as told in Albania.

The meaning of the first two lines requires no gloss, and that of the third little; as her elder son's wife the woman is daughter-in-law to his mother, that is to say, to herself. Consequently, the baby is her daughter-in-law's child. The fourth line is extremely involved. As the mother of her married son, the woman is mother-in-law to his wife, again herself. As her husband, her elder son is father-in-law where she is mother-in-law, and since she is her own mother-in-law, he is her father-in-law. Consequently, the baby is the child of a man who is son, husband, and father-in-law to one and the same woman, and she again is her own daughter-in-law and her own mother-in-law.

The quatrain, as we shall see presently, is a well-known riddle in Albania, but it is even commoner as a lullaby. The first two words, which vary from *nina nina* in North Albania to *nani nani* in the south, are of the international type represented, for example, by the *nini, baba, nini* ("sleep, child, sleep") of Hindustani and the *nani nani* of Arabic. Mothers croon them over and over again until the repetition of the soft vowels and consonants—*neena neena* or *nahnee nahnee* as they are pronounced—sends the child to sleep.

Most surprisingly, Albanian mothers often add a line or more from the Oedipus quatrain. For example in Mrs. Tajar Zavalani's native town, Fier in Central Albania, they commonly sing:

> *Nani nani biri im!*
> *Vellaj i burrit t' em!*

> Hush thee, hush thee, my son!
> Brother of my husband!

Needless to say, they do not think what they are saying.

They know the story behind the words quite well, however. A sinister connotation deriving from the Oedipus legend attaches to the first two words, as Mrs. Zavalani further informs me. If a visitor inquires about a boy or young man who has gone wrong, his female relatives—possibly even one who has just sung her baby to sleep with the extraordinary couplet just quoted—answer with the first two words of the lullaby, without finishing the verse. So they give the inquirer to understand that he is a lost soul but that nevertheless they cannot pluck him from their hearts.

The quatrain is also a favourite riddle among Albanian small boys. But Albanian minds are subtle and shun the obvious. So there is a catch in the riddle, which Mr. Dervish Duma explains as follows. The woman has married, not her very own son as the Oedipus story requires, but her step-son. She was her dead husband's second wife, he had had a son by his first wife, and it was this son whom she married after his death. In so doing she only obeyed the law which enjoins a step-son to marry his father's widow.

It must be said that this solution of the riddle does hardly more than provide small Albanians with extra fun. It destroys all the drama of the old story—the unwitting incest, the horror at its discovery, and the tragic sequel. For if it had been lawful for the widowed Queen to marry the young King, there would have been nothing to prevent them from living happily ever after. It also runs counter to all Albanian laws. The customary law of Albania does not allow a man to marry his father's widow. Its religious laws are equally forbidding. The Christians must obey the injunction in such texts as Deuteronomy, xxii. 30 ("A man shall not take his father's wife") and the Moslems the command in the Koran, Sura IV, 26 ("Marry not women whom your fathers have married, for this is a shame and hateful and an evil way"); the latter reference was kindly sent me by Miss Margaret Smith. The small Albanians, spurred by the national propensity to seek the subtle rather than the simple, seem only to have exaggerated the relaxation of marriage rules which followed the introduction of Islam after the Turkish conquest of Albania in the fifteenth century.

II. The Story

The handiest version of the story as told in Albania is in Mr. Stuart Mann's *Albanian Grammar*, pp. 90–2. This comes from one of the Dukagjin tribes in North Albania and was first published at Shkodër (Scutari) in the Catholic periodical *Hylli i Dritës* ("Morning Star") about 1929. My translation which differs substantially from Mr. Mann's (pp. 136–8), runs as follows:

The Fairy's Curse

A man once went at the crack of dawn to an alp to cut some boards for a cradle, because his wife was about to be given a child by Our Lord. As he was chopping up a spruce-tree, he heard a fairy calling to her mate from that very mountain.

"Bless me!" she said, "that poor fellow has got a son. What name shall we give it?"

"Oh, never mind, dear," the other replied. "I haven't time to bother my head about all the people that are born."

But the one who first spoke would not let her be so lightly. She called two or three times more to her, and then in exasperation she replied:

"May he kill his father and marry his mother!"

When the man heard the fairy's curse, he got a shock at first. Then he paid no more attention to it and went on with his work.

After making the cradle he took it home and there found the child born. The mother laid it in the cradle and put the usual necklet on its neck as a token.

When the child had grown a little, the father, unable to put the fairy's curse out of his mind, talked things over with his wife and decided to expose the boy. So he made a box and putting the child inside, cast it into the sea.

The waves caught it up, bore it far, far away, and at last washed it ashore. There Our Lord provided a goat which came every day and let the boy suck her.

One fine day a passing traveller came on the child and pitying him, took him to his home. There he kept him as one of his own family.

When the boy grew to be a stripling of sixteen or so, he took it into his head that he was a King's son. So he refused to stay any longer with his benefactor and went wandering the world over to see if he could discover which king he was the son of—so as to go and live with his father.

A good many years passed while he wandered. Then he happened to light on a country where the inhabitants were murmuring very much against their king. As he knew himself to be very able, he joined the party in opposition to the king, thinking to find a way of thrusting him out of this world with his own hand and taking his place.

As he passed day after day wondering how he could carry out his wish, he encountered three carriages a little outside the town, quite unexpectedly. After some people had pointed out which the king was in, he went up as though he wanted to say something to him. When he came close, he struck him with his mace and killed him. He then got in to the carriage, put the horses to a gallop, and entered the town. Without more ado the people elected him king and gave him the widowed queen to wife as they liked each other.

Before a year had passed, Our Lord gave them a son, and they seemed happy. But there was one thing which worried them. Whenever the husband talked to his wife, he had a way of calling her "mother," and she had a way of calling her husband "son"! In order to discover what was portended by this business, which they could never understand however much they pondered it, they sent to inquire of a spaewife. She replied that they must be kith and kin to each other.

After being told this by the spaewife, they began one day to talk over their lives at great length. Especially because the husband showed his wife the necklet which his mother had put round his neck as a token of identity when he was small, they realised that they were indeed mother and son, and that he had unwittingly killed his father. In his despair the husband plunged his knife into his wife's heart first of all, then into his son's, and last of all into his own.

As his wife rendered up her spirit, she sang to her dying child:

> Hush thee, hush thee, son!
> Son of my son!
> Son of my daughter-in-law!
> Born to thy father-in-law!

Looking about her, she saw that the house was falling down and burying them.

III. Commentary

Such is the tale of Oedipus Rex in Albania. The weapon used to kill
the King in his carriage indicates that it is of some age. For maces, the
classic weapons of the janissaries and spahis of medieval Turkey,
went out when muskets came in.

The tale falls into three sections—the curse, the exposure, and the
incestuous marriage. Each section is a whole in itself and reappears in
other stories, the second one being particularly popular. But it does
not seem certain that the three had been linked together in popular
story in North Albania. At the time when the story as we have it was
published, several Albanians made a practice of writing fictitious
short stories round Albanian history and folktales. "The Dancing
Girl of Dukagjin" in Mr. Mann's book, pp. 92–100, is one example
and this version of Oedipus Rex reads like another. Unfortunately
neither Mr. Mann nor I remember who published it in *Hylli i Dritës*,
and owing to the advent of a communist government in Albania the
only copies of this periodical which remain accessible to foreigners in
Europe are in Rome where they are at present beyond Mr. Mann's
reach and mine. Our failure to identify its first publisher makes it
impossible to appraise exactly the folklore quality of the story as a
whole. But it may be fairly said that each section, taken by itself, is
genuine Albanian folklore.

The sections do not quite match. In the first the father is a
peasant born among the mountains of North Albania as the alp, the
spruce fir, the hewing of the cradle, and the Catholic phraseology all
tell us. In the third he is a king and rides in a kingly manner in a
carriage, which presupposes a country much flatter than North
Albania and so gives an agreeable sensation of the distance to which
the child was carried first by the exposure and then by his own
wanderings.

The sections are strung together on the thread of inexorable
doom. From the moment the petulant fairy speaks, the child must
dree his weird. The father, anxious to save himself from being
murdered but unwilling to do so by taking his dangerous offspring's
life outright, casts him into the sea, to die if God will or to be
rescued, just as, being a native of the Balkans, he would have
thrown out an unwanted puppy or kitten. Providence willed that the
castaway should be rescued, sending first a goat to feed him and

then a Good Samaritan to adopt him. In this way the peasant father escapes the curse, but it is really the son whom that concerns; the father's fate had been decreed at his own birth and unless he had been doomed to die by his son's hand, it was independent of his son's. At his foster-father's the youth conceives the silly idea that he is of royal blood and sets forth to find his royal father. He thinks only to live in peace with him until he dies and then to succeed him. But the curse wills that in mean ambition he shall change his course, taking an unknown king's life and marrying the widowed queen, to discover in due course that the King had begotten him and the Queen given him birth.

The Oedipus Legend in
South Slavic Folk Tradition

Friedrich S. Krauss

The Oedipus tale is reported in Yugoslavia as well. Friedrich Krauss (1859–1938) was a scholar who specialized in erotic folklore. He was the moving force and editor of the nine-volume Anthropophyteia Jahrbücher *(1904–1912) as well as the ten-volume accompanying series* Beiwerke zum Studium der Anthropophyteia *(1907–1931), a journal and monograph devoted to sexual folklore. Krauss's geographic area of research was Yugoslavia where he made several extensive field collections. Krauss, living in Vienna, was obviously familiar with Freud's work. (Freud accepted Krauss's invitation to write a short introduction to the German translation of John G. Bourke's* Scatalogic Rites of All Nations *which was published in 1913.) This is undoubtedly why Krauss published these Oedipus versions in* Imago, *an important psychoanalytic journal founded and edited by Freud. Krauss did little more than report the texts since he no doubt assumed that the* Imago *readership would interpret them in the light of psychoanalytic theory.*

The first of Krauss's three texts is unusual insofar as it includes the mutilation of the feet of the exposed child. This detail is a well-known motif in the ancient Oedipus story, but it occurs rarely in modern Oedipus folklore. Furthermore, the hanging of the infant by

Reprinted from *Imago*, 22 (1935), 358–367. We are indebted to classicist Janis Kreslins for translating this essay into English.

its feet from a tree is unexampled in the modern oral tradition although it does occur in medieval versions of the Oedipus story. (On these, see Lowell Edmunds, "Oedipus in the Middle Ages," Antike und Abendland, *25 (1976), 140–155.) The second text, "Simeon the Foundling," is a common guslar song in Yugoslavia. The third text is the Judas story, which belongs to the Oedipus tale type. (For the standard study, see P.F. Baum, "The Medieval Legend of Judas Iscariot,"* Publications of the Modern Language Association, N.S. *24 (1916), 481–632. For a psychoanalytic treatment, see Norman Reider, "Medieval Oedipal Legends about Judas,"* Psychoanalytic Quarterly, *29 (1960), 515–527.)*

Evil fate is already determined at birth.

Two vilas[1] were walking along between the peaks of two mountain ranges. One called out to the other: "Oh, Uvid!" The answer of the other resounded shrilly: "What is it, Uris?" "Is that mother's son already here?" "Not yet." "Oh, oh, he has let the auspicious moment escape him." "What sort of person was that mother's son?" The first answered: "He would have become the most important merchant in the entire world." The line of questioning was repeated anew. "Oh, Uvid!" "Why are you calling me, Uris?" "Is that mother's son already here?" "He's still not here!" "Ah, this time an even more favorable moment has escaped him." "What sort of person was this mother's son, then?" The reply: "He would have become the most important person amongst the rulers of the world." And again: "Oh, Uvid!" "Why are you calling me, Uris?" "Now has the son of that mother finally arrived?" "Yes." "Oh, unfortunately the moment was unpropitious for him." "And what would that be?" Answer: "He will become the husband of his own mother."

At the same time, the mother they were talking about was coming down the mountain with her child and she overheard the entire conversation. Since she had borne a boy, she took a small needle in her hand, threaded it with silk thread, and drew it through the boy's heels. And she hung him from a tree.

By chance an emperor on a hunt came upon this place with his servants and hunting dogs. The hunting dogs sniffed out and discovered the exposed boy. The vilas were sorry because the dogs could snatch the child, and therefore they called the emperor to that place: "You have not been given the luck of progeny. Take this small child and lift it up that he may become your son. Otherwise you will not be apportioned a child of your own." The emperor dismounted from his horse, looked at the child hanging in the tree, and ordered his servants to lower the boy. He took him into the lap of his dolman and turned homeward. He called his wife down into the courtyard: "Come out, my Lady, look here! God has bestowed upon us a son. I found him in the country." The empress hurried down into the courtyard, took the male child and said: "Blessed me! I have received an unhoped-for child." She wrapped the child up in velvet and linen, called for three nurses, picked him up, and then raised him.

When the boy reached adolescence, he could ride and he knew how to handle weapons. He was wont to hunt in the company of the emperor and considered himself the emperor's very own son. That did not please the other members of the hunting party, and from envy they began to find fault with him because of his bearing: "You are no real royal prince, rather the bastard of a prostitute, who was found hanging on a branch of a tree in the forest." Upon having returned home once again with the emperor, he fell into the lap of the empress and implored her: "Mother, I must know once and for all, tell me frankly, am I your real son or am I not? For somebody reproached me today, saying that I am not your son but the bastard son of a prostitute." The empress confessed that she had not given birth to him but that the emperor had found him hanging from a branch in the forest. "He took you along, I raised you. So I hope that you are today and forever will remain my son, as if I had in pain brought you into the world." He answered: "I can't stay here any longer. Well, I have belongings of my own. Give them to me, I'll go out into the world. This rabble should know no more of me." The empress cried and beseeched him to the heavens as she would her true child that he should not abandon her and the emperor. He didn't pay any attention to this, saddled a horse and rode away.

And so he wandered through the world, from one place of lodging to another until his unalterable fate guided him exactly to his mother. She was still young and vigorous. The youth was especially pleasing in her eyes and she said to him: "Listen here, young man! If it suits you, then let's get married." He responded: "I agree, if it is fine with you." So they slept with each other that night.

At first dawn they called the priest and neighbor and got married. After the marriage the young man began a life of hunting. Upon returning home in the evening, he was bathed in sweat. He undressed, took off his shoes and gave them to his wife to put away. As she picked up the shoes, something came into her mind and she stared horrified at the bare feet and remembered what the vilas had once announced at her delivery. Alarmed she then asked him: "What is your lineage? May God help you, confess to me." After he related all to her, the where, how, why, and that someone once found him in the woods, she broke out in tears. Terrified he called out: "So may God help you, why are you weeping?" "Ah, how should I not cry, my unhappy son." As he heard these words, he also began to moan: "My unfavourable fate and I are three times cursed." He jumped up right on the spot, saddled his horse and called out: "In the name of Allah, mother, your eyes will never again look upon me." And so he then proceeded weeping into the unknown world, but she remained behind lamenting and wailing. And so the mother never again received any news of him, nor did he receive any news of her.

Here we have a version of the Oedipus legend, as it has been preserved from the very oldest times all the way up to the present in the folk tradition of Montenegro. How a Sophocles with his *Oedipus at Colonus* guaranteed its dissemination throughout the entire world is known to us through his poetic adaptation. There is no room here to discuss the variations. The storyteller starts out with a belief in the inevitability of fate. According to old Slavic beliefs, there is an *usud*, a determiner, who determines the fate of each newborn child. In the version above a schism in this determiner's personality has taken place. One, the *uvid* (insight) determined the moment of birth, the other *uris* (destiny, allotment), the fate and fortune of the newborn child. The determiner of fate performs the duties of his job silently. The two vilas become his interpreter and thereupon assume the masculine names of the split character. What is new is that "Swollen foot" (Oedipus) is the child of a maiden, while in Sophocles's version he comes into the world as a prince. The emperor and empress adopt the foundling through a festive and symbolic action, drawing the child between the legs and then lifting him up. This custom can still be found today amongst a large part of the Slavic peasant folk. The Greek loan word, *mantulija* (*manteuein*, "to foretell, prophesy") perhaps points to a Greek tradition. The dictionaries do not contain this word.

This story is found in Novica Šaulić's distinguished collection of legends. However, it may have possibly become known to the narrator from a guslar song, since several widespread songs handle this subject matter and the narrator preserves several modes of expression in the verse form. An example of such a guslar poem follows. It was recorded by Alex Sandić around the year 1860 in the Danube region and it appeared in Zara, 1861 in the Festschrift commemorating the hundreth birthday of the folk-poet Kaćić-Miosić, pp. 132ff.

> The patriarch Sabbas was devoted to hunting,
> Three full days, even four he devoted to the hunt.
> He didn't even bag the smallest game,
> He pulled in only a chest out of the water.
> When Sabbas opened this chest
> He found therein a child, a small boy
> And an ornate white letter under his head.
> And the letter reported gloomily and sadly the following:
> "A sister with her brother gave birth to him.
> She forged out of lead a small chest,
> Threw the little chest into the blue sea,
> And addressed the cold water:
> Take away, oh sea, injustice from the world
> So that the black earth may not contaminate itself,
> And that she no longer may be a cause of outrage in dear
>   God's presence.
> Take the injustice, O water, out of this world
> In order that I may become delivered for good from sin."
>   When Sabbas had read through this letter
> He directed a prayer to dear God.
> He carried the child to the church at Hilendar,
> Marked the child with the holy cross,
> And gave to him the beautiful name,
> The beautiful name: Foundling Simeon.
>   He brought him up and raised him
> Until the child could mount a horse
> And was ready to ride, until he was sixteen years old.

Then the venerable Sabbas spoke to him thus:
"Oh, foundling, my dear child!
Son, I have raised you well.
I have raised you, but did not beget you.
But you now count sixteen years.
Take as much of my treasure as pleases you.
In addition I will also give you as a gift my riding horse.
Go from one town to another
And try to find your parents."
The youth became scared and alarmed in spirit.
The departure from the manor was a bitter shock.
Sabbas had raised him with full affection
And had never spoken a word
That he was not his own child by blood.
He took the treasures with him, as many as he could
carry.
He melted into tears and addressed Sabbas thus:
"My heart breaks, I must leave the manor."
And he continued speaking to Sabbas meekly:
"Towards which country do you direct me?"
Upon hearing these words Sabbas felt pity
And in tears he offered this answer to the child.
"O foundling, you, my most beloved little child!
Up to now I have fed you as well as possible
Now I will also advise you well with all my heart.
Now for a good departure in good time, with God's help!
Direct your prayer to God, our only refuge,
And go there, wherever you will.
Try to find both of your parents."
The youth took the advice to heart
And set off with God's blessing at a good hour.
He turned to the sun in the east
And directed a prayer to dear God
And made a cross with the ordained sign.
Soon he flew across the broad plain
Just as a falling star through the clear sky.
When he reached Pribintown
The empress there was just ready to marry.
Everyone from the nobility wanted to become emperor.
They could not arrive at a decision,
Could not choose an emperor from their ranks.
They held consultation all day long

To determine in which way they might do what was right,
In order to place the right man on the throne.
They deliberated and reached this decision:
    "The empress, the lady, should throw,
Should throw an apple of pure gold,
And upon throwing it should speak these words:
    'The one upon whom the golden apple should fall,
This person the empress will in love embrace,
And on his shoulders the kingdom shall rest.'"
    All the suitors approached her.
The apple, however, did not strike any of the nobles,
But rather fell on the last one in line, Simeon the
    Foundling.
    The herald announced in the court publicly:
"It does not matter from where the unknown champion
    hearkens.
From now on the kingdom rests upon his shoulders."
    They yielded calmly to divine judgment
And led to the court the foundling.
They married the empress to him
And then celebrated the wedding.
    The evening passed and night fell
And they led the couple into the bridal chamber,
On soft pillows and white arms.
    And so she passed the night with him.
Early in the morning she awoke early
And said to herself:
    "Oh, dear God, does it accord with your will
That an unknown conqueror is to be my husband,
On whose shoulders the kingdom should rest?"
    Secretly she searched his garments
And found therein the delicate white letter
Informing her of his lineage and relatives,
Namely, that a sister begat him with her brother.
She screamed, like the dark mountain in travail.
    "Oh woe to me, my God, how you punish me!
How have I, God, so seriously sinned
That I begat a child with my own brother
And that this child now embraces his mother at night?"
    Having dissolved into tears she addressed him:
"Oh, my child, you, Simeon the Foundling,
Raise yourself up, son, on your champion's feet,
And rush away to Patriarch Sabbas.

So will a mother greet him:
Let him throw you into the deepest dungeon
That nine years you may languish therein
That you may be free of your sin."
    Then swiftly he jumped to his champion's feet
And hurried away to Patriarch Sabbas.
He handed over to him the delicate white letter
Which contained the greeting of his mother.
    After Sabbas had read through the letter
He threw him deep down into the cell
Where he was to languish for nine years
And thereby perhaps become free of his sins.
The desolate prison he carefully locked up
And threw the key into the blue sea.
From then the time advanced again,
And soon nine years had passed by
When fishermen were fishing on the sea
And caught a fish from the river Mostar.
    Because they wished to give the fish to no one
They presented it to the venerable Sabbas.
    When Sabbas cut open the body of the fish
He came upon the prison key.
The Patriarch Sabbas spoke these words:
    "Woe to me, have pity, O God!
I have locked that desolate prison,
But have completely forgotten the young man therein."
    When Sabbas now unlocked the doors
He saw that the youth had long since passed away.
Passed away had he and attained salvation.
At his head there was an enormous candle.
He was absolved from his sins.

This song is mine, dear guest,
From God, however, comes health, peace, and happiness,
As well as holiness of the soul in Paradise.

   In the Narenta, which flows by Mostar, thrive huge trout, which are especially highly regarded delicacies. One such fish, having strayed into the Adriatic Sea, is captured by fishermen. Because they do not want to yield their valuable catch to one another, they agree to give it as a gift to the most venerable Patriarch Sabbas. Here the tale includes the motif of Polykrates' recovered ring.

The ancient Greek plays were rooted in the folk tradition and were, in accordance with their origin, representations of religious observances. The poet could not freely alter the legends preserved by the traditions among the people; he could only elaborate and offer reasons for them. In this manner he created from theater and drama a moral institution, to which the chorus, which moved back and forth in strophe and antistrophe before the stage, contributed by singing its commentaries in the vein of folk feeling. Sophocles also elaborated a folk legend in his *Oedipus at Colonus*. His innovations were restricted, first, to the introduction of the character of Antigone, the daughter, the fruit of the one regarded as a horror, repugnant to the gods, and, second, to the blinding of the weak victim of a dismal fate. The ability of Sophocles to embellish this material artistically makes him one of the immortal poets of all time. At the same time the basic conception is preserved in folklore. We have yet a third South Slavic version of the same Greek folk legend. This one distinguishes itself from the two previous ones through the important trait that at the birth of the child, at the decisive hour, two goddesses of fate pronounce the disaster with unalterable certainty. The parents learn the future of their offspring and then decide to avert the course of fate by throwing the child from a bridge into a river. Some monks, who are fishing nearby, take the child and raise him until he is a young man. He sets out into the world; just as in the guslar tale, he is taken in by his parents; unintentionally he kills his own father, marries his mother, is recognized by her as her son, and is expelled from the household. His fate is fulfilled in an even more horrible way. He goes to Jerusalem, enters into the service of the Savior and his disciples, and betrays for a base wage of sin his Lord and Master to the revengeful Jews. With the miracle which Jesus performs with drops of his blood at the very last moment, the criminal realizes that he has basely betrayed his Lord. He rushes into the mountains, notably into a fir forest, and there hangs himself. It is here that one should look for the origins of the Judas legend, since as we all know, there was no thirteenth apostle Judas, who could have committed the disgraceful action. Also the betrayer who condemns himself is one of the oldest characters in Asiatic folklore. The South Slavic folk poet is not satisfied with such an ending. His Oedipus, with his bones, brings about after his death an eternal evil. Tobacco leaves sprout from them.

The version in Novica Šaulić, *Srpske narodne priče iz zbirke narodnik pripovjedaka*, Belgrade, 1931, Book 1, no. 37, pp. 58–60, runs as follows in translation:[2]

The curse is ordained by fate.

A man and his wife were wandering through a desolate place in a high mountain range. His wife was far advanced in pregnancy. There in the dark mountain forest, the tired woman sat down under a tree. Her husband asked her: "Why are you sitting down?" She remained silent. "Why are you sitting there?" It weighed heavily on her to admit to him the truth. After a long time she moved a bit. "Don't you realize why I am sitting here. I'm going to have the child. Fate (*Bog*) has ordained this." "Of course, we have also strived for this," replied the man.

All at once a voice spoke up from the forest: "Has the child appeared?" "No, by God, not yet," the reply came. Again the voice sounded: "Is the child already here?" "No, it still isn't." For the third time the voice sounded: "Is the child finally here?" "By God, yes." The first voice spoke: "In the name of Allah, it has appeared at an unlucky hour." "In God's name, why is this so?" "If it had arrived when I asked you the first time, it would have become the ruler of half the world. If it had been born by the time of my second query, truly, a ruler of many peoples would have come from the new-born child. But now he has been born at an unlucky time. He will call himself the executioner of his own father, he will be the lover of his own mother, he will put forth his own hand against God, and worst of all, he will place a noose around his own neck."

The young mother picked up her child, took it in her arms, and went on with her husband. They reached a river, spanned by a large bridge. When they were at the middle of the bridge span, she suddenly tossed the child in a long arc into the water and exclaimed: "By Allah, I don't wish that he be my lover and the executioner of his father."

Exactly at the same time, near some bushes in a meadow on the bank of the river, a pious monk was fishing with his students. The fisherman noticed the child, and the current carried it to them. The monk pulled him ashore. He wrapped him up in the lap of his dolman, carried him to church, baptized him immediately, found a wet nurse for him, and raised him so that the child passed as his own son.

The child was extraordinarily beautiful, like a vila, and he developed splendidly. By his first birthday he was already larger and stronger than almost any three-year-old. He was an unruly, wild child, and had no peer in this respect. He tore up church books in sanctuaries, destroyed holy paintings, broke crosses that were set up, laid waste to gardens around the church. They thrashed him, but he was not in the least bit afraid, because he was and remained a rowdy child.

By his fifteenth year, the monk was already unable to exercise any authority over him. He was too much for him to handle. There remained nothing else to do but to dress and equip him anew from head to toe. In addition, the monk provided him with some money and said to him: "Go out into the world, I no longer can keep you here. You give me more trouble than I can handle."

The youngster now wandered around the world. He went from place to place, from here to there, until he ended up at his father's and mother's home. They were extremely rich people and lived in great abundance. He asked them: "Could you furnish me lodging?" "Surely, why not? You can spend the night here." And in the evening they talked. "Where are you going, young man?" inquired the father. He answered: "I think I want to go into service somewhere." "Why do you wish to go into service, you who are so young and fine a gentleman?" "By God, I want to do this, if only someone will take me on." "I am ready, if you are inclined to do the job." And so they agreed that he should become their vine-grower.

And thus he went up the steep-sloped vineyard in order to inspect it. The grapes suffered much destruction from the sweet-toothed birds, who were accustomed to frequent the vineyard and who could not be driven away by any means. The young wine-grower prepared a sling, placed a rock in it, ran with it between the vines, and chased away the pests.

One day, the father said: "I must once and for all go and check out what the young man is doing, whether he truly watches over my vineyard. Thank God that we have an overseer!" He crept up to spy out how he performed his duties. At the same moment, the young man picked up a stone and flung it in that direction. The devil directed the throw to the forehead of the father. The rock penetrated the forehead. Struck, his father yelled out in great pain: "Why are you killing me?" The young man took the injured one on his shoulders and rushed home with him. Many gathered around the injured one in order to see what had happened. The father related to them the entire incident and enjoined them: "That was an act of God. Do not place any blood-guilt on him. He inadvertently hit me, he has not in the least committed any crime against me." After saying these words, he died.

In the meantime, the young man managed the household and farm with the wife of the dead man, his mother. People urged her repeatedly and emphatically: "Look, woman, take this young man as a husband. Do not waste so much effort and your possessions, since this lad, God witness, is an excellent bridegroom."

And so she took him as her husband and they sinned. One night the wife asked before going to bed: "Unfortunate one, who are you really and what is your parentage? You came drifting out of nowhere, you killed my husband, I married you and to this present day I do not know who you are or where you come from." He confessed to her that a monk had fished him out of the water, had taken him in and raised him as his son—"And therefore I set out into the wide world to seek my fortune." Horrified, she remembered the whole story. "O, you unhappy man, how did Satan bring you here? May Satan lead you away from here. May no one find out that you set foot in this place." With that she chased him from the house, and he wandered again out into the world.

And so he reached Jerusalem, where he met Christ and the Apostles. He entered into their service, prepared meals for them, served them, washed their dishes, and cleaned house. No one could have done it better than he.

And the Jews tried to bribe him: "Hand Christ over to us." Thus they spoke to him.

"Allah, I'll do it, if you would fill this box of mine with ducats." They gilded twelve of the cheapest coins, added a real gold ducat and presented to him the filled box. He said to them: "Follow me." In the living quarters there were nine doors. He opened one after the other and they followed him step by step. When he came to the room where the holy ones dwelled, he put before them salt and bread on the table, to each the same portion. But he spoke to those accompanying him: "The one to whom I stretch out my hand, that one is the Christ." He put salt and bread on the table for them and pointed with an outstretched hand towards him. A one-eyed man stood with a lance at the door, saw the sign and hurled the spear into the left breast of the Lord. A drop of blood squirted up and struck the guard in his blinded eye. At the very same moment his eye could see again and he yelled out: "Forgive me Lord, I am yours, by God." You know, my dear listener, how they tormented him, how he was dragged before the court and how horribly they finally dealt with him.

When Judas realized what he had set in motion, he yelled out bewildered: "By Allah and by God, what have I not done to myself? I became my father's executioner, am called lover of my mother, and now I have raised my hand against my God!"

And he bought himself a rope with his ducats and ran with it into a desolate mountain range. He wrote a short note from which people could discern who and what he was, climbed a tall fir tree, fastened around its tip the end of the rope, the other he cast around his neck and thus hanged himself on the tree.

And hanging there he decomposed. The people were greatly astonished because for three years they could not find out what had happened to his carcass, nor where he had hidden himself and what path he had taken. Some hunters got lost in that area and noticed the rope hanging from the tree. At the foot of the tree, directly under the rope, there lay scattered the bones of the hanged one. Tobacco leaves had sprouted from these bones. Because of this men should smoke tobacco. The sinner had done repentance, and this leaf should till the end of time in all the world perpetuate the memory of his offence.

NOTES

[1]Thomas Butler, *Monumenta Serbocroatica*, University of Michigan, Ann Arbor, Michigan, 1980, p. 475, n. 98: "A *vila* was a mythological being in South Slavic folklore. Similar to our fairies or spirits, *vilas* were said to be the spirits of unbaptized maidens, who lived in the woods, on mountains, and near bodies of water"—*ed. note.*

[2]Krauss presents his South Slavic texts in German translation. The English translations of Krauss' texts are from his German, not from the originals—*ed. note.*

An Oedipus Myth in Gypsy Tradition

Mirella Karpati

Not only is the tale of Oedipus demonstrably an oral one, but it continues to be passed on, as a Gypsy version collected in 1971 attests. The commentary offered on the tale takes Propp's essay on Oedipus as a point of departure with special reference to Propp's assumption that the tale reflects an evolutionary changeover from matriarchy to patriarchy. For additional writings on Gypsy culture by the same author, see Mirella Karpati, Ròmano Them (Mondo Zingaro), *(Rome, 1963), and Mirella Karpati and Renza Sasso,* Adolescenti zingari e non zingari: Un approcio sociologico con il test del villaggio, *(Rome, 1976).*

There once was and was not a woman who was, to speak frankly, pregnant. She dreamt that she had married her son. So when her son was born, what did she do? She put him in a wooden box and wrote a note: "Whoever finds this baby, let him keep him as his own and rear him." She put in also a hundred florins and then threw the box into the river. Well, it went downstream on the water for four days and four nights.

There was a fisherman near the water and he heard someone cry. He saw the box and the baby inside and read the letter. So he took

Reprinted from *Lacio Drom*, 12(1976), 5–9. We are grateful to Professor Ruth Scodel of the Department of Classics at Harvard for translating this essay from Italian. (We did not translate the initial part of the essay, which consisted of the text in Romany.)

the baby home and gave him the name Janos. Janos became big and strong and one day, when he was eighteen, he found under a cabinet that letter which said, "Whoever finds this baby, let him keep him as his son and rear him." Then he understood why the boys at school used to say to him: "That man is not your real father; you came from the water." He decided to go upriver to find his own family.

He walked and walked days and months along the river, until he saw ahead of him a bridge which was blocked. He went up onto the bank to wash his feet, because he was tired. And behold, a hostess from the nearby inn saw that he was a fine young man and asked him: "Are you looking for work?" "Yes" said the young man and he went to live with the woman. So they fell in love, and were always together.

One day that landlady looked through the young man's things and found that letter and realized that he was her son. What could she do? Well, she went to him and said, "Listen, I cannot be your wife any more, because I am your mother, your true mamma." She wanted to embrace him, but he with great horror repulsed her, climbed on the bridge, and threw himself down into the water. But he did not sink. He walked on the water, until he came to an old castle on an island. He closed himself inside and threw the key into the river. And he lived there many years.

Someone heard how he cried and told others. Then many priests came and with benedictions prayed that the door open, but to no avail. Then they said to a fisherman: "May God give you luck, we must make a journey of four or five days home and we are famished. Give us something to eat." Immediately the fisherman went to fish and he caught a fish eight meters long. And what was in its belly? The key. So they opened the door and had Janos come out and they went with him to his mother, because he forgave her. Then those priests made him Pope and he—Janos, that is John—was the first Pope after St. Peter.

All this is written in the Bible and they tell it in Hungary.

This story was told to me the 26 of July, 1971, by Milan Petrov, a Lovari gypsy of the Pluχačešti tribe.

We find ourselves faced with a gypsy version of the Oedipus myth, in which two basic types are mixed, that of Andreas of Crete and that of Gregorius, as they have been catalogued by Propp. Andreas too, in fact, is thrown into the water and reared by fishermen. When he learns that he is a foundling, he leaves to find his family and becomes guardian of his parents' garden; he kills his father and marries his mother. As soon as the truth of his condition is known, he goes under the earth and dies like a saint. In the Gregorius-type the father (himself incestuous husband of his sister) is already dead during an expiatory pilgrimage to Jerusalem; therefore the parricide is eliminated. The penitence consists in the retreat into a cave on an island, from which Gregorius is miraculously freed to be chosen Pope. That of Andreas is a democratic version, according to Propp, while in that of Gregorius is recovered, though at different times, the historical dimension of the rise to power, which in Oedipus adumbrates the moment of transition from matriarchy to patriarchy. The gypsy version, though it simply repeats traditional elements, has nonetheless variations which it is interesting to look at in the light of the culture.

What is striking, above all, is the complete absence of the father. There is never any reference to him and the plot of the story pays attention only to the mother-son relationship. Why? It could be to keep Janos from staining himself with an unpardonable crime (parricide), given his destiny as pope. Frequently, indeed, in fairy tales— as Propp observes—the plot is determined in a functional relation to the end. For the gypsy, to offend, much less to kill, one's father is a very serious offence. One could object that incest also—committed by Janos—is an offence. It is so also for the gypsies; just during these days Kako Slato told us a fairy tale which makes this point. Only in this myth the incest is committed unknowingly. In the Greek tradition there is no distinction between objective and subjective guilt, and Oedipus, victim of his fate, must expiate it nonetheless; this is the nucleus of the tragedy. For the gypsies, on the other hand, Janos is innocent and the moment of "recognition," with its immediate reaction of horror, is only the pretext for the beginning of the second movement. As proof of his innocence, "He did not sink. He walked on the water. . . ." Destiny exists and is accepted as ineluctable by the gypsies, but for this very reason there is nothing to do but accept it and thus it cannot constitute tragedy.

To this first hypothesis (innocence of Janos of a sin which the "Rom" could not justify, given the patriarchal family structure) one could, however, oppose the hypothesis of the existence of an earlier matriarchy, nor are elements to sustain this thesis lacking. Apart from the fact that the tribe of Milan takes its name from a woman, the less obvious, but more significant aspect seems to me to be the inversion of two traditional elements. In the common tradition it is always the father who exposes the son, who is then reared by an animal or a foster mother. All this signifies an initiation rite and especially the consignment to the waters is the initiation of a future leader: the examples of Moses, Cyrus, Romulus teach this. The animal nurse is the totem animal; when in fairy tales she is replaced by a woman, often the woman has an animal name. In the gypsy version, on the other hand, the woman is the protagonist, in the sense that it is she who receives the prophecy and decides on the exposure of her son. Also on his return she appears alone and free to accept him as her husband.

Likewise, it is she who takes the initiative in sexual advances. We now know that, where matriarchy thrives, the woman can freely change husbands or even have more than one (polyandry). This point is corroborated by the figure of the fisherman, who, himself alone and a man, rears and educates the baby. Here can be seen a hint of the institution of the avunculate, so important in a matriarchal structure for the basic role entrusted to the maternal uncle in the education of sons. Only with the coming of patriarchy does the absence of the father begin to be felt as a shame, and Janos suffers not so much in not having a father as in not having a family, that is in not being part of that network of relations characterized by the blood-tie which is the social reality of gypsy culture.

To these motifs a further element can be added, somewhat obscure in truth: "They went with him to his mother, because he forgave her." Why forgive her, if the incest was committed without knowledge and if she, on the contrary, had done everything to avoid it, while on the other hand securing a chance of survival for her son? Perhaps her offence was precisely that of keeping to a role no longer acceptable in gypsy social structure, and the "pardon" suggests exactly the passage from matriarchy to patriarchy.

In the myth there is another cultural feature of interest: the woman's reaction when she learns that she is Janos' mother. While he in horror tries to kill himself, she on the other hand exults "because I am your mother, your true mamma" and wants to embrace him. This is explained because being a woman and having sexual relations is of minimal importance compared to the fact of being a mother: only then does a woman enjoy esteem and prestige in gypsy society.

All other features and the plot itself belong to tradition[2]. Even the contradiction between the voyage of the newborn on the river for only four days and the return along the river for days and months is only apparent: the return is nothing other than the difficult task which in every fairy tale the hero must accomplish in order to get the longed-for prize, which for Janos is to find his family, truly essential in gypsy culture.

NOTES

[1]Cf. Vladimir Ja. Propp, *Edipo alla luce del folclore*, Einaudi, 1975. [Propp's essay on Oedipus is reprinted in this volume. Ed. Note]

[2]Cf. V. Propp, *Morfologia della fiaba*, Einaudi, 1966; B. Niccolini, *Composizione delle fiabe di magia zingare*, in "Lacio Drom," 1973, N. 1/2, pp. 31–95.

The Legend of Oedipus

James G. Frazer

In addition to fieldworkers who collected texts of the Oedipus story, there were library scholars who read such field reports with great interest. Among library scholars, surely one of the most celebrated was James G. Frazer (1854–1941), author of the monumental twelve-volume Golden Bough *(1911–1915). In this work and his other writings, Frazer displayed an uncanny ability to ferret out fugitive sources on a staggering variety of topics in the areas of myth, ritual, and magic. Thanks to a graceful writing style, Frazer's works have remained popular even though the nineteenth century evolutionary frameworks in which he wrote (from magic to religion to science and from savagery to barbarism to civilization) have long since been abandoned.*

Frazer's intellectual interests ranged from anthropology and folklore to the bible and the classics. One of his projects was a translation of and commentary on The Library *of Apollodorus which is the major ancient compendium of classical mythology. In the appendix of this edition, Frazer penned a brief note on Oedipus pointing out oral parallels which he had come upon during his reading. In the Finnish, Ukrainian and Javanese texts cited by Frazer we find the most common forms of the Oedipus tale in oral tradition. The setting of the parricide in a garden (as opposed to a carriage) is typical. The possible metaphorical or symbolic significance of the*

Reprinted by permission of the publishers and the Loeb Classical Library from *Apollodorus: The Library*, Vol. II, translated by Sir James George Frazer, Cambridge, Mass.: Harvard University Press, 1921.

hero's killing his father in a garden or orchard will not go unnoticed by psychoanalytically oriented readers. In reading Frazer's texts, one should bear in mind that they are polished literary translations from what were originally oral sources. One may compare, for example, Frazer's rendering of the Judas tale from the Golden Legend *with the oral version reported by Krauss. Readers should not miss Frazer's lighthearted summary and dismissal of solar mythological interpretations of Oedipus in his final footnote.*

For some details of Frazer's life, see R. Angus Downie, Frazer and the Golden Bough (*London, 1970*).

According to the legend, Oedipus committed a twofold crime in ignorance: he killed his father and married his mother. The same double tragedy meets us in a Finnish tale, which runs as follows:—

Two wizards arrived at the cottage of a peasant and were hospitably entertained by him. During the night a she-goat dropped a kid, and the younger of the two wizards proposed to assist the mother-goat in her travail, but the elder of the two would not hear of it, "Because," said he, "the kid is fated to be swallowed by a wolf." At the same time the peasant's wife was overtaken by the pangs of childbirth, and the younger of the two wizards would have gone to her help, but was dissuaded by the elder, who told him that the boy who was about to be born would kill his father and marry his mother. The peasant overheard this conversation and reported it to his wife, but they could not make up their minds to kill the child. One day, when they were making merry in the peasant's cottage, they put the kid to roast on a spit, and then laid the roasted meat near the window; but it fell out of the window and was devoured by a passing wolf. Seeing that one of the two predictions made by the wizards was thus fulfilled, the peasant and his wife were sore afraid and thought how they could get rid of their child. Not having the courage to kill him outright, they wounded him in the breast, tied him to a table and threw him into the sea. The forsaken child drifted to an island, where he was picked up and carried to the abbot of a monastery. There he grew up and became a clever young man. But he wearied of the monastic life, and the abbot advised him to go out into the world and seek his fortune. So he went. One day he came to a peasant's cottage. The peasant was out, but his wife was at home, and the young man asked her for work. She told him, "Go and guard the fields against robbers." So he hid under the shadow of a rock, and seeing a man enter the field and gather grass, he struck and killed him. Then he returned to his mistress, who was uneasy because her husband did not come home to dinner. So they discovered that the supposed thief, whom the young man had killed, was no other than the husband of his mistress; but as the homicide had not been committed with any evil intent, the widow, after weeping and wailing, forgave the young man and kept him in her service; nay, in time she consoled herself by marrying him. However, one day she noticed the scar on her second husband's breast and began to have her suspicions. Inquiry elicited the fatal truth that her husband was also her son. What were they to do? The woman sent him to seek out wise men, who might teach him how to expiate his great sin. He went and found a monk with a book in his hand. To him the conscience-stricken husband put his question; but when the monk, on consulting his book replied that no expiation was possible for guilt so atrocious, the sinner in a rage killed the holy man. The same thing happened to another monk who had the misfortune to receive the confession of the penitent. But a third monk proved more compliant, and answered very obligingly that there was no sin which could not be atoned for by repentance. Accordingly he advised the repentant sinner to dig a well in the rock till he struck water; and his mother was to stand beside him holding a black sheep in her arms, until the sheep should turn white. This attracted public attention, and passers-by used to stop and ask the pair what they were doing. One day a gentleman, after putting the usual question and receiving the usual answer, was asked by the penitent, "And who are you?" He answered, "I am he who makes straight what was crooked, and I summon you to the bar of justice." Seeing no hope of escaping from the arm of the law, the penitent took the bull by the horns and killed the gentleman. At the same moment the rock opened, the water gushed out, and the black sheep turned white. But his fourth homicide lying heavy on his soul, the murderer returned to the monk to learn how he could expiate his latest crime. But the holy man reassured him. "The gentleman whom you killed," said he, "offended God more than you by his professions. Your penance has been shortened; no expiation is required." So the repentant sinner was able to pass the rest of his days in peace and quietness.[1]

The same story is told, with some variations of detail, in the Ukraine:

There was a man and his wife, and they had a son. One day they dreamed that when their son should be grown up, he would kill his father, marry his mother, and afterwards kill her also. They told each other their dream, "Well," said the father, "let us cut open his belly, put him into a barrel, and throw the barrel into the sea." They did so, and the barrel with the boy in it floated away on the sea. Some sailors found it, and hearing the squalling of a child in the barrel, they opened it, rescued the boy, sewed up his wound, and reared him. When he was grown to manhood, he bid the sailors good-bye and went away to earn his bread. He came to the house of his father, but his father did not recognize him and took him into his service. The duty laid on the son by the father was to watch the garden; and if anyone entered it, he was to challenge the intruder thrice, and if he received no answer, he was to fire on him. After the young man had served some time, his master said, "Go to, let us see whether he obeys my orders." So he entered the garden. The young man challenged him thrice, and receiving no answer, he shot him dead, and on coming up to his victim he recognized his master. Then he went to his mistress in her chamber, married her, and lived with her. One Sunday morning, when he was changing his shirt, she saw the scar on his body and asked him what it was. "When I was small," answered he, "some sailors found me at sea with my belly cut open, and they sewed it up." "Then I am your mother!" she cried. He killed her on the spot and went away. He walked and walked till he came to a priest and asked him to inflict some penance on him by way of atonement for his sins. "What are your sins?" asked the priest. He told the priest, and the priest refused him absolution. So he killed the priest and came to another priest, who, proving equally recalcitrant, was disposed of by the young man in the same summary fashion. The third priest to whom he applied was kind or prudent enough to explain to him how he might expiate his sins. "Take this staff of apple-tree wood," said the priest; "plant it on yonder mountain, and morning and evening go to it on your knees with your mouth full of water, and water the staff. When it shall have sprouted and the apples on it are ripe, then shake it; as soon as the apples shall have fallen, your sins will be forgiven you." After twenty-five years, the staff budded and the apples ripened. The sinner, no longer young, shook the tree, and all the apples fell but two. So he returned and reported to the priest. "Very good," said the priest, "I will throw you into a well." He was as good as his word, and when the sinner was at the bottom of the well, the priest shut down the iron trap door, locked it, covered it up with earth, and threw the keys into the sea. Thirty years passed, and one day, the priest's fishermen caught a jack, cut it open, and found the keys in its belly. They brought the keys to the priest. "Ah!" said the priest laconically, "my man is saved." They ran at once to the well, and on opening it they found the sinner dead, but with a taper burning above his body. Thus all his sins were forgiven and he was gathered to the saints in bliss.[2]

The same double crime of parricide and incest with a mother, both committed in ignorance, occurs in a very savage story which the Javanese of the Residency of Pekalongan tell to account for the origin of the Kalangs, an indigenous tribe of Java. In it a woman, who is a daughter of a sow, marries her son unwittingly and the son kills a dog, who is really his father, though the man is ignorant of the relation in which he stands to the animal. In one version of the story the woman has twin sons by the dog, and afterwards unwittingly marries them both; finally she recognizes one of her sons by the scar of a wound which she had formerly inflicted on his head with a wooden spoon.[3] According to the Javanese, such incestuous unions are still not uncommon among the Kalangs: mother and son often live together as man and wife, and the Kalangs think that worldly prosperity and riches flow from these marriages.[4] However, it is to be observed that the story of the descent of the Kalangs from a dog and a pig is not told by the people themselves, but by the Javanese, who apparently look down with contempt on the Kalangs as an inferior race. Similar stories of descent from a dog and a pig are commonly told of alien races in the Indian Archipelago, and they are usually further embellished by accounts of incest practised by the ancestors of these races in days gone by. For example, the Achinese of Sumatra tell such a tale of the natives of the Nias, an island lying off the west coast of Sumatra; and the natives of Bantam tell a similar story of the Dutch.[5] Probably, therefore, many stories of incest told of alien peoples, whether in the past or in the present, are no more than expressions of racial hatred and contempt, and it would be unsafe to rely upon them as evidence of an actual practice of incest among the peoples in question.

In the Middle Ages the story of Oedipus was told, with variations, of Judas Iscarioth. It is thus related in *The Golden Legend*:

There lived at Jerusalem a certain Ruben Simeon, of the race of David. His wife, Cyborea, dreamed that she gave birth to a son, who would be fatal to the family. On waking, she told her dream to her husband, who endeavoured to comfort her by saying that she had been deceived by the evil spirit. But perceiving that she was with child from that very night, she began to be very uneasy, and her husband with her. When the child was born, they shrank from killing him, but put him in a little ark and committed it to the sea. The waves washed up the ark on the shore of the island of Iscarioth. The queen of the island found it, and having no child of her own, she adopted the little foundling. But soon afterwards she was with child and gave birth to a son. When the two boys were grown up, Judas Iscarioth behaved very ill to his supposed brother, and the queen, seeing that expostulations had no effect on him, upbraided him with being a foundling. In a rage, Judas murdered his brother and took ship for Jerusalem. There he found a congenial soul in the governor of Judea, Pontius Pilate, who appointed him to a high office in his court. One day the governor, looking down from his balcony on the garden of a neighbour, was seized with a great longing to eat some apples which he saw hanging from the boughs. The obsequious Judas hastened to gratify his master's desire by procuring, not to say stealing, the apples. But the old man who owned the garden, and who chanced to be no other than Judas's father, resisted the attempt, and Judas knocked him on the head with a stone. As one good turn deserves another, the governor rewarded Judas by bestowing on him the property of the deceased, together with the hand of his widow, who was no other than Cyborea, the mother of Judas. Thus it came about that Judas, without knowing it, killed his father and married his mother. Still the widow, now again a wife, was not consoled, and one day Judas found her sighing heavily. When he questioned her as to the reason of her sadness, she replied, "Wretch that I am, I drowned my son, my husband is dead, and in my affliction Pilate gave me in marriage against my will." The answer set Judas thinking, and a few more questions elicited the melancholy truth. Struck with remorse and anxious to comfort his mother, Judas flung himself at the feet of Christ, confessed his sins, and became his disciple. But being entrusted with the bag, he allowed his old evil nature to get the better of him, with the tragical consequences with which we are all familiar.[6] This monkish legend may have been concocted by a mediaeval writer who, having read the story of Oedipus, turned it to the purpose of edification by casting a still deeper shade of infamy on the character of the apostate and traitor.

It has been argued that traditions of incest, of which the Oedipus legend is only one instance out of many, are derived from a former custom of incestuous unions among mankind, such as some inquirers believe to have prevailed at an early period in the evolution of society.[7] But this interpretation, like another which would explain the legend as a solar myth,[8] appears to be somewhat far-fetched and improbable.

NOTES

[1]L. Constans, *La légende d'Oedipe* (Paris, 1881), pp. 106–108. The story is told more briefly by Gustav Meyer, in his preface to E. Schreck's *Finnische Märchen* (Weimar, 1887), p. xxv., referring to Erman's *Archiv*, xvii. 14 *sqq.*

[2]Eugene Hins, "Légendes chrétiennes de l'Oukraine," *Revue des Traditions Populaires*, iv. (1889), pp. 117 *sq.*, from *Traditions et Contes populaires de la petite Russie*, by Michel Dragomanof.

[3]E. Ketjen, "De Kalangers," *Tidjschrift voor Indische Taal-, Land- en Volkenkunde*, xxiv. (1877), pp. 430–435.

[4]E. Ketjen, *op. cit.* p. 427.

[5]J.C. van Eerde, "De Kalanglegende op Lombok," *Tijdschrift voor Indische Taal-, Land- en Volkenkunde*, xlv. (1902), pp. 30 *sq.*

[6]L. Constans, *La légende d'Oedipe*, pp. 95–97.

[7]L.J.B. Bérenger-Feraud, *Superstitions et Survivances*, iii. (Paris, 1896), pp. 467–514.

[8]This explanation of the story of Oedipus, put forward by the French scholar Michel Bréal, has been criticized and rightly rejected by Domenico Comparetti in his essay, *Edipo e la Mitologia Comparata* (Pisa, 1867). It was not to be expected that the parricidal and incestuous Oedipus should escape the solar net in which Sir George Cox caught so many much better men. According to him, Oedipus was the sun, his father Laius was the darkness of night, and his mother Jocasta was the violet-tinted sky; while his daughter Antigone may have been, as M. Bréal thought, "the light which sometimes flushes the eastern sky as the sun sinks to sleep in the west." Thus the old tragic story of crime and sorrow is wiped out, and an agreeable picture of sunrise and sunset is painted, in roseate hues, on the empty canvas. See Sir George W. Cox, *The Mythology of the Aryan Nations* (London, 1882), pp. 312 *sqq.*

Oedipus in Alur Folklore

A. W. Southall

Although this tale has an Oedipal theme, it does not belong to the Oedipus tale type. The complicity of the mother is noteworthy. The tale was reported from Uganda by anthropologist A.W. Southall of the University of Wisconsin.

There was a youth called Uken. He was having playful argument with his mother. "Now you are old, mother," said he. "But was I not a girl once too?" countered his mother, "surely if I dressed up the men would look at me still!" "Really, mother," answered Uken, "you who are all old now, who do you think would look at you?" Now when his mother heard what he said, his words sank deep in her heart. The next morning Uken was exchanging promises with a girl friend, and the girl promised that she would come to him that day. Then Uken's mother devised a trick. She stripped off all her old skin and there she was with complexion as clear as long ago when she had been a girl. By the time the youth came back from his walk it was night. He found his mother lying on his sleeping place. She was beautiful from head to foot, glistening with the oil she had used to anoint her body, and wearing beads of many kinds.[1] There she was lying relaxed on the sleeping place. So when her son came and entered the hut his eye lit up at the thought that perhaps the girl who had made him promises had really come. And so he lay with his

Reprinted from the *Uganda Journal,* 22 (1958), 167–169.

mother that night. At first light his mother went out and left him on the bed. She returned to her hut and put on her old skin. Then when morning came Uken got up and went to his mother's hut to ask her for food. She said "Your mother, your mother, just now you were lying with your mother there—did you know that you have a mother?" When Uken heard his mother speaking to him in this way, rage seized him and he went back to his hut without a word. Next he got out his spear and his arrows. He whetted their blades keenly. Then he set out aimlessly into the bush, with his horn to his lips blowing on it the while.

> "Mother, you have dishonoured me, mother you have
> dishonoured me.
> To whom will my wife fall now? Mother you have
> dishonoured me.
> To whom will my child fall now? Mother you have
> dishonoured me.
> To whom will my granary fall now? Mother you have
> dishonoured me."

So he went far away. He went and found a great tree, then he planted his spear and his arrows in the ground under the tree. And after that he climbed to the top of the tree and threw himself down on to the spear and it stabbed him to death. When he had died, then his body began to decay and when it had decayed completely, mushrooms sprouted from the spot. An old woman came to uproot the mushrooms and they said to her "Ah! uproot us gently! Don't just break us!" Then old woman uprooted the mushrooms and returned to her village with them. The mushrooms said "Don't cook us! just store us away in a pot." So the old woman stored them in a pot. Then the mushrooms rotted and bore maggots. The maggots changed into flies. The flies changed into baby rats, and those rats into a big mother rat. Then the rat turned into a baby boy. The child began to grow bonny until slowly he began to walk. The old woman was rearing him on cow's milk. He grew up and began to herd cattle. Little by little Uken became a youth just as he had been before. When Uken saw that he was full grown he began to consider: "What shall I do to make my people recognize me?" He told the old woman to brew beer, then he held a dance. This dance gathered together many people and his own folk also came to it. Then, when the dance was in full swing, Uken began to blow his horn, singing:

> "Mother you have dishonoured me, Mother you have
> dishonoured me.
> To whom will my wife fall now? Mother you have
> dishonoured me.
> To whom will my child fall now? Mother you have
> dishonoured me.
> To whom will my granary fall now? Mother you have
> dishonoured me."

When the people of Uken's home heard the way he blew his horn they said "But this child is like our child Uken." Then they told him that he should go back with them, but he refused and said "If you want me to go back with you to our home, you just go and kill my mother and I will go back with you tomorrow." Then those people went back and killed Uken's mother. The next day they came back to the dance. When the sun set and the dance was over they went back with Uken to their home and the old woman who had brought him up went with him also.

This story was told by Juliano Nanu the son of Bazilio of Panyidwar lineage in the sub-county of Angal, Okoro County, West Nile district, in July 1950.

Being a strongly patrilineal society, with authority concentrated in the hands of the father, the expression of the Oedipus complex in Alur folklore will cause no surprise. A few divergencies from the classical Greek form of the myth are worth noting. The essentials of the Oedipus story in the Homeric myth were that, through a series of coincidences which were both fatal and tragic in the original meaning of these words, Oedipus unwittingly killed his father and married his mother Jocasta. When he discovered the awful truth he put out his own eyes. Freud adopted this myth as the nearest counterpart of what he considered to be the nucleus of all neuroses and the fount of religion, morals, society and art. It represented the simultaneous existence of love and hate for the same object, the sexual rivalry with the father, whose death opens the way for the fulfilment of incestuous desires towards the mother, and the remorse occasioned by these feelings.

For Freud it was immaterial that Oedipus only discovered afterwards the identity of the father whom he had killed and the mother with whom he had been living. But the story of Uken departs even further from the orthodox pattern. We hear nothing of the existence of Uken's father, and Uken himself is tricked not by a tragic coincidence but by the purposeful action of his mother into sleeping with her. It therefore seems more like a case of a Jocasta complex.

Uken never falls in love with his mother as a person, in the way that Oedipus does, he simply makes a horrible mistake in the dark. After he has secured his revenge on his mother, the episode ends happily, for the Alur version seems to exonerate the son and put the whole blame on the mother.

It is in the light of these shifts of emphasis that the comparative study of folklore among the people of Uganda could be most rewarding. It is a great mistake to think that because a particular story has been recorded from one group there is no value in recording it from another. On the contrary, there is more to be gained from relating minor variations in the same story to other associated factors, than in collecting endless different stories for their own sake. What is the story of Oedipus-Uken in Buganda, Teso or Ankole?

NOTES

[1] *apaya, sinda* and *wang ujwiny* beads.

Oedipus in Bushman Folklore

Megan Biesele

This tale was collected from the !Kung, who are a linguistic subdivision of the San (formerly called the Bushmen) who inhabit the Kalahari. The narrator was !Kun/obe N!a of Kauri, Ngamiland, Botswana. She is a Naron woman married to a !Kung husband.

The central character is Kauha, a trickster figure. We present here the concluding portion of a longer narrative which consists largely of tricks played upon Kauha by his wives and vice versa. For more details about the Bushmen, see Elizabeth Marshall Thomas, The Harmless People *(New York, 1958), Lorna Marshall,* !Kung of Nyae Nyae *(Cambridge, Mass., 1976), and Richard Lee,* !Kung San *(Cambridge, 1979). For an introduction to Bushman folklore, see Megan Biesele's essay in Richard Lee and Irven DeVore, eds.,* Kalahari Hunter-Gatherers: Studies of the !Kung San and Their Neighbors *(Cambridge, Mass., 1976), pp. 302–324.*

The wives lived in discontent for some time. Kauha was satisfied and fed them well, but they were discontented just the same. One day one of the wives said "I think I'll go visit my family." Kauha refused, and said "No, you're not: we're staying here. Why should we go visit them—they never visit us." So they stayed. But the wife

Reprinted from Marguerite Anne Biesele, "Folklore and Ritual of !Kung Hunter-Gatherers," unpublished doctoral dissertation in anthropology, Harvard University, 1975, Vol. I, pp. 266–270.

grew restless. "How can I get away?" she wondered. One day when Kauha and his son went hunting, she simply ran off alone. The other wife sat in the camp alone and waited for her husband to return.

The wife who had left did not return. The other wife stayed at the camp alone, waiting for her husband. He was off hunting but he did not bring home anything for her to eat. Hunger began to work upon her, and she grew very thin. Soon she had no fat on her buttocks—they were nothing but skin.

One day Kauha killed a fat eland far from his camp, and came home at last to bring the news. "Hai? Where's my other wife?" he asked. "Oh, she's left," sniffed the wife who had stayed. "And you?" asked Kauha, "why do you look so terrible?" "Hunger, obviously," she replied. "Well, if you're going to look like this I'm leaving," said Kauha. "You're probably just starving yourself so you'll have an excuse to leave me and run after other men. I'm leaving, and you'll just have to sit here. I'm not interested in a woman who's so thin. You're awfully thin and ugly and you don't interest me at all." With that, Kauha took his son and began packing up their belongings. The wife just sat there. Kauha packed all his things into a string carrying bag. As they were leaving, his son put out his hand and drew his mother to her feet. "Please, mother, follow us, I beg you," he said. So she walked secretly behind them when they left.

After they had walked a long while, father and son sat down to rest. The son sneaked to where his mother was and found her a comfortable place to sit. Kauha rested and ate something and then they traveled further. After a while the son asked his father "Are we almost there?" "Don't worry—the meat is there. We'll come to it," answered Kauha.

When they came to the dead eland, Kauha and his son began cutting it up right away. Kauha skinned it and broke its body open. Then he took out its intestines. He dipped out the chyme with his cupped hands and dumped it on the ground. He was still dipping out the chyme when his son said to him "Father, let me take the chyme and throw it away for you. I want to watch the dung beetles eat it." (The son wanted the chyme to smooth on the ground for his mother, so she would have a nice place to sit.) So the father gave it to him and the child sat his mother upon it. Then he came back. "Father!" he said, "Won't you give me that bit of fat so I can watch the dung beetles eat it?" Kauha cut out the piece of fat for him and he went and gave it to his mother to eat. The son went back and forth between his father and his mother. He spent the whole day taking bits of food to his mother one by one. He and his father would eat a little and then he would take something like the bladder and go to his mother. "I'm going to go play with the dung beetles and eat my meat over there," the son would say. Then he would go give whatever it was to his mother.

At last the sun hung low in the sky. Kauha said "Since it's so late already, I think we'll just go to sleep and wait until morning to fetch water." "All right," said the son. He went and told his mother. Then they all went to sleep. The wife slept in one place and her husband and son slept together not far away. In the night the son went to check on his mother several times. In the morning Kauha went off to fetch water, leaving his son in their new camp. When he was gone, the son told his mother to come sit with him in the camp. Today she was fat, and *very* beautiful! She sat with her son in the camp as if she were a lovely python girl.

When a little time had passed, Kauha returned and saw her. "Hai? Is this my son who's sitting with such a beautiful woman? Who can it be?" he asked his son, "Has your mother returned?" "Yes, mother has come," he answered. "What has she been eating that makes her look so good?" "I don't know: she looked like this when she got here," he said.

Kauha dropped his water containers and ran to his wife. He climbed on top of her and right away he began screwing her very hard. Her son cried "Hey! Didn't you nearly kill my mother with hunger, and then abandon her so that I had to feed her myself? Who do you think made her beautiful again? If you think you're going to screw her now, I'll fix you!" Kauha was still lying on top of his wife and refused to get off. "Father, give me your axe so I can sharpen it and eat the eland bones," said his son. "Hand me the whetstone too." All the while Kauha lay on top of his wife and continued to screw her. Suddenly . . . (snap!). The boy had chopped his father in two with the axe! He did it to get him off his mother. (He no longer wanted his mother to be his mother: he wanted to marry her.) Then he lifted up his father's body. He took the top half and threw it one way and threw the bottom half the other way. "When did *you* suddenly grow up?" asked his mother, as she sat up.

"Will you make a fire so we can warm ourselves, mother?" he asked. "Certainly, my son." "I'm not 'your son' any more." "Well, what am I going to call you now? How about 'my little brother'?"

But he refused that name too. "My nephew?" But he refused again. "What am I going to call this child?" she wondered out loud. "My husband?" (Snap!) That was all he wanted. He jumped up and ran to the fire. He was looking for *tutus*, these little black insects that smell bad and crawl around near the fire. When he saw some he lay down in their midst. He wanted them to bite his penis so it would swell up and he would be able to do what he wanted. Well, the *tutus* bit him nearly to death. His penis swelled up until it was enormous. It was so big he couldn't take his mother with it. He had spoiled his own chances! The things that went on long ago. . . . ! This is what the old people tell, and this is what I have heard.

Oedipus in Papuan Folklore

F.E. Williams

Here is an Oedipal story from the Papuans of New Guinea. The characters in the tale include Kambel, who is also known by other names, including Gainjain, his wife Yumar, and his son Gufa. Kambel is the Papuan Originator who lived in the gainjan time, the time of the beginning of the world. The story does not belong to the Oedipus tale type. For further consideration of the rationale for ritual homosexuality as a means to promote phallic growth in young men, see Alan Dundes, "A Psychoanalytic Study of the Bullroarer," in Interpreting Folklore *(Bloomington, 1980), p. 196. For an appreciation of F.E. Williams (1893–1943) who served as "government anthropologist" in Papua from 1922 to 1943, see Erik G. Schwimmer, "F.E. Williams as Ancestor and Rainmaker," in Francis Edgar Williams,* "The Vailala Madness" and Other Essays *(Honolulu, 1977), pp. 11–47.*

Gufa, despite good feeding and attention, was a wretched undersized little boy, described as pot-bellied and constipated. He was the despair of his father until one day, ostensibly with the sole idea of promoting his growth, he conceived the idea of sodomizing him. He took him apart from his mother during the night and put his idea into effect, rubbing semen over the child's body.[1] The result was a

Reprinted from F.E. Williams, *Papuans of the Trans-Fly* (Oxford, 1936), pp. 308–309, 312–314.

miraculous increase in growth. The boy was instructed to keep this a dead secret from his mother, and when she next saw him she was delighted at the change but attributed it wrongly to the good food which Kambel must have given him, just as nowadays mothers are supposed to attribute the size of initiates to the special feeding they have had at the *waramongo*[2]. . . .

Kambel once went to work in his garden leaving his wife and son alone in their village. During his absence Gufa entered Yumar's house and saw her lying asleep without her skirt. His passions were aroused and he woke his mother up and had connection with her. Then he went off into the bush.

When Kambel returned he also wished to approach Yumar, but found evidence that some one had been with her shortly before. He suspected his son and decided to hide and watch for further developments. In due course he saw Gufa return and repeat his offence, and allowed him to go off without interfering. He then charged his wife with infidelity and she answered, "You fool, to leave me here alone! Your son has possessed me!"[3]

Kambel now proceeds to his revenge. He takes a taro of the kind called *bonjikaka*, cooks it, and affects to share it with his son. He refrains from eating his own share, but Gufa eats his and dies in consequence. Then Kambel goes off to his garden.

The dog Natekari has meanwhile missed the boy Gufa and gone in search of him. Natekari was the first possessor of a *moin*, or crocodile tooth, such as has since been used by many Keraki sorcerers. Now he has swallowed it and shot it forth from his body and, following its lead, is thus brought to Kambel sitting in the garden. Natekari in this *gainjan* time has the power of speech and he immediately accuses Kambel of having done his son to death, and tells him to give up the pretence of weeping. Kambel is alarmed. Taking some feathers of the owl (*burere*) he stuffs them into the dog's ears, and transfixes its tongue with a cassowary quill. Then he cries "Now you know me for what I am! Go and tell Yumar!" Natekari speeds off, bursting with his news of what Kambel had done to Gufa and, when he opens his mouth to tell it to Yumar, emits only the howl of a dog. Since that time dogs have lost the power of speech.

But Gufa has in the meantime come to life again. He leaves Kuramangu and goes to his maternal uncle in the Kaunje tribe. His *bava* asks why he has come and the boy answers, "My father hit me." But when asked why his father has so treated him he refuses to answer. His *bava* then tells him to go back and Gufa obeys.

When Gufa shows himself again at Kuramangu Kambel exclaims "Why have you come back? You are dead," and then in his annoyance turns his back and will not speak further. But presently, planning his second revenge, he alters his manner and pretends to welcome his son. He gives him a coco-nut to drink and goes off ostensibly to prepare food. But while the food is cooking he digs a pit and covers it with one of the huge *woratar* leaves. Then he places the food on top of the leaf and summons Gufa to sit down and eat. As the boy does so the leaf collapses; he is thrown into the pit and there speedily buried by his father. From this second death Gufa does not rise.[4]

Kambel waits awhile and hears the spirit of Gufa going down to the sea. But some time after, while he sits brooding over what has happened, a little *siroro* bird comes and perches overhead, crying, "Sirorororo!" It is Gufa's spirit returned and trying to talk; but he can no longer speak intelligibly. Kambel, unrepentant, looks up and answers, "Good! You are finished now. It was your fault!" And the little bird flies away.

After the death of her son, Yumar went away to the west. One version implies that she departed in grief and anger at her son's death, leaving Kambel behind; another that she waited and waited for her husband, and when he did not return from the garden finally went in search of him. At any rate she left Kuramangu, carrying with her a bag filled with every kind of yam and taitu. Thus she travelled farther and farther, singing a mournful song as she went, until she reached the Morehead River, at Garechita or Saraiam.

Meanwhile Kambel had risen into the sky and followed. Overtaking her at Garechita he attracted her attention by making a faint noise, "sip, sip," and there descended, greeting her affectionately with a "kiss," i.e., by placing her face against hers in a gesture called *tegerua*. He bade her leave some of the most important yams and taitu in the west, and bring back the remainder with her to Kuramangu.

This is the last we hear of Kambel and his wife on earth. Informants are rather vague as to his ultimate end. Some declare that he died and was buried at Kuramangu; but despite this rationalistic version he is also identified with the moon, Bangi (sharing that character, and the name also, with his son Wambuwambu), and it is said that when he travelled through the sky after his wife towards the west he was really pursuing her in her character of Eram, the sun.

NOTES

[1]Gambadi informants describe the initial occasion more vividly. The father bids his son stoop to drink at a pool and as he does so catches him at a disadvantage.

[2]It is to be noted that nowadays boys are not sodomized by their own fathers. The restriction of moiety exogamy is observed in sodomy as it is in marriage, Bangu consorting with Sangara and *vice versa.*

[3]The mother is represented as fully consenting to incest with her son. In one Gambadi version the son sits in front of his mother while she plaits the grass streamers in his hair and his desire is roused. He then makes an assignation with her for the evening and she waits "trembling and with cold hands. Will he come or not?"In another she is actually the temptress. Admiring the size of the boy after initiation she asks him to lie with her, saying that her husband is too old.

[4]In a Gambadi version the son actually has his head cut off in the first death. In the second he is killed by sorcery, his father causing a black snake to bite him.

The Dragon of Tagaung

R. Grant Brown

The following text from Burma was evidently not easy to elicit. R. Grant Brown's engaging account of his fieldwork including a search for someone brave enough to tell the story suggests that some informants may not feel comfortable relating incest tales to inquiring outsiders. Brown, a British magistrate and revenue officer in Burma from 1889 to 1917, makes no comment whatsoever about the tale's incestuous content, confining himself instead to speculations concerning a possible thematic parallel to the poison damsel element in the book of Tobit. (For Brown's discussion of this parallel, see his "The Pre-Buddhist Religion of the Burmese," Folk-Lore, 32 (1921), 77-100 (esp. pp. 92-94). For the poison damsel motif, see N.M. Penzer, Poison-Damsels and other essays in folklore and anthropology (London, 1952), pp. 3-71.)

The text is also of interest because of its use of a "neck riddle." The queen makes hairpins and a pillow from the body of her slain dragon husband and then asks the hero to guess the answer to a riddle based on her actions. This would seem to be an example of motif H 805, Riddle of the murdered lover, in Stith Thompson, Motif-Index of Folk-Literature, 6 vols. (Bloomington, 1955-1958). The riddle may be related to the famous Ilo neck riddle, one text of which is "I sat wi' my love, and I drank wi' my love, / And my love she gave me light; / I'll give any man a pint o' wine / That'll read my

Reprinted from the *Journal of the Royal Asiatic Society of Great Britain and Ireland*, (1917), 741-751.

riddle aright." [Answer: *I sat in a chair made of my mistress's bones,
drank out of her skull, and was lighted by a candle made of the
substance of her body.*] *For numerous Ilo texts, see Roger Abrahams,* Between the Living and the Dead, *Folklore Fellows Communications 225 (Helsinki, 1980), pp. 59-68. For an analysis of how the
solving of riddles in folktales leads to winning a spouse with a
particular reference to the Oedipus story, see Lowell Edmunds,* The
Sphinx in the Oedipus Legend, *Beiträge zur klassischen Philologie,
127 (Königstein/Ts., 1981), reprinted in this volume. For the psychological significance of Oedipus stories in Burma, see Melford E.
Spiro, "The Oedipus Complex in Burma,"* Journal of Nervous and
Mental Disease, *157 (1973), 389-395. In this essay (also reprinted in
this volume), Spiro discusses a version of the tale presented here but
a much less explicit one.*

Tagaung lies on the Irrawaddy River 124 miles north of Mandalay in lat. 23° 30', long. 96° 2', and is regarded by the Burmese
generally as their most ancient capital.[1] There are remains of other
cities in the neighbourhood, and to at least one of these, Tonngè,
local tradition assigns a still greater antiquity.

The Maha Yazawin, or royal chronicle, records that Dhajaraja,
a king of Sakya race, conquered Tagaung in the sixth century before
Christ and married its queen, Nagachinna.[2]

At the south end of the present village, in a grove of banyan-
trees, is the shrine of Bodawdyi, "The Great Father." A huge log
rises from the ground, the upper part of it carved into a head
measuring, with the headdress, over 4 feet in height, and covered
with gold-leaf. Over this a wooden building is erected, a small room
being provided for the image while the rest is left for worshippers.
The features are grotesque in the extreme: bulging eyes, a long-
bridged nose with exaggerated nostrils, a very short chin, and no
mouth. Between the eyes, one below another, are three leaf-like
ornaments curling forwards and suggestive of a dragon's crest.
Below the chin is what may be the conventional representation of a
beard. The ears are also conventional, somewhat in the shape of
tails. The headdress is a five-storied tiara.

Before the annexation a *nattein*, or guardian, was regularly
appointed by the local representative of the king, but the office has

fallen into abeyance, and the image is now looked after by the headman's wife and another woman. An annual festival in its honour is also extinct. Once a year, however, the doors, which are at other times always locked except on such an occasion as my visit, are thrown open, and adults permitted to see the image (if they dare to look) and make offerings to it. Children are not allowed to see it at any time, lest its grotesque features cause their sense of humour to overcome their fear, and the god be offended. The headman's wife who opened the door for me averted her face, and when asked the usual question, who the spirit was in life, said she did not know, an answer plainly dictated by fear. Villagers take off their shoes or dismount from their ponies when passing the shrine, and it is said that those who omit to do so are thrown violently to the ground, their fall being followed by vomiting and sometimes death.

At a shrine at Myadaung, some miles upstream, where Bodawdyi is worshipped, I tried to find out who he was, but was told I should hear all about him at Tagaung. Now that I was at Tagaung itself it seemed the very last place to obtain information on the subject, and none of those who accompanied me from other parts of Burma could tell me anything. I directed a search to be made for some one who was not afraid to tell the story, and at last a brave man was found, a fishery lessee of the name of Maung Ka. He came to my launch, and told the following tale.

"There came from the land of Thingatha[3] six brothers of royal birth, and founded the city of Tonngè and afterwards that of Tagaung. One of the brothers, Thado Saw, became king of Tagaung, and his queen was Kin Saw U. Now the foundation-post[4] of the palace was brought from Momeik, and from a knot in it sprang a dragon,[5] which took the form of a man; and he was loved by the queen, and slew her husband with a prick from his poisoned fang, and the king's brother Thado Pya reigned in his stead, and took Kin Saw U to wife. But he also was slain by the dragon, and likewise all the rest of the brothers in turn. Then Tagaung was a kingdom without a king, and the ministers sought for a king, and sent out a magic car[6] to bring him. Now Kin Saw U had a son Pauk Tyaing, who was lost in the forest when a boy, and was brought up by Po Byu and Mè I. His foster-parents would have taught him his letters, but he was too dull to learn aught but these sayings from them[7]:

> Thwa: ba mya: 'kǎyi: yauk.
> Me: ba mya: zǎga: ya..
> Mǎ eik mǎ ne ǎthet she.
> Keep going, if you want to get anywhere.
> Ask questions, if you want to learn.
> Wake, if you want to live long.

"With this learning Pauk Tyaing set out in obedience to the first precept, and he was met by the magic car and taken to the palace and offered the kingdom. But he bethought him of the second, and asked what had become of the former kings and husbands of Kin Saw U; and he learnt that the reason of their death was unknown, but each one had the mark of a single tooth upon him. And he waited seven days, and accepted the kingdom and Kin Saw U as his queen. Then the dragon came to him in the night to kill him like the others, but he was awake and ready for him in accordance with the third precept, and slew him with his sword. So the dragon became a *nat*,[8] and is worshipped under the name of Bodawdyi, "the Great Father.""

"Then the queen made hairpins of the beast's backbone, and a pillow of his skin. And she paid a thousand pieces for stripping off the skin, and a hundred for making the pillow; and she asked her husband this riddle, and they made covenant that she was to die if he guessed it, and he if he could not:—

> 'Taung pe : lo . 'sok.
> Ya pe : lo . chok.
> Chit-tè . lu ayo : sado : lok.
> Give a thousand for flaying :
> Give a hundred for binding :
> Hairpins of the loved one's bones.

"Seven days were given to Pauk Tyaing to guess the meaning of this riddle. Now his foster-parents had come in search of him, and rested beneath a banyan-tree near the palace. And they heard a crow say to her mate (for they understood the language of birds), "For to-day we have enough, but to-morrow where shall we get our food?" to which he replied, "Be not anxious. To-morrow Pauk Tyaing will die, being unable to guess the queen's riddle, and there will be a great feast." And he told her the riddle and its answer. Then fear filled the hearts of Po Byu and Mè I, and they hastened to the palace, where they found their foster-son and told him what they had overheard from the crows. So he gave the true answer to the riddle, and lived: yet he spared the queen, and she bore him sons, called Maha Thanbawa and Sula Thanbawa, whom the emanation[9] of the dragon within her womb caused to be born blind. They, when they became youths, were set adrift on a raft down the river; and upon it they caught an ogress stealing their food,[10] and she gave them their sight because they spared her life. At last they reached the place where is now the city of Prome. Here lived as a hermit Maung Dwe, brother of the queen Kin Saw U, and his daughter Ma Be Da by a *thamin*[11] doe, which had conceived by lapping that which ran from the hermit's body. And because it was not right that a woman should be seen at a hermit's dwelling he sent her every day to the river to fill with water a gourd having a hole no bigger than could be made by a needle. Here the young men met her, and enlarged the hole, so that Ma Be Da returned early to her father. And he questioned her, and heard the reason, and he sent for the youths, and knew that they were his kin, and gave the elder his daughter in marriage. Thereafter Maha Thambawa founded the city of Tharekittara,[12] and his brother was king after him when he died, and he also took Ma Be Da to be his queen."

The story narrated above is said to be told in the Tagaung *yazawin*, or history. If such a history exists in writing I have not been able to find it. In the *Maha Yazawin*, or State History of Burma, there is merely a passing reference to a king who rid the country of evil beasts. In any case I prefer to give such legends precisely as they come from the mouth of one of the local people, as the style of narration is more piquant and graphic than in the written histories, even if the latter do not suppress or gloss over the more primitive details, which are of course the most interesting to an anthropologist. The legend, despite its importance, is not given in the *Upper Burma Gazetteer* or the gazetteer of the district. Bodawdyi is not even allowed a place in the list of thirty-seven *nats* in the *Upper Burma Gazetteer* and Sir Richard Temple's sumptuous volume. He is quite distinct from the Bodaw of Mandalay and Taungbyon, who was put to death by King Nawrata in the eleventh century. The legend of the wicked queen and her dragon paramour is, however, very well known, and I heard it many years before my visit to Tagaung. A version of it, which I had not seen when the above was written, appears in Mr. Taw Sein Ko's *Burmese Sketches* (pp. 146–9). The author says in a footnote: "The Nagas play an important part in Burmese folklore. They are represented as huge serpents; but as a matter of fact they are the indigenous Naga races inhabiting the country." There may be some connection between the two, and it is possible that historically the queen's paramour may have been a man of Naga race; but no evidence is adduced, and the name Naga for the people now occupying the country between the upper reaches of the Chindwin and Assam is unknown to the Burmese, who call them Chins, though the Chins are quite a distinct race. The late Mr. Colston, I.C.S., in an interesting version or rather interpretation of the legend (*Journal of the Royal Society of Arts*, June 10, 1910, p. 709), was equally positive. "In Burma each pagoda had its own history, which had been carefully written up, and incorporated much legend with popular facts, which were unattainable in the formal histories of the country. These pagoda histories, known as *Thamaings*, had a remarkable characteristic in common, that they represented the people as moving down the country, colonizing it from India through the mountains, instead of moving up through the mouths of the rivers according to the version of immigration which was generally accepted. The most important legend connected with these Thamaings was that of Maung Pauk Gyaing,[13] which revolved, like other Burmese legends, round the old city of Tagaung, a city standing not in the delta, but far away on the highest reaches of the Irawadi near the barrier of hills which separates Burma from Assam (Kamarupa). In that legend, as in others, the principal actors go to India for their education. Janathedi, otherwise known as Maung Pauk Gyaing, had studied in Taxilla and came to Tagaung as an adventurer and married the queen after killing her husband, a Naga, who had followed her on her return from India through the Naga Hills, and the upshot of the tragic happenings at Tagaung was a move down the river and the colonization of the city of Prome. The name of Prome was not changed, but there were many other names in Indo-China which were of pure Indian ancestry, only to be explained by wholesale colonization."

Mr. Colston propounded the fascinating theory that the Indian colonizers of Burma were really people of Tibeto-Burman race who had overrun the plains of India and were gradually expelled therefrom. This hypothesis, which he thought was supposed by the types seen in early Buddhist sculptures, would account for both the evolution of Buddhism in India and for its almost total disappearance at a later date from the Indian plains. As regards the reference to Taxilla, Sir Richard Temple pointed out that names of places in India were often applied by these colonists to settlements in the country of their adoption, just as we have a London in Canada and a Worcester in the United States. See n.3.

The similarity of the legend in some respects to that of Asmodeus in the book of Tobit can hardly, one would think, be accidental. "In Ecbatane, a city of Media, Sara, the daughter of Raguel, was also reproached by her father's maids because that she had been married to seven husbands, whom Asmodeus, the evil spirit, had killed, before they had lain with her." (Tobit, iii, 7, 8). Maung Pauk Tyaing's part is there played by Tobit's son Tobias, who, when advised by the angel Raphael to marry his cousin Sara, demurred on account of the death of his seven predecessors. Raphael told him to take the heart and liver of a fish and make a smoke with it on the ashes of perfume, "and the devil shall smell it, and flee away, and never come again any more" (v. 17). These instructions Tobias carried out with complete success. "The which smell when the evil spirit had smelled, he fled into the utmost parts of Egypt, and the angel bound him" (viii, 3). The legend and the name of Asmodeus, which appear to be of Babylonian origin, are fully dealt with in the *Jewish Encyclopedia*, pp. 217–20.

NOTES

[1]See *Upper Burma Gazetteer*, vol. ii, pt. i, p. 193. A warning is necessary here. Mr. Duroiselle, Epigraphist to the Government of Burma, informs me that the stone inscription mentioned in the passage cited is a myth, the invention of a German archaeologist, Dr. Führer, who was removed from Government service for a similar hoax in India. Some tablets have been found similar to those in Pagan, but they contain no inscriptions.

[2]See n.5. The meaning of "chinna" can only be conjectured.

[3]"Saṅkassain, name of a town in India." (Childers, Pali Dict.). Mr. Duroiselle tells me it is "the name of a city in the north-west of India, only traces of which now

exist." It was a common practice, however, among Indian immigrant settlers to name towns founded by them in Burma after their former homes, and the place referred to may be a town in Burma which has disappeared. The name is not given in the *Imperial Gazetteer*.

⁴Burmese *u: yu daing*. I call it foundation-post (for want of a better term) because it is the post which, when a monastery or other public building is erected, is always set up first and dedicated to the guardian spirit of the building, offerings of fruit and flowers being placed on its summit. Doubtless it was under this post that a human victim was once buried in the case of important buildings (see Sir Richard Temple's article "Burma" in the *Encyclopaedia of Religion and Ethics*, p. 26). Every house, however, has its *uyudaing*. "In the houses of some Burmese families cocoanuts with a fillet of white muslin or red cloth tied round them are suspended by a cane support from a special post called the *uyudaing*. The Burmans have forgotten the origin of *uyu*, but the word or its synonym *kun* is still used in the Chin language to signify the guardian spirit of a family" (Taw Sein Ko, *Burmese Sketches*, p. 159). See also Stevenson's Burmese Dictionary, s.v.

⁵Burmese *nagá*, Pali and Sanskrit *nāga*. "Dragon" is properly, perhaps, a winged serpent, but the word is used as a synonym for "serpent" in Ps. xci and Rev. xx, 2. Snake-worship, whether indigenous or imported with Northern Buddhism, was prevalent in Burma at least up to the eleventh century, and survives in many practices, of which the homage paid to the image at Tagaung is the most remarkable. It will already have been guessed that the Great Father is none other than the dragon. "Among the Buddhists the Nâgas were counted as gods, ranking eighth in the list of beings." (Sir George Grierson's review of Winternitz on Snake Worship, *Ind. Ant.*, February, 1890).

⁶The Burmese expression is *p'okthwin: yat'a:*, which appears to mean a car (*yat'a:*, Pali *ratho*) used at the conjunction (*thwin:*) of the moon with the constellation Phussa (*p'ok*). The Pali compound *phussaratho* is used to mean merely a ceremonial car or pleasure-carriage.

⁷In the spelling used, which is practically that adopted by the Government of Burma, and is phonetic without any attempt at transliteration, the symbols *a, e, i, u, a, aw* have approximately the values in f*a*ther, m*e*n (F. *été* when final), mach*i*ne, r*u*de, *a*mong, s*aw*. Pronounce *th, ch, sh, ng* as in English, and *y* as in "yes." The forms *k', p', s', t'* are aspirated as in English, and *k, p, s, t* unaspirated as in French. A falling tone is indicated as in Burmese by (:), and a glottal check by (.). The level tone, as in Burmese writing, is left unmarked.

⁸Spirit. The souls of the departed do not necessarily become *nats*. They may enter other bodies or wander about as ghosts (*natsein*).

⁹Burmese *angwe.*. This interesting word seems to denote a quality in matter of permeating and influencing other matter. If bread and guavas are placed together for a time the bread will taste of guava, owing to the strong *angwe.* emitted by the guavas.

¹⁰In Burmese *bilu:ma*, a female *bilu:*. Bilus are represented in Burmese art as creatures of human form with grotesque features and tushes, and in legend as living on wild fruits and flowers and sometimes as cannibals. They are also credited with superhuman powers, and the Taungbyon Brothers, who may almost be regarded as the Burmese national heroes, are said to have been the progeny of a Muhammadan

(Arab?) and a *biluma*. See *Journal of the Royal Anthropological Institute*, July–December, 1915. It has been plausibly suggested that the word represents some race less civilized than the givers of the name. Its etymology is doubtful.

[11]The brow-antlered deer.

[12]The Pali name of the ancient city near the site of the modern Prome.

[13]The *gy* is meant to represent the sound of English *j*, and is an inconsistent attempt to preserve the Burmese spelling, which corresponds to *ky*. The modern pronunciation is neither *ky* nor *j*, but *ty*.

Oedipus-Type Tales in Oceania

William A. Lessa

When William Lessa, Professor Emeritus of Anthropology at UCLA, spent nine months on Ulithi Atoll between 1947 and 1949, he collected stories. One of these, Sikhalöl and his mother, bore a striking resemblance to the classical Greek Oedipus story. His interest piqued, he published the following essay in 1956, in which he sought to explain this apparent parallel. In his later monograph, Tales from Ulithi Atoll: A Comparative Study in Oceanic Folklore *(1961), Lessa expanded on his argument that both the Greek and the Oceanic Oedipus plots stem "ultimately from a Sargon-like progenitor." He concluded that the geographic spread of Oedipus stories in Oceania is to be explained not by independent invention (psychogenetically caused by a universal Oedipal situation) but by means of diffusion from a common source.*

The tale of Sikhalöl is one of the finest nonwestern Oedipal stories. It is one which invites comparison with European texts. Lessa reported that his informant for the tale, Melchthal, first heard the story on Mogmog early in the century, when he was a young boy, from an old man by the name of Thau. Later, the informant heard the same story several times from both men and women. Lessa remarked that "the story is told without any apparent emotion, either of approbation or condemnation." We have taken the liberty of extracting the text from Lessa's monograph and inserting

Reprinted from the *Journal of American Folklore*, 69 (1956), 63–73, and *Tales from Ulithi Atoll*, pp. 49–50.

it in his preliminary article. For Lessa's longer discussion, see his Tales from Ulithi Atoll, *Folklore Studies 13 (Berkeley and Los Angeles, 1961), pp. 172-214. For further consideration of Lessa's position, see Roger E. Mitchell, "The Oedipus Myth and Complex in Oceania with Special Reference to Truk,"* Asian Folklore Studies, *27 (1968), 131-145. For an anthropological treatment of a Micronesian text, see John L. Fischer, "A Ponapean Oedipus Tale: Structural and Sociopsychological Analysis,"* Journal of American Folklore, *79 (1966), 109-121.*

My interest in Oedipus-type tales derives from a story I collected on Ulithi Atoll which proved on closer inspection to be remarkably akin to the Greek story of Oedipus the King.[1]

A very beautiful young woman by the name of Lisòr was married to a chief by the name of Sokhsùrum. She became pregnant, and the child was born prematurely at seven months. The infant was still covered by the amniotic membrane, and the mother did not know there was a baby inside. She put the membrane in a coconut spathe and set it adrift on the ocean.

On the east end of the island, separated from the main village, there lived about ten people. One of them was Rasim, a man who had a large stone trap for catching fish. The spathe with the baby drifted against the sides of the trap and one day when Rasim went out to see if he had caught any fish he saw the infant lying on the coconut bract. He lifted it up and took it home. He then performed some magic so that it would grow up. Every day he would repeat the magic, at the same time giving the infant nourishment. This went on for many days and in a month the baby had grown to be a young man. Rasim had guessed the identity of the child from the beginning, for he knew that a girl from the village had been pregnant and had had a premature baby at the same time he had found the infant on the spathe.

Rasim made a small canoe for the youth, whose name was Sikhalòl. One day, Sikhalòl went sailing on the reef with some youths from another village. Their canoe passed by the menstrual house where his mother happened to be confined because she was menstruating. Lisór saw her son and said to herself, "Who is this handsome youth?" She waded out into the water and caught hold of the canoe, which was being pushed near shore by the wind while the boys swam playfully after it. Sikhalól told her to give him back his canoe. She told him to come over to her as she wanted to tell him something. He replied, "I cannot come ashore as I do not have on a loincloth." Lisór walked over near to him, still holding the canoe, and said, "Come and see me tonight and we shall spoon." The youth told her he did not know where she slept and Lisór told her she was staying in the menstrual house. Sikhalól said he would come. Then he sailed away with the other boys who were with him.

Sikhalól waited for darkness to fall. When nighttime arrived he went to see the beautiful young woman in the menstrual house. They made love. About four in the morning he returned to his house. These visits were repeated for several days in succession. After the tenth day, the chief, Sokhsùrum, went to see his wife at the menstrual house to find out why she was staying there so long. She did not want to return with him so she lied and said her period had not yet ended. The truth was that she wanted to continue making love with the handsome youth.

Sikhalól's foster father, Rasim, suspected that the youth was visiting a girl each night so he asked him if he had a sweetheart in the village. Sikhalól replied that he had. Rasim asked him where the woman lived and he answered that she lived in the menstrual house and was the wife of the chief. Rasim told him he was making a great mistake, for the woman was his own mother. Then he related the story of how he had removed him from the sea and raised him.

When Sikhalól went the next night to see Lisór he revealed to her that he was her son—the child she had set adrift on the sea. He said they had better stop their love-making. But his mother did not care and said they should continue, and so they did. When Sikhalól returned home in the morning he had a talk with his foster father, telling him he had spoken to his mother but that she did not care and wanted to go on making love. Rasim replied, "All right. I don't care, either." Sikhalól returned to his mother the next night and many nights thereafter, making love to her for three more months. On one of these occasions he happened to scratch her with his fingers on the side of her face.

The chief had meanwhile become very impatient with Lisòr and one day he went to see her and demanded that she leave the menstrual house, saying she was lying to him since she had been there for four months. She refused to leave, whereupon Sokhsùrum became angry, so she returned with him.

Lisòr's face still bore the scratches that she had got from Sikhalòl. She was afraid her husband might see them and guess their origin, so in order to conceal them she kept her hair, which was long, close to the sides of her face. But Sokhsùrum knew she had the scratches and had made up his mind how she had got them; therefore one day he suddenly pulled back her hair away from her face and exposed them. He demanded, "Have you been making love to someone else?" Lisòr replied, "No!"—but he did not believe her. He took a conch shell and blew it. All the men of the village assembled to see what was the matter. The chief told them to step up one by one and put their fingers near his wife's face so that he could see which ones fitted the marks. As each man did so Sokhsùrum held an ax poised to strike him down if he were the guilty one. When they had all submitted to the test he realized that none of them was responsible for the scratches.

The next day he sent word for the handful of men in the nearby village where Rasim and Sikhalòl lived to come to see him. Rasim told the men to go one at a time and return. While they were doing so, he told his foster son that he was going to teach him to wrestle, and Sikhalòl learned how to protect himself. When all the other men had completed their tests Rasim himself went and then returned. Now only his foster son was left and all the people in the little village surmised that he was the guilty one. Thinking he was about to be killed they decorated him with turmeric, arm bands and anklets of young coconut palm leaves, and a sweet basil wreath, and dressed him in a new hibiscus-banana fiber loincloth. Then they accompanied him to see the chief.

As the group approached the chief's house, Lisòr looked at Sikhalòl and began to cry. The other people sat down near the house. Sokhsùrum called over to the youth to come and put his fingers alongside his wife's face. He told him as he held up the ax that he would kill him if he were guilty. When the youth put his fingers near the scratches Sokhsùrum saw that he was the guilty one.

He began to swing the ax on Sikhalòl but the youth knew how to defend himself, for his foster father had taught him. He seized the ax and with it cut off the head of the chief—his real father.

Sikhalòl then took Lisòr back to his village, and they lived together there from then on.

Having speculated that the resemblance of this story to the Sophoclean tragedy is either (1) fortuitous, (2) the result of a universal psychological situation, or (3) the result of diffusion, I set about trying to discover what I could from a consideration of Oedipus-type tales in general. I found that aside from Europe, the Near East, and southern and southeast Asia, the story type seems to occur only in Oceania. Specifically, an examination made of several thousands of stories in connection with a broader survey of Oceanic folklore shows it to be present in twenty-three narratives from the islands of Sumatra,[2] Java,[3] Lombok,[4] Ulithi,[5] Truk,[6] Ponape,[7] Kusaie,[8] the Marshalls,[9] Kapingamarangi,[10] New Guinea,[11] and the Marquesas.[12] I am convinced that there are several more occurrences but that most of them would merely turn out to be no more than slightly differing local variants.

In the Aarne-Thompson classification of folktales the Oedipus story is labeled Type 931. The essential points are: (A) A prophecy that a youth will (B) kill his father and (C) marry his mother. He is (D) saved from being exposed to die and is (E) reared by another king, (F) the prophecy being fulfilled with tragic consequences.[13] Of these six motifs I consider prophecy, parricide, and incest as the most essential.

Of the various stories in my collection it should be pointed out that none meet all three of the major criteria or all three of the minor criteria. In fact, only a third of them mention even the combination of parricide and incest. In one case all three of the major criteria are missing! As for the minor motifs, all three are absent in half the stories. Most often lacking from this group of criteria is the motif of the fulfillment of the prophecy, which in view of the fact that usually there is no prophecy to begin with need not surprise us. This, of course, does not mean that in these cases parricide and incest are lacking, for they are often present without having been foretold.

I have taken further liberties with the criteria of the Oedipus stories. Not only have I welcomed tales in which both major and minor motifs are deleted with abandon, but I have used very liberal definitions of the motifs themselves. They do not always occur in traditional form. Yet I am sure that I can show elasticity is amply justified. In fact, one of the major goals of this paper is to demonstrate that despite what seem to be serious differences in the tales they are essentially of one type.

One way to indicate the over-all similarity of the tales in the collection would be to describe all of them—obviously impractical. But another way is to give concrete illustrations of various types of tamperings and substitutions to show that in the light of local cultural conditions they are quite reasonable. This is what I now propose to do.

The first type of change is in the *dramatis personae*. In the story from Truk the father is replaced by the mother's brother, a change that would have delighted the late Bronislaw Malinowski, for he had argued that in matrilineal societies having the avunculate the maternal uncle and not the father has the stern repressive role that antagonizes his nephew towards him.[14]

In this same story the mother's brother's wife is substituted for the mother. Perhaps this change is understandable if we view it as a way of retaining the wife of the hated man as the object of the incestuous relation.

On Ponape, there is another replacement in the cast of characters. The father's sister replaces the mother.

This brings us to another change, namely, in the gravity and nature of the act of incest. There seems to be a general tendency to play down the incest motif, which, in some instances, is altogether omitted. Alterations can involve simply a change in personnel, as in the substitution of the uncle's wife or the father's sister for the young man's mother. It should be observed that these sex partners cannot in a matrilineal society such as Truk and Ponape belong to the same clan as the youth, so the act of incest is rendered less fearful, for in most unilinear societies it is strictly forbidden to have relations with a clan mate. In short, the idea of incest is retained but it is attenuated by selecting relatives outside the clan group.

In addition to changes in personnel, the incest motif is minimized in other ways. In two Indonesian stories it is done by having the act of incest merely threatened instead of consummated.[15] Sometimes the motif is so drastically altered as to be almost unrecognizable. For instance, the act that enrages the husband may merely be an unerotic fingernail scratch on his wife[16] or it may be protracted breast feeding.[17] In the story from Kusaie the mother and son never display amatory interest, but they do unite to do battle against a party led by her husband, who is enraged because she has defied him and brought back to life the son whose skull he had crushed.

I can assign no reason for the wish to minimize the incest motif, except perhaps that in tales told to explain the origin of ruling families it may be felt necessary to play down the gravity of the violation of the taboo. At any rate, where incest is eliminated or minimized, parricide is the major theme of the story. Where incest is the dominant motif, such as in Ulithi and most Indonesian Oedipus-type tales, there is no substitution for the mother.

Another common change in Oceanic Oedipus-type tales is to be found in respect to the exposure of the child. Again these changes are to be seen as adjustments to local situations and do not vitiate the Oedipal character of the tales. For example, in Oceanic stories the child is never abandoned to die, as was Oedipus in the Greek tragedy, yet all the incidents attendant upon his birth are seen on scrutiny to be mere variants of abandonment in the literal sense.

One variant is to have the father try to kill his son outright at birth instead of having him left to die of exposure. This is what we find in specimens from the Sundas,[18] Truk, Ponape, and Kusaie. Another variant is to have the king remove the child from the scene by ordering his pregnant wife banished from the land because her unborn child has insulted him. Later, to be sure, after the child is born the king's other wife puts the neonate in a box and throws him into a river.[19] Another substitution for abandonment involves a miscarriage or stillbirth. There is no hostility towards the baby; he is merely left by his mother to float in the sea because of her ignorance of his viability or even his very existence.[20]

I am convinced that the reason why the abandonment motif is so distorted or even absent in most Oceanic tales of the Oedipus type is that the idea of prophecy and relentless fate, so important a feature of the Greek and closely allied stories, is absent from all Oceanic specimens except three cognates from Sumatra and Java.[21] If the near-elimination of the child at birth is not to be motivated by a prediction, then his narrow escape from death must be attributed to other causes, as we shall soon see.

Why is the prophecy motif usually absent in Oceania? Let us observe first of all that when it does occur it is present only in those islands of Malaysia most strongly subject to Hindu influence. We know that Java and Sumatra were centuries ago the seats of powerful Hindu-Buddhistic empires, and were later subjected to Islamic influence. The prophecy element is completely absent where there are no influences from the Indian and Moslem worlds, although the case of Lombok, just east of Bali, illustrates that the presence of either of these influences is not a guarantee that the prophecy motif will necessarily be present in a story.

In my opinion the reason for the absence of the prophecy element is that while divination is a world-wide phenomenon, the idea of relentless fate is not. The concept of fate is what gives the prophecy its special character. Divination is common in the unacculturated islands of the Pacific, yet it does not have the fatalistic quality seen in the systems of supernaturalism of the Indo-European and Semitic-speaking peoples. Therefore the threat to the life of the newborn babe must come from some other source than a desire to thwart fate.

On Kapingamarangi and Ulithi, where the idea of prophecy cannot very well be invoked as a motivation for the near-death of the newborn child, a miscarriage is substituted. This takes away the purposeful threat to the child and substitutes a fortuitous, impersonal one. On Ponape the story-tellers handle the fatalistic aspect of the story by offering no reason at all for the attempt to kill the child. We are simply told that when a certain chieftain departs from his house he leaves orders with his wife that she is to spare the newborn child if it is a girl and to kill it if it is a boy. On Kusaie, the implication seems to be that girls are more desirable than boys, for when the husband leaves his wife to go to the mountains he says that if she should give birth to a boy he will make a hole in the boy's skull so he can drink out his brain, but if the child is a girl then they shall keep her and in time she will become a woman and likewise have children. Only on Truk is a clear-cut explanation for "abandonment," i.e., infanticide, offered without either invoking the idea of fate or hedging with a miscarriage. A chief orders all the women to kill their newborn babes (male) because he fears that they may grow up to "speak" to his wives. But on most Pacific islands no attempt is made to do something about the prophecy motif. It is simply ignored.

The final kind of major change that we shall consider is the deletion or substitution of the parricidic motif itself. In instances where it is absent there are ample cognates to suggest that it was once an integral part of the story. On Truk a substitute is found in the form of the avunculicide, or the killing of an uncle. Here, as we have seen, the antagonism is between a boy and his mother's brother rather than him and his father.

The idea of parricide should be defined elastically enough not only to include avunculicide but to make it optional whether the youth or his father takes the initiative in expressing the antagonism between them. In the story from New Guinea, there is sexual jealousy between a father and son, and the father eventually kills the son instead of the other way around. In the Trukese story, we have an attempt at nepoticide, for the uncle tries to kill his nephew. On Kapingamarangi, the eventual outlet for sexual jealousy is banishment, a substitute for the killing of the youth. In short, parricide can have four equivalents: avunculicide, filicide, nepoticide, and banishment.

An interesting lesson can be learned from studying the occurrence of these various substitutions and deletions, and that is that within any group of cognates there can be greater differences in the constituent motifs than between widely separated stories that differ in the specific but yet minor details. Thus the Ulithian story is closer to the Sophoclean drama in such essential elements as the *personae* of the triangle, the abandonment, the act of incest, and the act of parricide, than it is to its Trukese cognate, where the mother's brother replaces the father, the mother's brother's wife replaces the mother, an antagonistic scratch on the hand replaces incest, and attempted nepoticide and effected avunculicide replace parricide.

Before leaving the matter of changes and substitutions, it is interesting to note that in one respect at least, there is remarkable consistency in the attribution of "royalty" to the father in the Oceanic tales, as in the Greek stories. These fathers are usually chiefs, but they may even be kings or princes.

Consistency is also to be found with respect to the presence of an adoptive parent of the hero. A foster parent usually appears not only where there is an instance of "abandonment" but also where there is the threat of actual infanticide. Except for the case from Truk, the adoptive parent is always a man. On Truk such a parent is a female moth or bird. In one case, just as in Greece, he is a king.

If the reader has become persuaded that there is a unity in the Oceanic tales under discussion, then an important point has been made, and we can proceed to further considerations.

One cannot help but interpret the significance of Oceanic Oedipus-type stories for psychoanalytic theory. Orthodox Freudians are constrained by the dictates of their theoretical position to adhere not only to a pan-Oedipus complex but to a pan-Oedipus folklore as well.[22] On both counts they can be shown to be wrong, for neither situation is universal. Where one is present the other may be absent, and vice versa.

Let us consider first the alleged ubiquitousness of the complex itself. The newer generation of depth psychologists has shown a tendency to rectify some of the fanciful dogmas of the past, involving as they did such ideas as the primal horde, race memory, group mind, and collective unconscious. Long ago Alfred Adler made a radical departure from Freud in suggesting that the Oedipus complex arises in special cases where a child has been so pampered by his mother that he cannot cope with the outside world and so returns to her and takes gratification in dominating her. While his sexual fantasies and desires are directed towards her, they are subordinate to the craving for power over her.[23] Franz Alexander, even though he tends to disparage the new sociocultural emphasis, says that the Oedipus complex is not necessarily universal itself and may even be lacking in cultures other than our own. He thinks the jealousy aspect is the infantile situation which is universally present, and that the child will manifest hostility and aggressiveness against what he considers to be any competitor who arrives on the scene in the long period of his postnatal dependence on parental care.[24] Karen Horney minimizes the role of the Oedipus complex in neuroses and substitutes "basic anxiety." She stresses the social environment. The Oedipus complex, she says, arises not from ultimate biological causes at all but from certain family relationships, and in any case is not ubiquitous.[25] Harry Stack Sullivan emphasizes parental roles, asserting that a parent of opposite sex will be turned to by the child because that parent treats it with greater indulgence than does the other.[26] Erich Fromm, despite certain limitations involving his Bachofen-like interpretation of Oedipus motifs as being symbolic of the struggle between democratic, matriarchal principles and authoritarian, patriarchal ones within a society, keeps in step with the current trend not only by saying the Oedipus complex is not universal but that the sex aspect must be removed from it and that the rivalry between father and son is really due to a struggle over authority.[27] Abram Kardiner believes that society creates the individual and hence also the Oedipus complex; therefore only through comparative sociology can we discover the sociocultural forces which create it.[28]

The importance of these retrenchments for the interpretation of Oceanic folklore is so self-evident that it would seem redundant to dwell upon the freedom they provide in the modification of the motifs in question. It is lamentable, however, that little effort has been expended by psychoanalysts and anthropologists towards inquiring as to the presence or absence of the Oedipus complex in non-Western societies. We, of course, do have Malinowski's classic insistence that at least for the Trobriand Islands there is no mother-son incest longing and no antagonism between father and son, and that the definition of the Oedipus complex must be dropped for matrilineal societies and replaced by a more elastic "nuclear family concept," which varies with social factors and provides a place for the antagonism between nephew and uncle.[29] Neither ethnographic materials nor Thematic Apperception Tests revealed the presence of the complex on Ulithi Atoll.[30] The complex is not reported in a personality study made of the Truk archipelago, where Rorschach and Thematic Apperception Tests were applied.[31] Nor is it mentioned in a personality study made of the Chamorros and Carolinians on Saipan, in which Rorschach tests, psychiatric interviews, and other approaches were used.[32] It is not discussed in a personality study of the Balinese, in which photographic analysis was employed.[33] It is said to be "decidedly not" present in the Marquesas, although the same source mentions it as present among the Tanala of Madagascar.[34] It is also described as present on Alor, where the Rorschach, children's drawings, autobiographies, and other approaches were used.[35] However, in all fairness to both sides of this question, it should be pointed out that in almost all the cases mentioned, which are limited to Oceania, there was either no conscious effort to look for the complex or else very little is said as to how conclusions regarding it were arrived at. On the other hand, this may reflect a growing unconcern on the part of the modern investigator towards the complex itself.

We may now briefly examine the old Freudian notion that, since there is a basic impact on culture by the infantile situation, the Oedipus-type tale should be found universally. The fact of the matter is that unless, like Róheim and other extremists, we are willing to accept fantastically compounded symbolisms,[36] we find such stories limited to a continuous belt extending from Europe to the Near and Middle East and southeastern Asia, and from there into the islands of the Pacific. It seems to be absent from such vast areas as Africa, China, central Asia, northeastern Asia, North America, South America, and Australia.[37]

There are those who might take the stand that granted neither the complex nor the tale-type are universal, they at least occur concomitantly. This is not the case. The design for living of a people cannot be said to provide the proper climate for harboring the tale, even though it may have an effect on the particular form it takes. There are many societies in Africa and Asia where the complex has either been declared present or where there is every reason to believe that, on account of the "patriarchal" character of the social organization, it is probably present; yet the story is missing. Conversely, the story exists where the predisposing cultural conditions which make the normal Oedipal situation a subject of concern in our own society do not exist. Ulithi is a case in point, and we may proceed to explore the conditions to be found on that atoll.

The child is not raised in a milieu in which attachment to a parent of the opposite sex can become a cardinal problem, for the nuclear family does not exercise the intense inward relationships common in the Euroamerican situation. This is because the nuclear family, consisting by definition of a married man and woman with their children, has a strongly dependent character, being subject to competition from three other kin groups—the extended family, the commensal unit, and the lineage.

Extended families, which consist of related nuclear families domiciled together, are on Ulithi only about one-third as frequent as independent nuclear families, but the latter have attached to them, for purposes of residence, one or more other individuals, e.g., a parent, sibling, cousin, nephew, niece, lineage mate, or other relative of either the husband or wife. Complicating the picture of the nuclear family and detracting from its functions is the fact that its members do not always eat together, even when living under one roof. A commensal unit may be constituted of individuals of several nuclear families. All this reduces and disturbs the family as a system existing in isolation with strong internal interaction. Husband-wife and parent-child relations yield much of their intensity. Further competing with the nuclear family is the lineage. The kinship system is a modification of the "Crow" type, resulting in non-localized groups of lineally related persons who trace their descent matrilineally through a common female ancestor. Every individual belongs to one of the many lineages now extant on the island. Each lineage normally has a head man, a head woman, its own traditional lands, a common cooking hearth, a traditional "house," a canoe shed, and even a set of ancestral ghosts. The individual in Ulithian society carries on much social interaction with this kin group. He calls all the members of generations above him "father" or "mother" and carries on relationships with them which to some extent parallel those with his real parents.

But there is much more that makes us wonder how an Oedipal tale can appear in such an unoedipal environment as we find on Ulithi. The extremely common practices of adoption and remarriage further weaken the internal relationships within the nuclear family. Forty-five per cent of all Ulithian babies are adopted, usually before birth, and share in two families—that of their biological parents and that of their adoptive ones. While the biological mother ordinarily nurses and trains the child for the first two years, there is nevertheless much sharing of these duties with the adoptive mother, who usually lives nearby. Both sets of families grant much attention to the child through feeding, fondling, and play. The child cannot maintain the habitual and intense interactions possible in a single family.

As for remarriage, many children are raised in nuclear families that have been reconstituted through divorce, which is very common. Because of divorce and death, the average number of marriages for persons over the age of fifty is almost two and a half. This reduces still more the rhythmic character of interaction within the family. In view of the decentralized nature of the nuclear family, then, there is not much opportunity for the rise of an Oedipus problem.

I see that I have already digressed far from the main purpose of this article and do not have space to discuss matters of authority, discipline, and training, but anything I would have to say in this regard would show that the permissiveness present on Ulithi is in direct contrast to the more rigid training which many psychoanalysts hypothesize as being concomitant with the "patriarchate" and predisposive to Oedipal problems. I could demonstrate that Ulithian society is closer to the so-called "matriarchal" type than it is to the "patriarchal" one, which some analysts, such as Fromm, say goes hand in hand with the Oedipus complex.

Of course, there are many who feel that it is useless to insist upon an intimate connection between the Oedipus complex and the Oedipus plot. In the last century the naturistic school of folklorists were firmly convinced that the tale symbolizes natural phenomena; and so we find, for instance, that Michel Bréal explains Oedipus as the personification of Light, the chief event in the drama being his struggle with the Sphinx—the storm cloud—and his blinding being the disappearance of the sun at the end of the day.[38] Domenico Comparetti sees the drama as a moral tale depicting man's inability to escape his destiny.[39] Similarly, the more conservative contemporary folklorists, such as Stith Thompson, insist that the dominant theme of the Sophoclean play is not incest and parricide but prophecy and relentless fate.[40] Many of the more recent psychoanalytic interpretations depart from Freud's original emphasis and make outstanding revisions and re-evaluations. Otto Rank says the story is an attempt by the hero to retain his immortality through incest and at the same time satisfy society's insistence upon fatherhood.[41] Erich Fromm finds that the drama is a vehicle for expressing not what Freud called the Oedipus complex, which is based on incestuous striving, but the conflict between father and son over authority, as well as the conflict between the patriarchal system and the matriarchal order which it defeated.[42] A.J. Levin, a lawyer well grounded in psychoanalytic doctrine, says that Freud skims over the fact that when Oedipus was three days old his ankles were riveted

together and he was hung upside down to die of exposure, and that
the real appeal of the *Oedipus Rex* of Sophocles to the Greeks is its
expression of infantile resentment against abandonment, as well as
the psychological effects of rejection.[43] H.A. van der Sterren finds
that the emotions of the positive Oedipus complex are not as clearly
expressed in the drama as Freud would have us suppose, and that
emphasis should be given to the pre-oedipal elements, for Oedipus
harbored much enmity towards his mother, Jocasta, who has some
identity with the Sphinx.[44] George Devereux says that we must
credit the Greek poets and dramatists with more psychological
acumen than we have so far done, for what they called "Fate" was
merely the personification of man's character structure and latent
conflicts. The Oedipus stories express the male child's tendency to
view his father as a homosexual ogre, and also his desire to exchange roles with the father in this respect. Using materials derived
from many Greek sources, most of which he claims have been
scotomized, he maintains that the terrible curse uttered against
Laius by Pelops was brought about as the result of homosexual rape
by the former against Chrysippus, the latter's son, with whom Laius
had fallen in love, and that later Oedipus killed his father on the
road in a jealous quarrel over this same Chrysippus. Devereux even
suggests that Oedipus' cohabitation with Jocasta should be viewed
primarily as a homosexual act.[45]

One could cite various other such exegeses, but the point I want
to make is simply that a single story can mean all things to all people
and that the Oceanic peoples have as much right as sophisticated
Western intellectuals to interpret the Oedipus-type tale to fit their
own tastes and values. Thus, looking back on the various omissions,
tamperings, and changes in emphasis discussed earlier in this article
I would say there is nothing puzzling, unfair, or immoral about the
way they depart from the central plot.

How then are we to account for the presence of Oedipus-type
stories in non-oedipal societies? I believe that at least for most cases
the answer lies clearly in diffusion. The fact of the matter is that the
stories in my collection nearly always occur in contiguous areas and
often bear striking resemblances to one another, sometimes in specific details not connected with either the major or the minor motifs.
In fact, I could show that the twenty-three stories from Oceania are
definitely reducible to but seven or eight. Thus, the Ulithi, Truk, and

Kapingamarangi tales are all very similar in general outline as well as in some highly specific details. The three stories from Ponape form a definite group of cognates of their own. The Kusaie story is generally independent of the Ponapean group but contains a specifically similar introduction that makes us wonder if it is not linked to them. The Marshallese tale seems independent. Of the thirteen Malaysian stories, all are reducible to two groups of cognates. In the first group, a king learns from a diviner that the son which his wife is about to bear will slay him and win his kingdom. To prevent a fulfillment of the prophecy the king orders the baby put into a box and abandoned, but the baby is found and is raised by another king. The boy grows up and lives to kill his father and rule in his stead. In the second group, a girl has intercourse with a dog and becomes pregnant. She bears a son, who kills his father, the dog. The son marries or tries to marry his mother. The single Melanesian specimen seems unrelated specifically to any others from Oceania. The lone specimen from Polynesia is a weak one and comes from the Marquesas, thus making it the easternmost of all Oceanic examples.

I do not wish to imply that the above evidence shows that seven or eight separate stories diffused throughout the Pacific. I merely point out that it is possible on a simple level to demonstrate that a group of stories can be reduced to one third their number. It is not at all unlikely that these stories all had a single prototype and that the tales which have been derived from it have become too altered by retelling to be recognizable as cognates.

My conclusion is that, while it is possible that an original Oedipus story arose in the remote past, in connection with an oedipal situation in a "patriarchal" type of society somewhere in a broad belt from Europe to south Asia, one cannot say that wherever such stories are found they offer proof of the underlying presence of an Oedipus situation, or that wherever the complex occurs the story will arise out of it. The oedipal situation is one that is culturally determined and culturally modified and is not the result of instinct, racial memory, or engrams of the past. It is not universal, for there are many social systems not conducive to its development. Therefore, it is hardly to be expected that the Oedipus-type tale would be universal. In fact, within Oceania it is surprisingly sparse. There is good evidence to show that, at least in this area, the presence of the tale type is mostly the result of diffusion and not of some psychological mechanism inspiring people independently to create it. As the story diffused it lost its original oedipal implications and became altered for use either as an explanatory myth or an interesting yarn. There is no evidence that Oceanic peoples attach much importance to the story. True, in the Sundas one group of cognates takes the form of an origin myth, but it is always told about some group of people other than that of the storytellers.

NOTES

[1]This article is an extension of a paper given before the American Folklore Society in New York, December, 1954, and represents a preliminary version of a detailed study to be published in the University of California monograph series, *Folklore Studies*. The author wishes to acknowledge the research assistance of Gerda Herritt and Hal Eberhart.

[2]Christiaan Snouck Hurgronje, *The Achehnese*, trans. A.W.S. O'Sullivan (Leyden, 1906), I, 20, which deals with an Acheh version; Anonymous, "Legenden van Djambi," *Tijdschrift voor Nederlandsch Indië*, VIII (1845), 34–43, which deals with a Djambi version, the highlights of which are summarized by Ph. S. van Ronkel, "Catalogus der Maleische Handschriften van het Kon. Instituut voor de Taal-, Land- en Volkenkunde van Ned.-Indië," *Bijdragen tot de Taal-, Land- en Volkenkunde van Nederlandsch-Indië*, LX (1908), 211.

[3]Tammo J. Bezemer, *Javaansche en Maleische Fabelen en Legenden* (Amsterdam, 1903), pp. 173–188, and *Volksdichtung aus Indonesien: Sagen, Tierfabeln und Märchen* (The Hague, 1904), pp. 97–100; Hendrik H. Juynboll, *Supplement op den Catalogus van de Sundaneesche Handschriften en Catalogus van de Balineesche en Sasaksche Handschriften der Leidsche Universiteits-Bibliotheek* (Leyden, 1912), pp. 25, 54; J. Knebel, "De Kalang-legende, volgens Tegalsche lezing, uit het Javaansch," *Tijdschrift voor Indische Taal-, Land- en Volkenkunde*, XXXVII (1894), 489–505; Jos. Meijboom-Italiaander, *Javaansche Sagen, Mythen en Legenden* (Zutphen, 1924), pp. 48–61; Winter, "Oorsprong van het zoogenaamde Kalangs-Volk," *Tijdschrift voor Nederlandsché Indië*, II, Part 2 (1839), 578–588.

[4]J.C. van Eerde, "De Kalangslegende op Lombok," *Tijdschrift voor Indische Taal-, Land- en Volkenkunde*, XLV (1902), 36–39, 43–45, 46–47.

[5]Author's unpublished field notes from Ulithi Atoll.

[6]John L. Fischer, unpublished field notes from Truk, MS in Bernice P. Bishop Museum, Honolulu, pp. 1011–23. I wish here to acknowledge Fischer's great generosity in letting me make full use of his rich data.

[7]John L. Fischer, unpublished field notes from Ponape, MS in Bernice P. Bishop Museum, Honolulu, pp. 1043–46; Paul Hambruch, *Ponape: Die Ruinen; Ponapegeschichten*, in *Ergebnisse der Südsee Expedition 1908–1910*, ed. Georg Thilenius, II, B, VII, 3 (Hamburg, 1936), pp. 321–324, 325–330.

[8]Ernst G. Sarfert, *Kusae*, in *Ergebnisse der Südsee Expedition 1908-1910*, ed. Georg Thilenius, II, B, IV, 2 (Hamburg, 1920), pp. 438-439.

[9]August Erdland, *Die Marshall-Insulaner; Leben und Sitte, Sinn und Religion eines Südsee-Volkes* (Münster i. W., 1914), p. 258.

[10]Samuel H. Elbert, *Grammar and Comparative Study of the Language of Kapingamarangi; Texts and Word Lists*, mimeo. (Washington, 1948), pp. 112-115. A briefer version appears in the same author's, "Uta-matua and Other Tales of Kapingamarangi," *JAF*, LXII (1949), 245.

[11]Francis E. Williams, *Papuans of the Trans-Fly* (Oxford, 1936), pp. 312-314.

[12]Samuel H. Elbert, "Marquesan Legends," unpublished MS in Bernice P. Bishop Museum, Honolulu, pp. 325-327.

[13]Stith Thompson, *The Folktale* (New York, 1946), p. 141.

[14]Bronislaw Malinowski, *Sex and Repression in Savage Society* (London, 1927), pp. 9-11, 13, 44-47, 79, 120-121, 258-259, and *The Sexual Life of Savages in North-Western Melanesia* (New York, 1929), I, 6-8, 18, 20-21.

[15]Bezemer, *Volksdichtung*, pp. 97-100; Juynboll, p. 54.

[16]Fischer, Truk MS, pp. 1011-23.

[17]Erdland, p. 258.

[18]Bezemer, *Fabelen*, pp. 173-188; Meijboom-Italiaander, pp. 48-61.

[19]Juynboll, p. 25.

[20]Elbert, *Grammar*, p. 112.

[21]Anonymous, pp. 34-43; Bezemer, *Fabelen*, pp. 173-188; Meijboom-Italiaander pp. 48-61.

[22]Cf. Géza Róheim, "The Anthropological Evidence and the Oedipus Complex," *Psychoanalytic Quarterly*, XXI (1952), 537-542, where the author denies that it is possible for infants and children raised in a culture which inhibits sexual activity not to develop an Oedipus complex.

[23]Alfred Adler, *Social Interest: A Challenge to Mankind*, trans. John Linton and Richard Vaughan (London, 1938), pp. 21, 51, 213-214.

[24]Franz Alexander, "Psychoanalysis Revised," *Psychoanalytic Quarterly* IX (1940), 1-36; *Our Age of Unreason: A Study of Irrational Forces in Social Life* (Philadelphia, 1942), pp. 230-232.

[25]Karen Horney, *The Neurotic Personality of Our Time* (New York, 1937), pp. 20, 83-84, 160-161, 285; *New Ways in Psychoanalysis* (New York, 1939), pp. 12-13, 79-87.

[26]Personal communication from Harry Stack Sullivan to Patrick Mullahy, in the latter's *Oedipus: Myth and Complex* (New York, 1948), p. 315.

[27]Erich Fromm, *Man for Himself: An Inquiry into the Psychology of Ethics* (New York, 1947), p. 157; "The Oedipus Complex and the Oedipus Myth," in *The Family: Its Function and Destiny*, ed. Ruth Nanda Anshen, The Science of Culture Series, V (New York, 1948), pp. 334-358.

[28]Abram Kardiner, *The Individual and His Society: The Psychodynamics of Primitive Social Organization* (New York, 1939), pp. 67, 99-100, 133, 246, 383-389, 479-481, 485.

[29]Malinowski, *Sex and Repression*, pp. 4, 5-7, 14-15, 75, 80-82, 100, 137, 142, *et passim*.

[30]William A. Lessa and Marvin Spiegelman, "Ulithian Personality as Seen

through Ethnological Materials and Thematic Test Analysis," *University of California Publications in Culture and Society,* II (Berkeley and Los Angeles, 1954), pp. 243–301.

[31]Thomas Gladwin and Seymour B. Sarason, *Truk: Man in Paradise,* Viking Fund Publications in Anthropology, No. 20 (New York, 1953).

[32]Alice Joseph and Veronica Murray, *Chamorros and Carolinians of Saipan* (Cambridge, Mass., 1951).

[33]Gregory Bateson and Margaret Mead, *Balinese Character,* Special Publications of the New York Academy of Science, Vol. II (New York, 1942).

[34]Kardiner, pp. 246, 302, 349, 410.

[35]Cora Du Bois, *The People of Alor: A Social-Psychological Study of an East Indian Island* (Minneapolis, 1944).

[36]Róheim, *Psychoanalysis and Anthropology* (New York, 1950), pp. 175–192; *The Riddle of the Sphinx,* trans. R. Money-Kyrle (London, 1934), *passim.* While Róheim does not actually claim to have Oedipus-type stories among primitive peoples, he discovers the presence of Oedipal elements in the folktales of such peoples as the Australians, Melanesians, Alorese, Marquesans, Yurok, and Navaho. This he does by recourse to a point of view which makes him look for and accept "unconscious ideas," and "real motifs." Thus (*Psychoanalytic Quarterly,* IX [1940] p. 542) he takes Malinowski to task for not recognizing the following story, which appears in the latter's *Sexual Life of Savages* (pp. 411–412), as being an Oedipus tale: a man named Momovala has intercourse with his daughter, and the girl commits suicide by persuading a shark to eat her up. He then kills his wife by coitus, and finally cuts off his own penis and dies. Róheim (*ibid.*) offers the following, too, as an example from Malinowski (pp. 405–408) that has been overlooked: a woman has five sons and five clitorises. Every time the stingaree comes to have intercourse with her, he cuts off one clitoris, and each time one of four sons who try to fight the monster runs away. Finally the youngest son rescues the last clitoris from destruction by spearing and cudgeling the stingaree to death. An extremist, Róheim believes that the primal horde posited by Freud did really exist in the past as an archaic form of human social organization, but "myths of the Primal Horde type may be based not on the unconscious memory of primeval tragedies but may be actual narratives of events in human times." In short, the primal horde is still with us in the ethnological present, and in substantiation of this Róheim offers some seeming instances of it in Central Australia ("The Primal Horde and Incest in Central Australia," *Journal of Criminal Psychopathology,* III (1942), 454–460.) His documentation and interpretations are questionable.

[37]While I am not prepared to document my sources, I have found authorities who claim that Oedipus-type stories are to be found in England, France, Finland, Lapland, Lithuania, Hungary, Roumania, Russia, the Ukraine, Albania, Greece, Cyprus, Egypt, Iran, and India.

[38]Michel Bréal, *Mélanges de Mythologie et de Linguistique* (Paris, 1877), pp. 163–185.

[39]Domenico Comparetti, *Edipo e la Mitologia Comparata* (Pisa, 1867).

[40]In a letter to the author from Stith Thompson of Indiana University, 31 October 1952, there is this declaration of his viewpoint: "Certainly the Oedipus story of Sophocles involves only quite accidental events and, so far as I can see, has no bearing whatsoever upon the so-called 'Oedipus complex.' The only enmity Oedipus has is toward an unknown man who tries to drive him off the road. From the Greek point of

view, the fact that this man happened to be Oedipus' father came entirely from the workings of Fate and not from any psychological law. The same is exactly true of the unwitting marriage with his mother." See also Thompson's *Motif-Index of Folk Literature*, V (Bloomington, 1935), 46–47, for a description of motifs M343 and M344.

[41]Otto Rank, *The Trauma of Birth* (New York, 1929); *Modern Education*, trans. Mabel E. Moxon (New York, 1932).

[42]Fromm, *Man for Himself.* . . . (Above, note 27.)

[43]A.J. Levin, "The Oedipus Complex in History and Psychiatry: A New Interpretation," *Psychiatry*, XI (1948), 285–289.

[44]H.A. van der Sterren, "The 'King Oedipus' of Sophocles," *International Journal of Psychoanalysis*, XXXIII (1952), 343–350.

[45]George Devereux, "Why Oedipus Killed Laius: A Note on the Complementary Oedipus Complex in Greek Drama," *International Journal of Psychoanalysis*, XXXIV (1953), 132–141.

Oedipus in the Light of Folklore

Vladimir Propp

The name of Vladimir Propp is well known to folklorists for his pioneering work of 1928, The Morphology of the Folktale, *which brought structuralism to the study of folk narrative. Few people realize that Propp, Professor of Folklore at the University of Leningrad, also wrote the first major folkloristic essay on the Oedipus story. Published in 1944, it was translated into Italian in 1975, but it remains largely unknown.*

In reading Propp's essay, one must keep in mind his theoretical bias. Propp accepted the notion of a universal evolution of human society. According to his views, society progressed from a primitive state to a civilized one. This unilinear evolutionary theory, so popular in Europe in the late nineteenth century, assumed that modern "primitive" peoples, e.g., in Africa, represented earlier stages in the evolutionary scale. This is why Propp attaches special significance to a Zulu Oedipal story (though the story's relationship to Aarne-Thompson tale type 931 is tangential). For Propp, the Zulu version represents a form of the Oedipus story earlier than the ancient Greek. Propp also assumes that human societies evolved from an initial state of matriliny to a later state of patriliny. Propp's view of Oedipus is that the tale represents the historical clash of two con-

Reprinted from *Učenye zapiski Leningradskogo gosudarstvennogo universiteta,* Serija filologiceskich 72 (1944), fasc. 9, pp. 138–175. We are greatly indebted to folklorist Polly Coote for translating Propp's essay into English. We also appreciate Johanna Albi's translation of the Italian version of the essay into English.

flicting social orders, one matrilineal, in which succession to the throne is achieved by the son-in-law who kills his father-in-law, the old king, and the other patrilineal. Accordingly, in the later evolutionary stage, it is a son who succeeds his father rather than a son-in-law who replaced his father-in-law. Regardless of the validity of such theories that matriarchy everywhere precedes patriarchy, Propp's skillful and magisterial application of the comparative method is a landmark in Oedipus scholarship.

We present here a translation from the original Russian with the addition of slight changes made by Propp for the Italian translation. For details of Propp's life, see Reinhard Breymayer, "Vladimir Jakovlevic Propp (1895-1970)—Leben, Wirken and Bedeutsamkeit," Linguistica Biblica *15/16 (April, 1972), 36-66, and Isidor Levin, "Vladimir Propp: an evaluation on his seventieth birthday,"* Journal of the Folklore Institute, *4 (1967), 32-49.*

Methodological Premises

The relationship between folklore and historical reality is one of the most important problems in folkloristics. The object of studying this relationship, however, is not to discover correspondences between particular elements of folklore and individual events in the historical past, but rather to find in history the causes that produced folklore as a whole as well as individual tale types.

The problem of finding historical origins is relatively easily solved if an item in folklore such as a tale directly reflects the past. For example, in many cases one can successfully show that forms of wooing in folklore correspond to forms of marriage that previously existed and have since disappeared. The problem becomes more difficult when we encounter motifs and tale types in folklore that clearly cannot be traced directly to historical reality. Such things as winged horses, magic pipes, clashing mountains, one-eyed giants, and so on, never existed. In these cases either the past has been obscured and deformed, or the motif has been created by some processes of imagination as yet insufficiently investigated and understood.

The broad study of folklore in historical perspective shows that as in the course of time the new ways of life created by historical development, new economic conditions, and new forms of social relationships penetrate into folklore, the old does not always die out and is not always supplanted by the new. The old continues to co-exist with the new, parallel to it, or forming with it various imaginary hybrid combinations impossible both in nature and in history. While these combinations appear to be pure fantasy, nevertheless the same ones come into being completely independent of one another wherever the historical advances that produce them take place.

Thus, for example, the winged horse represents a combination of bird and horse that occurred when the cultic role of the bird was transferred to the horse following its domestication. As another example of such a combination, a fairy tale tells that the hero sees a house in the forest that has no doors; there is no way in. But then he spies a "tiny, almost invisible door in a post"[1] and enters through it. What has happened here? At one time houses were built on piles. It is fairly easy to find traces of such dwellings in folktales.[2] The pile dwellings were eventually replaced by ordinary buildings built upon the ground. While one type of building replaced the other in real life, in the imagination they were combined; the new was super-imposed on the old. The ordinary door is superimposed on the pile, resulting in a door in a post.

Essentially the same process takes place in pictorial art, in real life, and in language. Marr[3] has shown, for instance, that the most ancient draft animal, the deer, was in time replaced by the horse. The substitution of one for the other in life resulted in their com-bination in the imagination. In the human mind the deer met the horse and the two formed a hybrid deer-horse. Although such a combination is impossible in nature, the hybrid was so real and powerful in the imagination that it was given concrete form and created artificially. Although Marr did not know it, people did adorn horses with antlers and ride on them. There is a model of a horse adorned in this way in the Hermitage Museum.

Hybrids of this kind not only form the basis of individual words and visual images in real life and in folklore, they also explain folklore motifs, episodes in tales, and entire tale types. In particular, the story of the hero who kills his father and marries his mother is based upon such a hybrid formation. In undertaking research on such phenomena, it is essential to define what elements are being combined and what kind of form results. Moreover, any contentions regarding combinations of old and new, such as the ones suggested above, must be supported with ample concrete data from history and folklore.

The Folkloric Character of the Story of Oedipus

This study does not cover all the problems connected with the Oedipus story, a task that would require a large work of research. Here we more modestly limit ourselves to tracing the conflicts of historical contradictions reflected in the tale.

The existing literature, extensive as it is, cannot suffice for our purposes. Since up to now no compendium of all the Oedipus material has been made, studies have been carried out on limited corpuses, without reference to comparative folklore. Moreover, these studies are unsatisfactory in their method and in their definition of the problem. If one leaves aside the works of the Freudians and of the mythological school, the basic question debated in the literature is whether or not a given tale is borrowed from ancient sources. But this question does not touch on the essential point. Even if borrowing (or the lack of it) were proved conclusively, the problem of the origin of the tale would not be solved.

In order to answer the question we pose, it is not sufficient to draw upon evidence from one or two peoples. All available material should be brought into consideration. The story of Oedipus is known in folklore in the form of folktale, legend, epic song, lyric song, and chapbook. In written literature based upon folklore it is cast as tragedy, drama, poem, and novella. It occurs among all the peoples of Europe and also among the Zulu in Africa and among the Mongols. A catalogue of all the material would be too long to include in a brief article; a survey of the data could form the subject of a special study in literary history.

Indexes of folktale types list two major types for the Oedipus story, AT 931 and AT 933. In fact one can define four types of the story into which almost all the European Oedipus material can be classified.

The story of Andrew of Crete always opens with a prophecy. The hero is set adrift in the water and is raised in a monastery or by boatmen, fishermen, or the like. He discovers he is a foundling and leaves his guardian. He is hired as a watchman in the home of his real parents; in performing the job he kills his father, who has come to test him, and marries his father's widow. Afterwards he learns the truth and imposes on himself or accepts the penance of going under the earth (he buries himself in a well, etc.). When people remember about him later, he is already dead but has become a saint, or he dies then and there as a saint, upon completing his famous hymn, the canon of Andrew of Crete. This type is the fullest and the closest to the Oedipus story, with the one exception that the hero does not become king. It is known among the Russians, Ukrainians, and Belorussians, and in a slightly shortened and different form among the Serbs.

The Judas type develops at the beginning like the Andrew of Crete type. While living with his guardian, Judas kills his foster brother and runs away. Unlike Andrew he sometimes is raised in a royal household, having been found by a queen. Back in his homeland he is hired by the governor, usually Pilate. To please his master he steals apples from his own father's garden. When caught in the act he kills his father. He marries the widow and, when he learns the truth, goes off to become a disciple of Christ. This type is very close to the Andrew type, differing from it only in some details of the development, in the ending, and in the treatment of the hero as a wrongdoer.

The story of Gregory begins with the incestuous union of a brother and sister. After the birth and removal of an infant, the father goes to Jerusalem to expiate his sins and dies there. The place where the hero is raised is subject to great variation. When he discovers his origin, he goes off to seek his parents. The timely death of the father obviates patricide in this story. As a rule, Gregory marries a queen whom in many versions he has rescued from persecutors. He usually becomes king, although there are versions that have a bourgeois rather than a royal setting. When he discovers that he has married his mother, he does not go under the earth like Andrew of Crete, but shuts himself in a cave on an island. He is found and becomes pope. The fame of his saintliness spreads through the world and reaches his mother. She comes to him for confession; they recognize each other. This type is common in Roman Catholic Western Europe and in Poland. It is also known among the Czechs and in manuscript tradition among the Russians.

The story of Alban begins with an incestuous union between a king and his daughter. Their child is carried off to a foreign country and thrown on the highway. Some beggars find him and take him to the king of that country. There he is raised. The king claims him as his own son, marries him to the daughter of a neighboring king, and dies. The second king's daughter is none other than the boy's mother. But since he was born of father-daughter incest, his wife is at the same time his mother and his half-sister, and his father is also his maternal grandfather. When the truth is revealed, the wife summons her father and all three withdraw to the desert. But the devil again tempts the old father. Again he sins with his daughter. The young son finds them out, kills both parents, and goes off to the desert alone. Subsequently he becomes a saint and miracles are worked by his body. This story type is relatively rare and is found mainly in Latin manuscripts rather than in a folklore tradition. There are, however, traces of it in the Arabian Nights.

This cursory description of the main types of the tale is sufficient to support the conclusion that the European tradition includes not only "Oedipus Rex" but also "Oedipus at Colonus." The hero withdraws to a cave, under the earth, or into the grave, and becomes a saint. While "Oedipus Rex" has given rise to much scholarly writing, the connection between data from European folklore and "Oedipus at Colonus" has gone completely unnoticed.

We shall examine the whole tale, motif by motif, using the method outlined above. The tale does not arise as a direct reflection of a social order. It arises from a conflict, from the contradictions that occur as one order replaces another. Our main task is to trace these contradictions to discover what elements are in conflict in historical reality and how the conflict gives rise to the tale.

To fulfill our aims we will refer not only to variants of the specific tale type, but also to the fairy tale in general, as in its structure the Oedipus story represents a typical fairy tale.

Prophecy

In Sophocles' *Oedipus* events unfold before the spectator from the end to the beginning. At the moment when the king appears on stage before the people, all the important events of his life are already in the past. The exposition does not proceed in chronological order. But if we rearrange the events in the order of their sequence in time, we see that the life of Oedipus was predetermined before his birth. According to Jocasta's story, his father, the Theban king Laius, received a prophecy:

> There was an oracle once that came to Laius,—
> I will not say that it was Phoebus' own,
> but it was from his servants—and it told him
> that it was fate that he should die a victim
> at the hands of his own son, a son to be born
> of Laius and me. (11. 711–714)

The second part of the prophecy, that the son will marry the king's widow, his mother, is revealed only much later after many years, and not to the parents but to the young Oedipus himself, when he is already in exile. From the same Delphic oracle Oedipus learns

> That I was fated to lie with my mother
> and to show daylight an accursed breed
> which men would not endure, and I was doomed
> to be murderer of the father that begot me. (11. 791–793)

Thus the father knows he will be killed by his son, and the son knows more than the father: he knows that he faces a sinful union with his mother. Such a disposition of the prophecy is not at all in keeping with folk tradition. Normally in folktales, prophecy, which-ever of its varied forms it takes, is given immediately and in full at the birth or even before the birth of the child. The parents know of the prophecy, but the child does not. By making the hero himself aware of it, Sophocles gives the whole story tragic meaning. If Oedipus did not know of the prophecy, there would be no tragedy; there would simply be an accident of fate, as usually happens in folklore.

Admittedly there are cases in folktales in which the boy knows of his fate. Thus in a Romanian tale when, after being raised by a miller, the boy meets an angel who tells him, "Beware of the king's daughter and do not appear before her. She will demand you as her husband although she is your mother."[4] He does in fact marry her but does not share her bed. Such cases are innovative reworkings of the tale that seek to mitigate the horror of the sin. In Russian and Belorussian tales even before birth the boy calls from the mother's womb: "I will marry my mother and kill my father with a weapon," (Smirnov, 186), or, "I'll kill my father and take my mother to wife," (Dobrovol'skij, *Smolenskij sbornik*, p. 270). But still there is no tragedy: the hero makes no effort to escape his fate as Oedipus does in running away from his supposed parents. The hero of the folktale is unaware of any impending fate.

In Sophocles' play the foreknowledge is organically linked with the entire plot, while in the folklore material the prophecy is only loosely connected to the internal psychological structure and to the external compositional structure of the tale. The prophecy may be left out without any damaging effect on the plot. It serves as only one of the ways the departure of the youth from home may be motivated. In the stories of Gregory and Alban, in which there is never any prophecy, the departure is motivated instead by the incestuous union of the parents. These types of the Oedipus tale alone are evidence that prophecy can be replaced by substitutes. Yet it is also frequently absent in other, extremely diverse and numerous versions. Characteristically, not one of the African texts includes prophecy. Apparently the more archaic form of the tale does not yet have the element of foreknowledge.

Prophecy in itself is not part of the complication of the plot. Though it occurs at the starting point of the narrative, it is actually a product of the end. Prophecy does not determine the outcome; rather the outcome determines the prophecy. Under certain conditions— which also pertain to our study—prophecy grows out of the denouement. In this light it becomes clear why, as Lur'e has observed, in folklore prophecies are always fulfilled.

However, when we compare the end of Sophocles' *Oedipus* with the prophecy, we see that the end nevertheless does not completely correspond to the beginning. The prophecy speaks only of patricide and incestuous marriage. But this is not all that happens. Oedipus takes what he supposes is another's throne, unaware that it is his father's. In marrying his mother he gains a throne. In other words, the prophecy does not include mention of his future rank as king and how he will obtain the throne. If we assume that prophecy is the product of the denouement, it should run thus: (1) Oedipus will kill a king and take his throne; (2) this king will turn out to be his own father; (3) he will receive the throne from a woman, the king's widow; (4) as a natural consequence of the preceding, this woman will turn out to be his mother.

Such a formulation is based on the assumption that the killing of a king, regardless of who he is, rather than the killing of a father, has primary importance. This assumption permits us to submit the hypothesis that the tale arose from historical forms of the struggle for power, or more precisely, from the conflict of two forms of inheritance of power. "Oedipus" was originally a tale of kings, and like a true fairy tale it ended with accession to the throne. Its descent to a middle-class milieu took place later in its development in Europe in the medieval legends about Judas, the merchant's son, and others. The story of Gregory preserved the royal form of the tale in Europe, thanks to the fact that the hero eventually becomes pope, a position entirely consistent with his royal birth, while the democratic Andrew of Crete becomes a simple popular saint. Alban and Paul of Cesarea are always of royal birth.

The content of the prophecy must be investigated before we turn to the fact of prophecy itself. We must therefore consider the element of accession to the throne, comparing it with historical forms of accession and tracing when and how prophecy could become connected with it. Since prophecy anticipates the end of the story, examination of it also sheds some light on the motif of patricide. The prophecy speaks of the killing of a father (a king) by his son (the heir to the throne). Inheritance from father to son is a relatively late form of inheritance. Power did not always descend in the male line, but at one time passed from the king to his son-in-law, the husband of his daughter, that is, it was conferred by a woman through marriage. Frazer says of this form:

> Thus it would seem that among some Aryan peoples, at a certain stage of their social evolution, it has been customary to regard women and not men as the channels in which royal blood flows, and to bestow the kingdom in each successive generation on a man of another family and often of another country, who marries one of the princesses and reigns over his

> wife's people. A common type of popular tale, which relates
> how an adventurer, coming to a strange land, wins the hand of
> the king's daughter and with her the half or the whole of the
> kingdom, may well be a reminiscence of a real custom.[5]

Frazer speaks here of half the kingdom. But this half is the fairy
tale's attenuation of the earlier forms that existed both in reality and
in folklore. Originally the hero kills the king and receives the entire
kingdom, a situation considerably modified in folklore, where the
old king remains alive and shares his kingdom with the hero.

Frazer has thoroughly researched the killing of the king by his
successor. The central point of *The Golden Bough* is that the king is
removed before his natural death. We need not go into an investigation of the whole of this complicated phenomenon. We are concerned with a single instance of such killing in folklore, namely the
killing of a king by his future son-in-law.

Frazer establishes the various lengths of time after which the
king might be supplanted and killed. Folktales show clearly that one
of the possible terminations for a king's reign could be when the
king's daughter reached the age of marrying (a point Frazer overlooked). Her betrothed is the deadly enemy of the king—he is the
heir and the one who will kill him.

Why was the king killed? This is a question for historical ethnography. One may suppose (judging by Frazer's evidence) that it was
to prevent the priest-king from falling into physical weakness or old
age, since not only human life, but also the welfare of the sun,
livestock, and harvest depended upon him. He ruled by virtue of his
magic endowments. The failure of his physical powers would signal
the weakening of his magic powers, and since the loss of his strength
would mean great disaster for his people, he was not permitted to
reach this state.

Examples of a son-in-law killing a king are not rare in folklore,
although the murder naturally has frequently been replaced by a
compromise in which the new king receives the daughter and half
the kingdom during the old king's lifetime and inherits the whole
after the natural death of the king.[6] In these cases there is as yet no
son. The tales reflect the historical epoch when inheritance passed to
the son-in-law. Thus hostility toward the son-in-law, and sometimes
toward the daughter, too, precedes hostility toward the son.

The presence of this motif in American Indian myths, in which hostility toward the son is completely absent, proves its archaic origin. "Oh, Tlaik is a very cruel man. He kills all his daughter's suitors."[7] Or, "'You have come to marry my daughter?' 'Yes, I came for that.' Then the chief made him sit next to him so as to burn him."[8] In another passage, an old woman (the equivalent of the witch in European tales) says to the hero. "The chief will give his daughter to one who comes to visit him. That is why he proposes they do something that will kill them."[9] These are by no means the only examples, but we need not cite them all. Our purpose is to establish the presence of this motif and the concomitant absence of hostility to the son among the totemistic peoples of North America.

It may be objected that the motif of hostility toward the son-in-law is of a completely different order than the motif of hostility toward the son, that the two are not comparable and have no relation to each other either in history or in folklore. But the relationship can be proven by the fact that the hostility to the son-in-law occupies the same place in the compositional scheme of the fairy tale as hostility toward the son. Fear of the son-in-law leads to setting difficult tasks that are intended to eliminate him but instead bring it about that he replaces the father-in-law on the throne—a motif present even in contemporary folktales. The motif of fear of the son functions in the same way in the plot among the more advanced Zulu as the motif of fear of the son-in-law does among the more primitive peoples of North America. In a Zulu tale we read: "They say there was once a chief; he sired many sons. But he did not like having sons, for he said it would come to pass that if the sons came to power they would take away his power."[10] We have the very same motif, although already in an obscured form, in a Malagasy story whose setting has descended from the milieu of chiefs and future chief-kings to the domain of the common people. "Then they agreed that they would throw the child, if it were a boy, into a pond for fear he would harm them when he grew up."[11]

What causes the replacing of fear of the son-in-law by fear of the son? It is caused by a change in the form of government: the son-in-law as heir is replaced by the son as heir. The motif of fear of the son, along with the motif of patricide, must have arisen among the Zulu just at the stage when this form of inheritance was coming into effect. "The theme of the wife being banished with her children or children being driven away by their father the chief is very widespread in Africa," according to Snegirev.

A comparison of these two forms of inheritance (through the son-in-law and through the son) reveals one essential difference. Inheritance through the son does not in itself involve conflict. At this stage of social evolution, the birth of a son is typically a joyful event for the royal father. The motif of desire for a son is very widespread in folklore, along with the motif of childless couples praying for children "to be a comfort in life and a replacement for them after death."

Although hostility between father and son did exist historically—fathers were killed by their sons and heirs as late as the nineteenth century—the tale type does not arise from this situation. New social relations do not create a new tale type; rather they transfer the old conflict to the new relations. The son and heir, replacing the son-in-law, assumes the function of hostility to the father and of murdering him. Thus the motif of patricide arises in folklore.

This explanation clarifies only one aspect of the prophecy, its content, and says nothing about the fact of prophecy itself. A study of various prophecies in our tales shows one remarkable regularity in their appearance: oracles, forewarnings and prophecies are completely absent when power passes from the king to the son-in-law, when the identity of the son-in-law is not known and he comes from another lineage.

In omitting prophecies when the hero kills his future father-in-law, tales reflect a historical situation. It was commonly known that the king would be killed and succeeded by his son-in-law; the king himself knew that he would inevitably be killed and frequently committed suicide. If the situation were to be formulated in an oracle it would run: "O king, a man of another lineage will come to you; he will marry your daughter, kill you, and take your throne." As a rule, there are no such oracles in folklore. The few exceptions prove that our hypothetical oracle is not a fiction, but rather given in the nature of things. For example, Oenomaus was forewarned that he would die if his daughter Hippodameia married.

Prophecy is also lacking in the early stages of the occurrence of the patricide motif, in the Zulu tale, for example. The banishment of the son is motivated by fear of him and not by prophecy. But in the patriarchal era, fear of the son ceases to make sense; now, on the contrary, sons are desired. The fear of the son must be motivated by the outcome, by the denouement. Prophecy arose and replaced direct fear of the son in the period when the father's authority not only was well established but also formed one of the bases of civil and national life.

In such an era, under such a system of government, a hero could not desire to kill his father, or he would be not a hero but a criminal. In time corrections are made in the tale, necessitating various accommodations in the plot. For instance, deliberate murder is replaced by unwitting murder, intentional murder by one's own will is replaced by murder willed by the gods, for gods, too, appear in this stage.

The Zulu tale shows clearly that deliberate murder preceded unwitting murder of the father. The prophecy of patricide is unknown in preclass societies; it appears with the rise of the patriarchal system. The son cannot even wish to kill the father. But, on the other hand, the father, possessed of all the fullness of power, is free to act toward the son as he chooses. Oedipus, the killer of his father, is a criminal, albeit an unwilling one. But the deed of Laius, who tried to kill his son, is never regarded as a crime. The picture is entirely different in the earlier versions of the tale, such as the Zulu, when there is as yet no state and patriarchal authority is just coming into being. Here the father who tries to murder the son is the criminal, while the son who kills his evil father is neither a wrongdoer nor a victim, but a popular hero.

All these facts explain not only the content of the prophecy but also the reason why there is no mention in the prophecy of accession to the father's throne: namely that there was nothing unnatural in the accession of the son which would require motivation by an oracle. Only the murder required motivation.

Hence the oracle never speaks of murdering a father-in-law, but only of murdering a father or a father figure. For example, it is foretold to Acrisius king of Argos that he will be killed by his grandson, the child of his daughter Danaë, who would inherit the throne. This child is Perseus. In this instance the grandson obviously replaces the daughter's husband, and with the appearance of a grandson in place of the son-in-law prophecy comes in. The Medean king Astyages dreams that danger threatens him from the offspring of his daughter. The child is Cyrus, who is condemned to death as soon as he is born but is saved, reared in obscurity, and later raises Persia in revolt and seizes the throne of his grandfather (Herodotus I, 107–28). Here the heroic nature of the ascent to the throne is noteworthy—as yet there is no sin in killing the grandfather. It is also significant that the rule is for power to pass not to the son but to the grandson, the daughter's child. The daughter still serves as the intermediary in inheriting the throne. In Sophocles' lost tragedy, *The Aleadai*, Aleus the king of Tegea in Arcadia is told by the Delphic oracle that his sons will perish by the hand of his daughter Auge's son, if one should be born. Her child is Telephus, who kills his uncles, substitutes in this case for the father, since the father is the semi-divine Heracles. These cases explain in addition the fear of the daughter and her banishment along with her son. It is foretold to Peleus that he will yield his kingdom to a hero with one sandal. This hero he recognizes to be his nephew Jason, his brother's son. At this point inheritance is in the male line, but not yet going from father to son.

Finally the son makes his appearance. Odysseus is told at Dodona that he will meet death at the hands of his son. For this reason he keeps Telemachus at a distance but perishes by the hand of Telegonus, his son by Circe. According to Aeschylus, Zeus himself is destined to be dethroned by his son by the goddess Thetis. Only Prometheus knows the secret and he does not tell Zeus.

Finally also Laius must die by the hand of his son; this death is foretold him by the oracle who, however, doesn't predict that the same hand will deprive him of power. Greece has drawn from it the tragedy of involuntary sin, the most terrible for a Greek: patricide. The prophecy isn't motivated by anything. The course of history motivates it.

The Marriage of the Parents

As we have seen, the Oedipus story in modern folklore by no means always begins with a prophecy; sometimes it can also begin with an incestuous union of the hero's parents. Opening with incest is characteristic of the legends of Gregory, Alban, and Andrea da Vergonia and completely unattested in the classical story of Oedipus, though not entirely unknown in ancient sources. In this motif, as in the motif of prophecy, the new is superimposed on the old.

In the medieval texts usually the father is led to commit incest by sinful passion. But this is not always the motive. We already know that originally the mortal foe of the king is the son-in-law. If the king himself marries his daughter, he averts this danger and preserves the throne for himself and his descendants. In a thirteenth-century Latin text it is stated directly: "nec volebat ex filia suscipere generum" (He did not wish to have a son-in-law from his daughter).[12] He refuses all suitors, although some are nobly born princes worthy of her hand, and marries her himself.

The motif of the father wishing to marry his daughter is characteristic of tale type 510B,[13] as well as of the Oedipus type. But here too the father acts on his own initiative only in a few variants. Normally he is indirectly fulfilling the will of his deceased queen. On her deathbed the queen commands her husband to marry only a woman who can wear her ring (Xudjakov 54, Smirnov 25, et al.). The king begins to travel the world over and finds in the end that the ring fits only his own daughter. So he plans to marry her. Thus even here there is no sinful passion.

The same situation can arise if a king and queen on their deaths leave a son and a daughter. It should be noted that the princess in fairy tales normally has no brother. The reason for this lack may be that she transmits the throne whether or not she has a brother. There is no brother in folklore as long as there is no role for him in history. In a new epoch the inheritor is the son, not the daughter, and the princess acquires a brother. The folk mind has a simple solution for the conflict between the daughter as heir and the son as heir: it marries the brother to the sister. In this way the old order is preserved—the princess still confers the throne and the son-in-law inherits—and the new order is introduced—the son inherits the throne. Again the new is superimposed on the old.

The combination of new and old is revealed still more clearly in an old Serbian text and an old Bulgarian text analogous to it. A brother and sister are left after the death of their father. Suitors come and demand to marry the sister and take half the kingdom with her. Another king wishes to have the brother as his son-in-law and half the kingdom as well. Here we readily recognize the folktale interpretation of the old order of inheritance. The old order cannot be reconciled with the new, for the son of the king, the brother of the princess, is appearing as the heir on the historical horizon. The brother and sister are in despair; the kingdom of the father will be divided. "The brother and sister counseled together and said, 'What shall we do?' and they agreed that the brother would marry the sister and keep the entire kingdom."[14]

Thus the interests of state and dynasty form the original basis for incestuous marriage. Of course none of this ever really happened; all these are phenomena from the realm of imagination and folklore, reflecting the change that has taken place. We find the motif of brother marrying sister in other types of fairy tale as well, and again we see that the parents are the instigators of the marriage. "Once upon a time there were a tsar and a tsarina. They had a son and a daughter. They told the son that he should marry his sister when they died."[15]

However tempting it is to explain such marriages as traces of the incestuous family, there are no grounds for this supposition. The motif in our tale, an incestuous marriage following the death of parents or one spouse, is a phenomenon of a completely different order. It is a reflection in the imagination of the conflict between two forms of inheritance. Even when the tale is set in a middle-class milieu, the old arrangement remains evident. For example, in an Italian tale there is a wealthy family. The father dies without leaving a will. Later the dying mother tells the son and daughter, "'All the money and all the goods—keep them in the family.' The son said, 'do not worry, we will do as you say.'" The mother died; the brother and sister were alone. They began to grow up. The brother wanted a wife, the sister wanted a husband. But their mother's last wish required that they should touch neither the gold nor the silver, nor the money. Afterwards the brother proposes to marry the sister.[16] Here the royal family has been replaced by a wealthy family, and, just as in the former case incest allows the preservation of the kingdom, in the latter it allows the preservation of the wealth. And if the churchly novella makes a sin of this motif and the literary tale makes it a story of passion, the guileless folktale preserves the motif in its pristine purity. It is significant that incestuous marriage always occurs after a member of the family has died. The father coerces his daughter into marriage after his wife dies, the brother proposes to his sister after the father dies, the mother to her son after the husband dies, that is, at a moment when the question of inheritance becomes critical.

Banishment of the Child

In order to escape the oracle, Laius pierces the feet of his child and orders a slave to expose him in a wild place in the mountains. In the play Jocasta says:

> And for the son—before three days were out
> after his birth King Laius pierced his ankles
> and by the hands of others cast him forth
> upon a pathless hillside. (11. 717–719)

Laius treats his child as parents often do in folklore and myth. Sophocles diverges from popular tradition only in that he chooses the more rare form of abandonment in the mountains rather than the usual setting adrift in the water and he avoids the inconsistency or contradiction typical of this motif, namely that the child condemned to death is at the same time saved from death (for example, the barrel in which he is set adrift is coated with pitch so that he will not drown, etc.).

This contradiction is most interesting for us. It has already been noted in the literature, but not explained. Thus Diederichs wonders why in the Russian version of the Judas tale a paper bearing a name is placed in the chest along with the baby. This is very strange, in his opinion, because "casting upon the water is intended to do away with the unfortunate child."[17]

Careful examination of the motif, however, shows that this is precisely not the intention. At first sight it does seem that upon hearing the prophecy the father desires to destroy the child. To do this he orders a special chest, a watertight box. "He placed money in the box, bedding over that, and thereon laid the child."[18] The compromise nature of doing away with the child is especially clear in this text. In other cases, too, money is placed in the box. One has the impression that the child is being equipped not for death, but for a long journey, and everything is being done to ensure that he survive and be properly brought up. Sometimes the contradiction is avoided by a division of roles: the father orders the child's death, and the mother, or a nurse entrusted with the evil deed, takes pity on the child and in every way tries to secure its life. "They commanded the nurse to cut the child's throat, place him in a little basket, and set the basket afloat in the river, but the nurse took pity on him and put a placard on him with the inscription: a child cast into the river from such and such a city."[19]

Here a contradiction occurs in the parents' command. If the child's throat is to be cut, then why order him to be put in a basket? The nurse displays in this case the true wisdom of folklore: she only cuts the child a little around the neck, that is, she inflicts on him the mark of death, simulating decapitation, and thereby reveal-ing the full meaning of the motif. The child bears the marks of death, but he does not suffer death itself. Here we have a child being sent off on a long journey to be brought up, with the marks of death on him; we have seeming death but not real death. This case discovers the significance of Oedipus' pierced feet, which are another, deformed mark of death.

Russian tales are in this respect more archaic and more consis-tent. They have not only the mark of decapitation; even more often they have simulation of disembowelment. "When they had heard the prophecy, the parents washed him, dressed him, and thought to themselves. They cut his tummy; they took a little raft and lined it with pillows and set it on the river, saying, 'Don't touch it; it will float where it will.'"[20] The tale teller is completely unaware of the contradiction between the disembowelment that should kill the child and the pillows, signs of parental concern for the preservation of his life.

Although the marks of death are most prevalent in tales found on the territory of the USSR, this is by no means a peculiarly Russian feature. In a tale from Cyprus a mother inflicts a few blows with a dagger on her child's breast and nails him into a box which she casts into the sea.[21] So we cannot agree with Robert that the pierced feet of Oedipus were specially devised to prepare for the discovery of his identity.[22]

In sending the child towards a presumed death and in his upbring-ing far from his parents it is easy to recognize traces of an initiation rite. The picture of the upbringing will show this more clearly. For now it suffices to recall attention to the fact that the signs made on the child's body are signs of death. From the point of view of the literary composition of the tale, these marks are the tokens by which the child will later be recognized. It matters little whether the token is a kerchief, ring, red hair, a brooch, or an icon hung on the neck, or finally pierced feet.[23] Besides, the mark of the feet is encountered in Ukranian folklore as well: "They impressed a mark on his right thigh, prepared a little chest, and put the child inside; they then sealed the chest and with Judas inside cast it into the water." But this token is originally a mark of death, transferred from the slit stomach, severed head, or stabbed breast to the pierced feet. In these marks, as well as in the following motif of upbringing, it is easy to see traces of the rite of initiation.

It would be impossible to present here a comparative study of all the variants of the motif of casting on the water. Such studies in the folklore of the world reveal one salient recurrent feature: children cast into the water are the future leaders of their people. Thus Moses begins his career, so also Cyrus starts out by being thrown as a child into the Tigris; so, too, the Babylonian king Sargon I begins, and thus Oedipus, cast into the water, starts on his way to becoming leader, king, and demigod, or similarly in the Christian legends, Pope Gregory, St. Andrew of Crete, and others have their start. Stories of being banished by his mother are told also of Solomon, who is said to have spoken from the womb, accusing his mother of adultery. Among the Mongols, Genghis Khan is forced into exile as a child,[24] and in a Kirghiz narrative it is the mother pregnant with Genghis Khan who is cast into the water.

King Sargon is especially interesting for our purposes. In a cuneiform inscription in which he recounts his deeds and all his monuments and campaigns, he begins the story of his reign by telling how his mother placed him in a reed basket daubed with clay and set it in the river. This fact witnesses to his greatness as much as his monuments and campaigns; it proves the legitimacy and sacral authority of his kingly title.[25]

Passing through water is not only the beginning of a royal career; it is a precondition for accession to the throne. The marks of disembowelment, decapitation, or stabbing in the breast on the abandoned child reveal the significance of the whole motif. The king must be one who has passed through the rite of initiation and can display the marks of death, the equivalent of the ritual tatoo or seal.

Without discussing the essential significance of this motif in all its manifestations, we should add that the element of transporting the child in a boat or barrel derives from the archaic motif of transporting inside a fish. In American Indian narratives a youth is carried in the belly of a fish that has swallowed him; he cuts his way out. There is very clear evidence for the transference from fish to boat or barrel, from cutting oneself out of a fish to breaking out of the bottom of a barrel. We shall meet swallowing by a fish again in the discussion of the end of the tale.

All the evidence points to the conclusion that by being thrown into the water with the mark of death on him Oedipus enters upon the normal course of a popular hero in folklore. But if this is true, it controverts Robert's notion that Oedipus was thrown into the water in the role of a seasonal vegetation divinity (Jahresgott). As proof of this idea he refers to Aeschylus' mention that the child was abandoned in winter (fr. 122).[26] Study of the motif in the light of folklore shows that Robert's opinion is in error. The essential point of the motif of casting into the water lies in the preparation of the child for a career as a leader.

The Child's Upbringing

The hypothesis we have proposed concerning the origins and primary meaning of the motif of casting into the water is confirmed by study of the subsequent motif of upbringing. Here the Zulu material, coming from a society in the most archaic stage of development, offers conclusive evidence. Sikulumi, like the European hero, is condemned to death by his father because the father fears the son will kill him. But, again like his European counterparts, Sikulumi is spared by his mother or nurse. "It happened once that he fathered another son. The mother carried the baby under her arm to some old women. She gave them gifts and earnestly begged them not to kill him but to take him away to the mother's brother, for this was a son she loved very much. They took him to his mother's brother and settled him there."[27]

In this tale the child is banished twice. He soon returns from the first banishment but is driven away again by his father. This time the father "ordered his men to send him away; they set out and placed him far away in a large forest. For it was known that in that forest lived a huge many-headed beast—it was said to eat people."

The ritual of initiation consisted of an imitation of a totem animal swallowing and regurgitating a youth. The fiction of swallowing was regarded as death, the regurgitation as resurrection to life. Communion with the totem animal gave the initiate magic powers, made him a full member of the tribal society, and conferred on him the right to marry. Among the Zulu, a pastoral and agricultural people, the ritual was no longer practiced at the time of the formation of the tale; the myth of the tribal hero Sikulumi retains only traces of it, such as sending the hero to a beast to be devoured.

The beast does not swallow Sikulumi as it does in the American Indian tales. Instead, as the boy is sitting there, the beast emerges from the water. "This beast owned all things. It took the youth, did not kill him, and took him and gave him food until he grew strong. It happened that after he grew strong and needed nothing more, he had a numerous tribe, for this beast ruled all things, food, and people; he desired to visit his father. He set out with his huge tribe, himself being the chief."

In this tale the beast feeds and raises the boy, makes him a chief, and gives him a tribe. Then the boy sets out to kill the old chief, his father. It is not only stated but also clear from the subsequent narrative that the boy obtained magic attributes from the beast, power and invulnerability. This extremely important text shows that the hero of narrative who is sent to be devoured by a beast falls into the same situation that we know in initiation ritual. He is sent away to the beasts and returns not only hale and unharmed, but also a hero. Devouring by a beast is the earliest form of the motif of upbringing, one that is not preserved in European folklore. Thus the marks of death inflicted on the child's body, his condemnation to death that is not death, the inscription containing an invitation to raise the child—all these elements of the tale become comprehensible. The boy is sent off to be brought up.

While the forest has disappeared from later tales, the beast does not fade out completely or all at once. The boy is no longer raised by a beast, but he is fed by forest animals which suckle the abandoned child. Klinger is right in saying that "the number of ancient tales that speak of children being left in the wilderness and fed by animals is almost unlimited. The list of relevant citations given by Usener and Bauer is far from complete."[28] Suffice it to mention here at least Romulus and Remus, who were suckled by a wolf, and the Cyrus cycle.

Nourishment on the milk of wild beasts is, as it were, the second phase in the development of the motif. From this point of view, Oedipus represents a further stage. Later on a woman enters the scene: the child is given to a wet nurse or to a woman who has just given birth. Traces of the transition from animal to woman nurse are evident both in ancient narratives and modern folklore. There is an interesting example in Herodotus' version of the Cyrus story, in which the wife of the shepherd who takes the child in is called in Median Spako, in Greek Cyno, meaning bitch; i.e., the child is nursed by a woman bearing the name of an animal held sacred by the Medes. In more modern folklore in the chapbook tale of Genevieve, the mother is driven out with her son. When the milk of the starving mother fails, a doe appears and suckles the child. Thus we have a continuum running from raising by an animal through suckling by forest or other animals to nursing by a woman with an animal name or by a woman and an animal together.

Before tracing the further development of this motif, we must dwell on one detail in the Cyrus story. The boy is raised by a shepherd's wife, that is, in a certain social milieu that must be discussed before we turn to the figure of the foster parent. The appearance of shepherds here is no coincidence. Shepherds figure frequently in ancient tales yet are completely absent from European folklore.[29] Even the Zulu Sikulumi pastures livestock in his first banishment. The Zulu are a pastoral people who had already passed through the totemistic stage of tribal society characteristic of hunters and were forming a permanent state organization with inheritance from father to son at the time when the tale was created. Archaic forms of the motif have only shepherds as the foster parents of the abandoned child, as in the case of Cyrus. But when class differentiation arises with the creation of the state, the democratic chief is replaced by the king. Since the purpose of the upbringing is now to raise a future king, a royal family appears in the role of foster parents, without, however, completely eliminating the shepherd.

Shepherds find the child, but bring him to a king who gives him a
royal upbringing. This is what happens to Oedipus in all versions of
his story. In Euripides' "Phoenician Women," shepherds find the
boy and take him to Periboea, the wife of King Polybus. A shepherd
brings the boy to a royal court also in Sophocles. Later on, this
bifurcation of the finder and the foster parent can be preserved in
other forms, but equally often it disappears. There are no shepherds
in modern folklore. They are replaced most often by fishermen,
millers, or sailors, also often by a monastery. The disappearance of
the split role is connected with the transfer of the tale to a middle-
class setting. The hero does not become a king and so is not raised
by a king. Nevertheless there may be bifurcation of roles: If the boy
floats to a monastery, he is found by washerwomen or by regular
monks or nuns and brought to the abbot or abbess. Conversely,
even in the royal setting sometimes the finder and the foster parent
are the same person: for example, a princess who goes to the sea to
bathe or to wash clothes, as we have in the version of Oedipus
preserved by Hyginus (Fab. 66: "cum vestes ad mare lavaret").

The question of the social milieu in which the boy is raised
returns us to another very complicated and difficult question we
have already touched on, the question of the role of women in the
child's upbringing. We naturally expect that along with the shift
from animal to woman nurses we noted earlier, the last traces of the
animal (the woman's name) will disappear and the wet nurse will
emerge on the scene. This is in fact the case, but the situation is
complicated by the combination of two motifs—the motif of raising
by a supposed mother and the motif of raising by the natural mother
or nurse far away from the father with the child ignorant of who his
father is.

This latter motif is found in the American Indian myths. Evidently it was formed in that stage of the transition from matriarchy
to patriarchy when the absence of the father was beginning to be felt
as a shameful lack. Originally when the head of the family was a
woman, the husband did not live with her in monogamous marriage.
Husbands could be replaced; they could return to their mothers or
go to another woman. Marriage could also be polyandrous. The
child stayed with his mother and did not know who his father was.
At this time there was nothing shameful in this situation. But with
the transition to the patriarchal family and patriarchal authority,

the situation changes. From the point of view of the new order, the old way is ludicrous and shameful. The self-consciousness of the child who in folklore so often suddenly discovers that he has no father and sets out to find one reflects the social consciousness of the new order that regards having a mother but no father as a disgrace.

The motif of the boy raised with his mother, ignorant of who his father is, is preserved in the tale of Rustem and Sorab, the *Hildebrandslied*, the Russian *bylina* of Sokol'nik and other tales. The *bylina* about the fight between father and son provides some highly interesting and significant evidence for the history of the motif.[30] Sokol'nik's mother Latygorka is an Amazon, a queen and a mighty warrior who does battle even with Ilya Muromets. In her, as well as in her son, it is easy to trace an association with totem animals (he is surrounded by snakes, has animals at his command, birds on his shoulder, etc.).

The antiquity of the motif is attested by its presence among American Indians and Pacific Islanders. In a Micronesian myth a maiden is carried off by a spirit, lives with him, and then is sent home. She gives birth to a son. But his companions jeer at him because he has no father. The mother sends him to the father.[31] This is the most archaic form of the motif, preserved also in the tale of the battle between father and son. The boy lacks only one parent, the father, and he sets out to seek him. In the words of the *bylina* he has "no tribe, no family." Or in historical terms, he belongs to no patriarchal family at a time when this family type has become an historical fact.

Later on, with the establishment of monogamous marriage, the old tragedy of being deprived of a father is adapted to new conditions—the child is deprived of both parents, not just the father. Oedipus does not live with his mother apart from his father as Sokol'nik does; he lives far from both parents. But just as Sokol'nik goes to seek his father, Oedipus in European folklore goes to seek his parents.

The transition is especially clear in the story of Odysseus. He has two wives and two sons, one, Telegonus, by Circe, who lives far away (the name itself means born far away), the other, Telemachus, by Penelope. The common opinion that this is a simple case of doubling, that one figure is a pale copy of the other,[32] is incorrect. The marriage with Circe is a marriage of the old order: She is a totemistic and matriarchal, self-sufficient head of the family, a sorceress and a mistress of animals. Her husband does not stay with her. The marriage with Penelope is a monogamous marriage of the new order.

While in the *Odyssey* the old and new orders co-exist side by side, in the Oedipus story the new order has triumphed. Oedipus is the child of a monogamous marriage. However, it is easy to discover traces of the original natural mother in the background behind the foster mother living far removed from the real mother. Sophocles reduces the role of Merope to a minimum. She receives only passing notice, in connection with Oedipus' fear that he will marry her, the foster mother he believes to be his real mother.

But there is an older version preserved by Euripides and others. The foster mother here is Periboea. Either she finds the child in the water herself, or stable grooms find him. She is barren and convinces her husband Polybus that the foundling is her own child. Robert is absolutely right in saying, "The tragedian did not invent this story. It bears the stamp of popular tradition."[33] In Plutarch's account of Romulus and Remus a shepherd finds the children and brings them to his wife. She has recently miscarried and so takes the children for her own. The shepherd's wife in Herodotus' story of Cyrus gives birth to a stillborn child and joyfully accepts the child her husband has found as a substitute. In the story of Moses the substitution of the natural mother for a foster mother develops differently: The mother comes to the princess as a wet nurse and nurses her own child.

From these examples it is clear how the old motif of the natural mother giving birth to her child independently of a husband, and sometimes even without apparent participation of a husband, and raising the child far from the father, underlies the new motif of the foster mother taking in a child of a monogamous marriage without, however, entirely displacing the real mother.

Furthermore it is possible to establish that through the role of the woman we have another connection with initiation ritual, which involved in some way the idea of woman. Admittedly, in the era of initiation rites all intercourse with women was forbidden for a certain time on pain of death. Nevertheless the ritual of initiation recognized the female principle. Often the initiates had some secret common mother, never seen by anyone, but spoken of. The masked figure who performed the rite dressed in animal guise can be regarded as a female animal. The youth himself sometimes was changed into a woman. Hence the female attributes of the shaman, hermaphrodite gods, etc. It is possible that Achilles' being raised in girl's dress among the daughters of Lycomedes is related to this phenomenon. Traces of taking on a woman's identity are rare in antiquity in general; in Sophocles' *Oedipus* there are none at all. Perhaps, however, it is significant that Auge's son Telephus, whose story is very like Oedipus', grows up on Mount Parthenion with his friend Parthenius or Parthenopaius. The etymology of these names is apparent: They are connected with the idea of a maiden. If this is not mere coincidence, but rather a trace of a previous custom of raising a youth not only by a woman but in the woman's domain, then this tradition is related to the form that recurs in Russian and Belorussian tales in which the hero is raised in a nunnery.[34]

From the examination of this part of the motif of upbringing we can conclude that the beast is gradually replaced by the woman nurse, but that behind the figure of the nurse lurks the figure of the natural mother. We have observed an intersection of two motifs—the motif of the boy raised apart from his real parents and a more ancient motif of a boy raised by his mother apart from his father. Such an intersection was made possible because the rite of initiation, which separated the child from his family for upbringing, also involved the idea of woman as mother. On the one hand, the hero of the tale may find a second mother in his foster mother, who is supposed to have borne him, and on the other hand he may be raised in the woman's domain, which in modern tales takes the form of a nunnery.

The first thing that the fisherman—or monk or whoever it may be—does on finding the boy is to give him a name. This would seem to be a normal act, not worthy of attention. If we look more closely at it, however, it does not appear so simple. Once having referred to initiation ritual we should recall that one of the important moments in the ritual occurred when the youth adopted a new name. The receipt of a new name as it were emphasized and confirmed his death and resurrection in new form. It is significant that in tales the parents who set their child adrift usually do not baptize him on the pretext that he is a child of shame or often without any reason given at all. He is to receive his name not at home, but in that mysterious

family to which he goes. Cases in which they do baptize the child
anyway and publish the name by putting an inscription with the
child may be regarded as variations. Most often it is stated, sometimes in great detail, that the boy is named upon reaching a foreign
shore:

> [The abbot] took the child from the chest,
> Christened him in his own monastery.
> A fine name was given him,
> The given name: Simeon the Foundling,

as it says in a Serbian song.[35] Similar references in greater or lesser
detail are found in numerous texts.

Let us now look more closely at the place where the child lands.
It is impossible to define this place exactly, as the folk imagination
allows the most improbable settings. In his work on Oedipus, Robert
labors in vain to locate the child's destination on a map. In ancient
sources the Sicyonian shore, Corinth, the city of Elaea in Asia
Minor or Mount Parthenion (in the tale of Auge), and other places
are named. But whatever the places are called, all variants share a
common feature: they are all cut off from the world. Most frequently the place is an island, as in the legend of Judas (Iscariot
Island); monasteries are also very common. If it is a kingdom, it is a
completely isolated kingdom where wars are unknown and no news
penetrates from the rest of the world. There is an air of unreality
about it. It lies far away, like Egypt, Assyria, or Hungary. The hero
is carried there by the waves of the sea and returns home in a ship
tossed up on land by a storm (especially in the Judas legend).

But this faraway and mysterious place turns out at the same time
to be nearby, sometimes in one and the same text. In such cases of
inconsistency, usually one form is older than the other. The Zulu
text reveals the most ancient and original form: The boy is sent to a
forest that is not far away. The place of upbringing turns out to be
nearby also in the Malagasy text. As ideas of distance develop, the
isolation and mysteriousness of the place are perceived and desig-
nated as removal to a distance. We cannot trace here how the place
becomes an island or what role water plays in the process. The
transformation into an island, a place visited by no ships, where
only a storm can land a tiny boat, takes place naturally. No one
knows the way to this place. The pretense of ignorance in ritual

takes on the character of genuine ignorance in the tale; the mysteriousness of the place is indicated by the fantastic names which the bearer of the tradition connects not with any idea of a concretely existing place but only with the idea of distance.

Besides the place of upbringing, we must also examine the surroundings in which the hero grows up. In his new home the boy almost always has companions of his own age. For example, after many years of being barren a queen takes in a foundling and then unexpectedly gives birth to a child of her own. If the child grows up in a monastery, unaccountably there are other boys there as well.[36] Sometimes he is raised by a miller or a fisherman with a numerous family. Or two fishermen find him and quarrel over who should take him. One is childless but refuses to take the child; the other has many children already, but his wife is good-hearted and the child goes to the large family. The intention to provide companions for the hero is obvious.[37] The boy is raised in a collective, either in a monastery or with a group of brothers, or even with one brother supposed to be his twin, or a playmate, or finally in a school. All these forms of collective, easily identified in modern folklore, have disappeared in Sophocles. Oedipus is the only son of his adoptive parents Polybus and Merope. Only the drunken feast where the insult is given suggests the presence of some undefined surrounding group of companions.

This feature can be explained in two ways: Either raising the boy in a collective is purely realistic (children usually grow up in groups), or there is some historical and folkloric significance to it.

As a rule we do not find collectives in folklore. If there are brothers, there are three of them, a purely conventional number. All the interest of the narrative focuses on the single hero. The one exception is the bands of seven, twelve, or so warriors who live as brothers in the forest. The connection between this motif and the initiation cycle has been demonstrated elsewhere.[38] Our hero is raised in different conditions. Nevertheless a form of brotherhood can be observed here, whether it be siblings (even if only supposed siblings) or a monastery or a school. Thus the old collective is adapted to new conditions of life, but the new forms do not create the collective.

On examining the growth of the boy, his stature and his amusements, we find a similar adaptation of old notions to new ways of life. Sophocles says nothing of how the boy is raised, how he grows and develops. In modern folklore he sometimes grows with marvelous speed and almost always surpasses his companions. He not only learns reading and writing and all sciences faster than anyone, in the monastery he not only masters all theology so quickly and well that he soon knows more than all his teachers, but he also acquires wisdom and authority. He is destined to become abbot. Sometimes he is even a "sweet singer."[39] "The lad was swift to learn and swift to become wise."[40] Reading, writing, and theology are later forms equivalent to the wisdom and experience acquired by the future leader. Even in antiquity the originally magic character of this wisdom, which is easily recognized in many types of the fairy tale, was lost. It is best preserved in the story of the lawgiver of Tartessus, Gabis, found in Justin's epitome of Trogus. This is the most archaic of the tales in the Oedipus cycle, but it has attracted no attention from scholars. Here the boy is thrown into the wilderness to be devoured by beasts. But the hungry dogs and swine not only do him no harm, they even feed him with their milk. A second attempt is made to do away with him by throwing him into the sea, but the waves carry him to shore. A doe nurses him, and he acquires extraordinary agility, equal to that of the deer with whom he courses over forest and mountain.[41] In other words, his power comes from a beast, just as in the African myth of Sikulumi. After becoming king, the boy is the first to give laws to his uncivilized people: He abolishes slavery and teaches them to plow the earth and plant wheat. It is clear from this that during the period of his unbringing the hero acquires the qualities of a leader, and that originally these qualities were connected with totemistic magic and with the training of youths during initiation.

The hero's playtime activity is evidence of the same connection. The boy surpasses his companions not only in theology and monkish knowledge but also in sports competitions. He hurls a stone farther than the others, jumps farther, etc. He is ambitious and sometimes even bullying. This last quality is exaggerated in the tales of Judas. He mocks his less able companions, beats them up, and finally kills his own foster brother, after which he runs away. Of course Judas does not become a leader or king. But the connection of this motif with kingship is clear in Herodotus' story of Cyrus. The boys are playing at being king. Cyrus naturally turns out to take the part of king. One boy, the son of a distinguished Mede, does not obey him. Cyrus flogs him severely, and from that point the rest of the events unfold. Similarly in the Zulu tale Sikulumi takes the lead over his companions, though in a completely different, purely African way. He orders them to slaughter a bull, which according to Zulu law is a right belonging only to grown men. By this action he shows the boys that he is already a man.

The happy life of boyhood could continue for a long time. In some cases, in fact, if the hero is raised in a royal family, he stays there to assist and later succeed his supposed father, as Alban does. But the fatal secret remains, the secret of the child's birth. He is not the true son. The secret is brought to light.

It makes no difference for the development of the plot which of the great variety of means is used to reveal the secret. In Sophocles' play, at a drunken feast someone calls Oedipus a bastard (line 779). This incident, unique among the versions of the story, is purely Sophocles' invention, yet at the same time essentially folkloric. We do not know who this drunk is, nor do we know how he learned the secret of Oedipus' birth so carefully guarded by his supposed parents. Oedipus rushes to see his parents but still does not learn the secret. He hastens on to Dodona and there learns his future, which impels him to flee Corinth. He is running away from his future. This touch derives from Sophocles' inspired tragic conception of the plot. In folklore events proceed differently, just as they probably did in Sophocles' sources. The hero quarrels with his companions at play, he injures and beats them, or they him, or they envy him his extraordinary successes, and someone drops the fatal word, "foundling." How they know the secret is again not explained. The revelation of the secret is motivated in folklore by a fit of rage, in Sophocles by drunkenness. After making inquiries, the hero discovers the fatal truth, whereupon he departs. Unlike Oedipus, he runs away from his past. In the saints' legends he usually knows nothing of a prophecy and cannot know of it. He sets out for the Holy Land to expiate the sins of his parents. But the waves carry him to his native city, or else he, like Rustem, sets out "to seek his family and clan." He runs away simply out of shame. "I am ashamed to hear your own little boy call me a bastard."

The variety of the reasons why the hero departs lead one to suppose that these are only pretexts. The real reason for departure is that the time has come for his upbringing to be ended. New adventures await the hero now that he has become a man. Folktales and legends of the Oedipus type often omit entirely the revelation of the secret of the hero's birth. They simply say, "So soon as he grew up, he took his leave." "They raised him until he was seventeen." "He grew up and the fisherman said, 'Be off now, my son, into the world'" etc.

For the same reason it is precisely at this point that the secret of his birth is made known. Speculation on how the companions found out the secret is pointless. The fatal word has to be let fall in order to give the hero a reason for leaving. The unvarying element of departure needs motivation of some kind. The motivation provided would itself require motivation from our point of view, but not from the point of view of the poetics of folklore, in which causal connections do not play a decisive role in the development of a plot.

In cases where the hero is raised in a nunnery, the reason for departure is different. It is said of the hero, "He began to keep company with the nuns, to flirt with them. The nuns complained to the abbess. The abbess decided, 'We can send him away; now he can win his own bread.'"[42] The abbess dismisses the hero with the same words that other foster parents use. The boy has reached maturity, as he shows in the Buslaev text by seducing three nuns and the abbess. In other words, the basic reason for the hero's departure, his having reached manhood, remains the same, while the immediate pretexts in folklore for his leaving vary widely.

Departure

Where does the hero go? The hero of the standard fairy tale first receives a magic gift, an agent or helper, and then goes to the kingdom of his future wife, where with the aid of his magic gift he performs the difficult tasks set by the princess and then marries her. Similarly the initiation ritual was intended to prepare the youth for marrying. The usual order of events in the fairy tale reflects matrilocal marriage, the entry of the bridegroom into the bride's family.

The norm for the fairy tale is that the newcomer should have no family when he arrives in the bride's kingdom. This is a reflection of a very ancient practice. The bridegroom, having received a new name (and we have seen that the heroes of Oedipus tales, too, are renamed), feigns ignorance of his family. He has left his father's family and has not yet entered into his wife's. The motif of "Know Nothing," the hero who remembers neither mother nor father, is based on this situation. The Russian tale of Oedipus contains clear examples of the motif. On arrival in a city where he is offered a wife, the Russian Oedipus answers a question concerning his identity: "I do not know my parents. I came from a certain monastery where I grew up."[43] Or, "I am a miserable orphan, I have no father or mother and know not my family."[44]

The future leader of men follows exactly the same path as the fairy tale hero. We have, for example, the unrecognized arrival in *Oedipus*. After leaving the country of King Polybus, Oedipus, though he believes himself to be a king's son, enters Theban territory not in a kingly manner, on horseback or in a chariot, but as a stranger, a foreigner, a lonely traveler acquainted with no one. There is no necessity in the course of events for him to arrive thus; he could ride in a chariot splendidly armed. But he does not come as a king's son because the tradition of "Know Nothing" is predominant at this point.

This small point throws further light on the connection which exists between Oedipus and the fairy tale, a connection so intimate that not only isolated details but also the very essence of the Oedipus tale became clear only through comparison with the fairy tale.

In order to understand the subsequent events in Oedipus' life, we must briefly sketch a picture of the adventures of the fairy tale hero after his arrival in the country of his future wife. After entering the bride's kingdom unrecognized, he learns that the king has proclaimed some kind of difficult task, such as freeing the city or the princess from a dragon. The reward for accomplishing the task is the hand of the princess and half the kingdom. The hero fulfills the task, thus completing his first adventure. In the second adventure, not met so frequently but nevertheless attested in folklore in various forms and with various motivations, he kills the old king, the bride's father. And for the third adventure he marries the rescued princess and becomes king. This is the usual fate of the fairy tale hero.

Now let us see what happens to Oedipus. Just like the fairy tale hero, he is sent away from home. But after his upbringing he does not go on to the country of his future wife. Rather, unbeknownst to himself, he returns to the home of his father. As a hero of the new patriarchal order he heads for his father's family, the family to which he belongs, rather than for his wife's family. This shift in Oedipus' destination represents a turning point in the history of the tale. At this juncture Oedipus diverges from the fairy tale and forms a new offshoot, a new tale within the framework of the same compositional scheme.

Oedipus goes through the same three adventures as the fairy tale hero: He unwittingly kills the king of the country he comes to; he solves the riddle of the Sphinx and thereby delivers the city from distress; as a reward he receives the hand of the queen. These adventures parallel those in the fairy tale but differ from them in several respects. First of all one notices a change in the order of events. In the fairy tale the difficult task precedes the killing of the king; in the story of Oedipus the events are reversed. Sophocles' *Oedipus* does not make clear that the riddle of the Sphinx is a difficult task. A scholium on Euripides' *Phoenician Women*, however, tells that the citizens proclaimed that whoever delivered them from the scourge would receive the hand of the widowed queen and the crown. According to patriarchal ideas, the heir could not ascend the throne during the lifetime of the old king. The promise of the kingdom could be made only after his death. Thus the king must be killed first, and then the promise of the kingdom and the queen's hand can be offered. Under the matriarchal system, on the contrary, the heir appears as the daughter's husband first, and then the old king is removed, or as the fairy tale has it, shares the kingdom with the son-in-law. Hence in the fairy tale the proclamation of the task comes from the old king himself, while in *Oedipus* it comes from the citizens of Thebes who have lost their king.

Now let us look at each of the events in this general sequence, in the order given by the fairy tale rather than that of *Oedipus*. This order will facilitate both exposition and comprehension of the argument.

The Sphinx

How and why the Sphinx appears in the city is not explained in *Oedipus*. The attribution to the wrath of Hera suggested by a scholium on Euripides' *Phoenician Women* is clearly secondary, as

Robert also has shown. Everything seems to happen by coincidence at this point. Oedipus happens to arrive at a city which for no apparent reason is beset by the anger of the Sphinx. The underlying motivation for the appearance of the Sphinx is clear in the fairy tale, in which the motivation of events is entirely consistent with the plot. The motive for the challenge to the hero is the testing of a suitor by means of difficult tasks set by the princess herself or by her father. As tests the difficult tasks are both motivated logically in the story and explainable in historical terms. We cannot pursue here an investigation of the Sphinx-woman, who in our view is the result of a combination of the princess who sets the task with the dragon who demands tribute in human blood. It is sufficient to establish that in terms of the fairy tale we have in the riddle of the Sphinx a difficult task. The actual substance of the task is irrelevant.

Originally the tasks brought no benefit to those who set them. Such tasks as hiding oneself, sitting through a hot bath, eating an enormous number of oxen, leaping up to the princess' window, and the like, had a magical character and were supposed to justify the hero's claim to the princess' hand. In *Oedipus* the task has a utilitarian character. The city is in distress; a hero appears, delivers the city and wins the right to the throne which he himself has cleared by killing his predecessor.

The riddle of the Sphinx was created by transferring the task from the princess to a dragon. The Sphinx clearly has the attributes of a woman, and in some versions Oedipus deprives her of her power just as the princess-sorceress in fairy tales is deprived of hers—by sexual intercourse. But the transfer of setting the task to a different figure introduces the element of coincidence into the plot: The Sphinx is motivated not by anything in Oedipus' past, but rather by his future, as preparation for his marriage and accession to the throne. If one takes Sophocles' *Oedipus* in isolation, there seems to be a lack of connection between Oedipus' past and the appearance of the Sphinx.

Why is Oedipus the only one who can solve the riddle and destroy the Sphinx? In Sophocles his success seems due to luck and nothing more. Or perhaps it is because he is especially intelligent, wise, clever, and skillful? As Robert points out,[45] in antiquity Oedipus was renowned for his wit; his sharpness became proverbial. According to Aeschylus, even the gods admired it. Comparative folklore, however, suggests a causal connection between Oedipus'

past and the defeat of the Sphinx. Oedipus overthrows the Sphinx
not because he has wit, guile, or skill, but because he is following the
course of the fairy tale hero and the leader: He has been set adrift in
the water, raised in a far-off, mysterious kingdom (rationalized in
Sophocles into Corinth), and now proves himself in fulfilling a
difficult task. Thus through comparison with the fairy tale of folklore it is possible to see a consistency in the sequence of events that
has been obscured in Sophocles.

Patricide and Marriage

The main points concerning patricide have already been made in the
discussion of the oracle. We were able to establish that regicide
preceded patricide, murder by the son-in-law preceded murder
by the son, and intentional, even heroic killing of the old king
preceded unintentional, involuntary killing. The reason for one
succeeding the other was seen to be that the son replaced the son-in-
law as inheritor of the throne. The reflection of this shift in the
Oedipus story is not incidental nor is it unique to this tale type. It
illustrates the natural process by which new tale types are created in
new social settings.

The arrival of the fairy tale hero in the country of his future wife
leads to the killing of the old king, the father. Originally no enormity
was seen in such an action. Our most archaic example of a patricide
in this system of tales, Sikulumi, remains a true hero, just as the
murderer of the father-in-law always does. Cyrus, too, remains a hero
despite killing his grandfather. But in the course of time this action
came to be regarded as an atrocity. With the new consciousness of
wrongdoing, tragedy was born.

In this connection, patricide must be examined as a compositional element. The killing of the father-in-law was fully motivated,
although modern folklore buttressed the motivation by making the
old king an evil-doer. The reason for the murder was lost when the
father became the victim in place of the father-in-law and fatherhood was invested with an aura of sanctity. As we saw, even in the
Zulu myth the father committed the crime of attempting to kill his
son, thus giving the son cause to kill him instead. In later tradition the
son kills the father accidentally and unwittingly. Two coincidences,

in themselves unconnected with anything, thus arise in the Oedipus plot: the overthrow of the Sphinx and the killing of the father. The whole tale acquires an air of fatality; consequently in all European scholarship *Oedipus* is treated as a tragedy of fate although in essence, and in historical terms, it is not. In origin the tale is one of winning the throne through murder and marriage; in substance it is a tragedy of patricide, of involuntary sin, of misfortune. Its hero is a hero in all respects and therefore becomes tragic. There would be no tragedy if the hero were a villain. Later tradition developed in this direction, associating the tale with the villain Judas. The tale plot remains the same but is no longer tragic.

Hitherto it has been impossible to interpret the coincidence of the patricide except as the working of fate, because the Oedipus tale has not been studied comparatively. Even Robert saw no connection between the patricide and the overthrow of the Sphinx.[46] The comparison with folklore reveals all the original connections and shows that they were lost when the action was transferred from one set of characters to another.

After fulfillment of the difficult task, the further progress of the fairy tale hero involves his marrying the king's daughter and succeeding to the throne. Oedipus, too, marries and becomes king. The events are the same as in the fairy tale except that the hero has arrived not at the bride's home but at his father's home, which is also the bride's home. This change involves not one but two alterations in the fairy tale sequence.

First, if the alteration were simply superficially carried out, we would expect Oedipus to marry the king's daughter, as the fairy tale hero always does. Theoretically, then, Oedipus should marry his sister. And in fact there is evidence that such a solution is not foreign to folklore. Bernhard Schmidt, a collector of contemporary Greek folktales, notes that he heard stories in which Oedipus marries his sister. Unfortunately he did not record or publish any of these tales. The putative role of the sister in the Oedipus system of tales is best supported by the story of Cronos, who castrates and succeeds his father Uranus and marries his sister Rhea.[47] Nevertheless, no such forms of the Oedipus tale are attested. In the extant tales a second alteration is made: Oedipus marries the king's widow.

The method of looking for reflections of historical contradictions in folklore that we have applied above can help also to explain this second alteration. The contradiction reflected here is a conflict between two female figures: the king's daughter and the king's wife. Under the old order, the daughter plays the decisive role in the transfer of power. The throne passes through her hands to a foreigner, while she remains in her place. Under the new order, the king's daughter marries someone who takes her away with him, rather than a new arrival who stays with her. These two possible orders are clearly reflected in modern folktales. Either the hero marries the king's daughter and stays with her, receiving her father's kingdom—the old original order—or, after marrying, the hero goes to his father's kingdom with her and takes the throne there—the new order. In the latter case the princess has lost her role as transmitter of the throne. She has been deprived of this role also in *Oedipus*, because the son now appears on the historical scene to replace the son-in-law. Oedipus son of Laius is the son, following the new order, and at the same time the suitor, following the old order. When the king's daughter disappears, her role passes to the king's widow. Oedipus marries his mother. The old role has been transferred to new characters created by changes in the social order.

The First Apotheosis of Oedipus

Having married and ascended the throne, Oedipus has completed the course of the fairy tale hero. The fairy tale normally ends at this point. The hero in the fairy tale is descended historically from the original creators of the world order, law givers, and founders of culture. Such, for example, was Gabis, the lawgiver of Tartessus, who was thrown out for beasts to devour and later returned, was recognized by brands on his body and by his facial features, inherited the kingdom of his father-grandfather and first gave laws to his people, founded cities, abolished slavery, and taught people to plow the earth and sow wheat.[48]

The later hero does not give laws or teach people to plow, sow, or forge metal. All this he finds already done. The fairy tale hero only ascends the throne, he does not reign. But Oedipus' story could not end with accession to the throne; Oedipus reigns. This element of reigning enters relatively late in the evolution of the tale through the elaboration and extension of the fairy tale's apotheosis of the hero. Oedipus not only reigns, he reaches sublime heights as king. He is a near divinity. "Oedipus whom all men call the great" (1. 8) is a king-god such as Frazer described in *The Golden Bough*. He can save the people from the plague and mediate between gods and men. The old priest says of him:

> Perhaps you'll hear a wise word from some god
> perhaps you will learn something from a man.
> God hears you from the heavenly height,
> to you the thoughts of men are open
>
> (11.42–43)

Likewise in the fourth ode the chorus sings:

> [He] ruled and reduced to nought
> the hooked taloned maid of the riddling speech
> standing a tower against death for my land;
> hence he was called my king and hence
> was honoured the highest of all
> honours; and hence he ruled
> in the great city of Thebes.
>
> (11.1198–1203)

Traces of Oedipus the magician-god-king-priest are scattered throughout the tradition.

Oedipus' reign contrasts with the following phase of the action when the tragedy begins. He might have reigned thus to the end of his days. But the fatal secret remains, demanding revelation.

Exposure

The last act of Oedipus' literary biography is also the first act of the tragedy proper. The exposure begins.

The narrative tradition of folklore again shows us the original form of the motif. Exposure takes place quite simply in the fairy tale and is recounted in two or three lines. The duration of the marriage varies from one night to a number of years and in some (very rare) cases children are produced. The incest in the marriage bed is made known by a scar on the stomach or neck, a seal on the feet, by an icon or a picture or a gospel that had been placed with the baby in the chest, or even by the chest itself which the hero carries about with him always, as Peleus and Neleus do in Sophocles' lost tragedy *Tyro*. Zelenskij notes that Peleus "for reasons unknown to us" brings with him a trough in which he and his brother were found by their foster father. We should speak of literary intentions rather than of reasons. The recognition is prepared by this somewhat naive device.

The physical evidence, the pierced feet, that plays a decisive role in folklore has only secondary importance in the play. In the fairy tale the mother-wife on discovering the scar on the wedding night at once reveals the truth to herself, the hero, and the audience. If Sophocles had handled the tale as modern tradition does by effecting the exposure instantaneously, his tragedy would have failed as an artistic whole. We need not speak here of the artistry with which Sophocles arranges the exposure. Beginning with the plague, which is itself an as yet unfathomed and mysterious revelation of some shameful deed, the truth is gradually unfolded. Tiresias reveals it to the audience. In telling of Laius' death Jocasta reveals the patricide to Oedipus without understanding its significance herself. The shepherd reveals the incest to Jocasta in Oedipus' absence, and then tells Oedipus, confirming at the same time the fact of the patricide.

Thus the whole tragedy grows out of a single incident in the narrative tradition, the exposure. The tragedy in fact consists in the exposure or recognition. All the other incidents recede to the background. They are essential to the plot, but they are introduced only briefly and in retrospect. They are necessary only insofar as they move the action toward the last terrible moment.

Oedipus' Second Apotheosis

Sophocles' tragedy ends at this point. The rest of the action— Jocasta's suicide, Oedipus' self-blinding and parting from his children —is an artistic elaboration of the situation, but not a further development of the plot itself.

The figure of Oedipus is clearly ambivalent. He is a great hero and benefactor to his city and kingdom and at the same time he is a great criminal. This incongruity demands a resolution. In the early versions of the tale type, when patricide is not perceived as shameful and no incestuous marriage is involved, the tale finishes with the hero's marriage and enthronement. The later notion of patricide as a crime committed involuntarily by a noble hero requires either the rehabilitation of the hero, that is, insofar as there is a sense of pollution involved the absolution or expiation of his sin, or conversion of the hero into a thorough villain. Folklore develops both possibilities, associating the tale on the one hand with saints, on the other hand with Judas. The criminal traits of the central character were developed and emphasized much later, because early epic tragedy demanded a noble hero, not an evil one.

Comparison of *Oedipus at Colonus* with modern folklore shows that *Oedipus Rex* and *Oedipus at Colonus* together form an organic whole; they are not two separate stories. Andrew of Crete, Gregory, Paul of Cesarea, and others undergo a second apotheosis that parallels *Oedipus at Colonus* not only in basic substance but also in details.

The folktale is constructed according to certain laws of composition that hold in all its parts.[49] If the hero undergoes further adventures after his marriage, these adventures are always ordered in the same way as in the first round of events. The story enters a second move. The second move, however, is not a repetition of the first. While the compositional framework remains fixed, it is filled out with the most varied content, so that only the trained observer can perceive the underlying repeated pattern.

In this way *Oedipus at Colonus* forms a second move following *Oedipus Rex*. Oedipus leaves his home once more, as he did before as a boy. Once more he is exiled, once more he faces utter neglect and obscurity. The departure of the hero from home is the first stage in the further development of the action.

The events the hero experiences fall into two groups, those that themselves determine the outcome of the action and those that result from determinative events. The essential determinative event in the most archaic versions of the hero's progress is the swallowing of the hero, subsequently recast in other forms and reinterpreted. Swallowing makes the hero. This is the course of the hero, put in the briefest schematic form, a course that has very complex historical origins.[50]

Oedipus the king has followed this course. We have already observed how the motifs of being set adrift and brought up in a foreign land are derived from ritual swallowing by beasts and how this act prepares for further events: marriage and accession to the throne. But we also saw how the old plot came into conflict with new social relationships and how Oedipus, while retaining the features of the great hero and leader, tragically became a dishonored wrong-doer. This situation requires a second move to follow. Oedipus leaves home again, to be swallowed again, not by a beast or by water this time, but—in accordance with the new agricultural religion—by the earth.

The cult of the earth was the vital religion of ancient Greece. Out of touch with this religion, in the later Christian tradition of Europe the tale lost the clarity characteristic of *Oedipus at Colonus*. For this reason it is not surprising that modern folklore, while it preserves the kind of details that clear up the obscurities in *Oedipus Rex* and permit the decipherment of much of the story, did not preserve such details relating to *Oedipus at Colonus*. On the contrary, the Greek material, rooted in a still living religion (Oedipus became the object of a cult) complements and illuminates material in contemporary folklore. Nevertheless we shall see that even in this part of Oedipus' story some details are clearer in modern folklore than in Sophocles.

The penance imposed on the sinner is best and most fully preserved in Russian, Ukrainian, and Belorussian material. The hero invariably goes under the earth in some way. For example, Andrew of Crete goes to the archbishop. "They came to a church where there was a well. The people had dug for seven years and found no water, so they had closed it up. It was of unfathomed depth."[51] Or in another case, "The bishop ordered a vault to be dug three sazhens deep and one-half sazhen on each side."[52]

The nature of the penance is explained by another form transferred from other legends and occurring alongside the form of burial, that of watering a burnt log until it grows and yields and bears fruit, and similar tasks. It is clear that this penance is a trial: If the log blooms, the sinner is forgiven; if not, he is condemned. Burying the hero under the earth also is trial as well as punishment. "He gave an order that if after thirty years the vault should fill with earth and the earth rise above the vault, then he would be forgiven." This passage must be understood to say that the hero is to be imprisoned for thirty years underground without food and that if the earth rejects him and throws him to the surface, he is forgiven, but if it swallows him forever, he is condemned. Also in a Belorussian story, "The earth began to rise in the well and by the thirtieth year it had outgrown the well so that he was right under the roof."[53] That is, the well filled up from the bottom and lifted Andrew from the bottom to the very roof. The notion is expressed still more clearly in a Russian tale: "Here a mother and son were thrust into the earth in two separate wells. When these wells fill up so that you come out, then God will forgive you."[54]

Just as the hero is being plunged into the earth, another incident takes place. The keys to the well or to the victim's fetters are thrown into the sea where they are immediately caught and swallowed by a fish. After the set term expires, a miracle occurs: the body of the hero emerges from the earth and the keys emerge from the water. Either they float up by themselves or the fish that swallowed them is caught. The keys thus are doubles of the hero, being swallowed by the sea and the fish as he is swallowed by the earth and returning home at the same time. In ancient stories only swallowing by the earth occurs.

The western versions of the tale type do not have the hero go underground. The sinner departs to a cave on an island or on the shore, often on a rocky, precipitous islet (whence the name "Gregory on the Stone"). As living in caves is customary for repentant sinners, one does not readily see in the western material any connection with *Oedipus at Colonus*. In Russian and other Slavic material the motif of the earth is very common. The earth plays a role even when the sinner builds a structure on it. For example, he finds an empty hut by the sea. "He went in and ordered them to lock him in and cover the hut with earth." Or a hermit advises him, "My child, make a wooden house and place a high mound of earth over it." The youth does so. "He heaped a high burial mound over it."[55]

The last quotation indicates that the victim enters a grave, just as Oedipus does. But he does not die in the manner of other men. Like Oedipus, he does not even die at all. The earth returns him, but not as he was. Rather he is transformed; a shining light and a fragrance emanate from him, the bread and water beside him are untouched, he is no longer an earthly, physical being. The popular imagination spares no colors in painting the picture of his holiness. It restores him in new and splendid shape. Regardless of whether he is actually alive or dead, his existence is perpetuated in one of two ways. If dead, he is immediately declared a saint and miracles are wrought by his body. If alive, he lives on also as a saint, or he becomes the Pope of Rome, that is, once more he becomes a ruler, but a ruler of a different order.

In this respect the stories of Oedipus, Gregory, and Andrew of Crete all develop in the same way. In Oedipus, the power of the earth makes the hero a cult hero, just as Andrew of Crete becomes a saint, though not a saint of the kind the church recognizes. The church's story of Andrew's life does not resemble our legend, for such a hero could not be canonized. The legendary hero, while he becomes pope, does not represent the ideals of the Catholic church. Behind the Gregory and Andrew of legend, the scholar sees the monumental figure of ancient Oedipus, whose remains also worked miracles—they defended the city from enemies.

After it had lost the sacred character inherent in its ritual origins, what attraction did the tale type have? Its appeal lay in one feature, the suffering of the hero. Individual suffering was foreign to ancient Greece, for the Greek was first of all a social being. Nevertheless, in Greece even at the height of its flourishing, when the first signs of decay were already evident, the suffering of Oedipus has a private character. Oedipus, the incarnation and heart of the city, of its achievement and its prosperity, suddenly is thrown out by this society and left alone with himself. He loses the crown, that he had never misused for personal ends but had used only in the service of his people. He loses the woman who was both wife and mother to him, who linked him with the pulse and current of life. It is no accident that he uses her pin to put out his eyes, to put himself in the darkness that is a symbol and expression of his separation from the world. He must lose his children too. The children also are presented in a way not entirely Greek. The Greek father, following a deep instinct molded by his society and state system, desired sons. Oedipus has daughters as well as sons. It is through the tenderness of the daughter that he later finds the way for a partial return to the world. The scene of his parting with the daughters is perhaps the most moving in all tragedy. At that moment Oedipus becomes truly human, and man enters European history.

The notion of suffering gives us the key to the acceptance of the tale by Christianity and its becoming a Christian legend. The tale had acquired a new kind of sacredness even in the Greek version, with the second apotheosis of Oedipus. The first apotheosis is the victory over the Sphinx and Oedipus' becoming king; the second is the swallowing of the victim by the earth and his becoming a god. But, characteristically, in the wholesome world of ancient Greece Oedipus the divinity is not a defender of the suffering. He becomes the defender of the city from the dangers of war—whichever side has his body will triumph. The medieval legend did not accept the first apotheosis and reinterpreted the second. But in studying this process of development we should not limit ourselves to analysis simply of the tale type; the tale should be examined within the framework of the course of history. Just as the pastoral Zulu, the nomadic Berbers, the mountaineers of the Caucasus, and the ancient Greeks all left their mark on it, so too the struggle between the church and the humanistic aims of the Renaissance, the gloomy seventeenth century, and the unrealized ideals of the peasantry are all reflected in the tale in ways that only an extensive historical study of human culture could show.

NOTES

[1]*Živaja Starina*, XXI, 1912, p. 346.

[2]V.Ja. Propp, "Mužskoj dom v russkoj skazke," (The Men's House in the Russian Folktale) *Učen.zapiski LGU* No. 20, Serija filol. nauk, vyp. I, 1939.

[3]N.Ja. Marr, "Sredstva peredviženija, orudija samozaščity i proizvodstva v doistorii," (Means of locomotion, tools for self-defense and production in prehistory), *Izbr. rab.*, vol. III, 1934, pp. 123–151.

[4]Obert, *Rumänische Märchen und Sagen*, 1925, No. 46.

[5]Sir James George Frazer, *The Golden Bough*, 1 vol. ed. (New York: Macmillan Co., 1963), p. 180.

[6]The king is killed: I.A. Xudjakov, *Russkie narodnye skazki*, St. Petersburg, 1861, Vol. III, 83; A.N. Afanas'ev *Narodnye russkie skazki*, 2nd ed., 1863 et seq., 122a, 123, 123 var.2; D.K. Zelenin, *Velikorusskie skazki Vjatskoj gub.*, St. Pet., 1915, 105; A.M. Smirnov, *Sbornik velikorusskih skazok arhiva RGO*, I, II, Petersburg, 1917, No. 4, 30, et al.

[7]Franz Boas, *Indianische Sagen von der nordpacifischen Küste Amerikas*, Berlin, 1895, p. 65.

[8]Ibid., p. 118.

[9]A. Kroeber, *Gros Ventre Myths and Tales*, Anthropological Papers of the N.Y. Mus. of Nat. Hist., Vol. I, Part II, New York, 1907, p. 88.

[10]Callaway, *Nursery Tales, Traditions and Histories of the Zulu*. Natal, 1866, no. 41. Russ. trans.: *Basni i skazki dikih narodov*, trans. from English, St. Pet., 1874,

pp. 50–55; *Skazki Zulu,* I.L. Snegirev, trans., Moscow-Leningrad, 1937, pp. 56–60. The son is sent away by his father the chief, who fears that he will usurp his power. The child is reared in the forest by a beast, acquires invulnerability, and returns to kill his father.

[11]Ferrand, *Contes populaires malgaches,* Paris, 1893, p. 93.

[12]Haupt, *Historia Albani aus ein. röm. Handschr.,* Monatsb. d. preuss. Akad. d. Wiss., Mai 1860, pp. 245–55.

[13]Bolte-Polivka, II, p. 65.

[14]Novaković, *Arch.f.slav. Phil.,* XI, 1888, p. 321. Lamanskij, *ŽMPN,* 1869, VI, p. 118.

[15]Afanas'ev, No. 164. Cf. Af. 65 and Af. 161 and the notes to them in the edition of Azadovskij, Andreev, and Sokolov (Vol. I, Leningrad, 1936, Vol. II, 1938, Vol. III, 1940).

[16]Finamore, *Archivio per lo studio delle trad. popol.,* V, 1886, p. 95.

[17]*Russische Revue,* 1880, IX, p. 122.

[18]Oniščuk, *Materialy po gucul'skoj demonologii* (Mat. po ukr. etnol., XI) 1909, pp. 12–15.

[19]Dobrovol'skij, *Smolenskij etn. sbornik,* 1891 (Zapiski RGO, otdelenie etn., XX), p. 269, No. 34.

[20]Smirnov, 186.

[21]Liebrecht, "Kypr. Märchen," *Jahrb.f.rom.u.engl.Litt.,* 1871, p. 351.

[22]C. Robert, *Oidipus. Geschichte eines poetischen Stoffes im griechischen Altertum,* Berlin, 1915, Bd.I-II.

[23]Incidentally, the mark on the feet turns up also in Ukrainian folklore. "They took him and put a seal on his right leg. They made a chest and put him in it and sealed the chest and threw the chest with Judas into the water." Gnatjuk, *Legendy,* II, No. 414 (Etn. Zb.XIII, 1902).

[24]G.N. Potanin, *Očerki severo-zapadnoj Mongolii,* 1883, IV, p. 802, 827.

[25]Gressmann, *Altorientalische Texte u. Bilder etc.,* 1909, p. 89.

[26]Robert, *Griech. Heldensage,* pp. 885–86.

[27]*Skazki Zulu,* pp. 56–57.

[28]V. Klinger, *Skazočnye motivy v istorii Gerodota,* Kiev, 1903, p. 38.

[29]The Byzantine texts form an exception: V. Istrin, "Die griechische Version der Judaslegende," *Arch.f.slav.Phil.* XX, 1898, pp. 605–620.

[30]For an index of the variants and a basic bibliography see A.M.Astaxova, *Byliny severa,* I, 1938, pp. 609–614.

[31]Frazer, *The Belief in Immortality,* III, p. 193.

[32]Robert, *Griech. Heldensage,* p. 1397. "Telemachos . . . ein abgeblasster Doppelganger des Telegonos."

[33]Ibid., p. 885.

[34]"The child floated to an island. On the island was a nunnery." Dobrovol'skij, p. 869. For example, the child's arrival at a nunnery is described with great detail and artistry in the Buslaev manuscript of the seventeenth century.

[35]Vuk St. Karadžić, *Srpske narodne pjesme,* II (Beograd, 1964), No. 13, 14.

[36]Karadžić, *Srpske nar. pjesme,* II, 1875, 2nd ed., No. 14, 15.

[37]Gnatjuk, *Legendy,* II, No. 327.

[38]S.Ja. Lur'e "Dom v lesu" (The House in the Forest), *Jazyk i mysl.*, VIII, 1932, pp. 159–95; V.Ja. Propp, "Mužskoj dom v russkoj skazke" (The Men's House in the Russian Folktale), *Uč. zap. LGU*, 20, Ser. Fil. nauk, I, 1939, pp. 174–99.

[39]N.I. Kostomarov, "Legendy o krovosmesitel'stve," *Socinenija*, vol. I, 1903, p. 179.

[40]Gnatjuk, *Etn. Mat.*, VI, No. 49, *Etn. zbirn.*, XXX, 1911.

[41]Klinger, op. cit., p. 41.

[42]Smirnov, 186.

[43]Ibid.

[44]Gnatjuk, *Etn. Mat.*, VI, No. 49.

[45]Robert, I, p. 859.

[46]"Ein kausaler Zusammenhang zwischen dem Vatermord und der Tötung der Sphinx hat schwerlich bestanden." *Oidipus*, I, p. 58.

[47]Hesiod, *Theogony*, 453ff.

[48]Klinger, op. cit., p. 41.

[49]V.Ja. Propp, *Morfologija skazki*, Leningrad, 1928.

[50]V.Ja. Propp, *Istoričeskie korni volšebnoj skazki*, Leningrad, 1946. (In preparation at the time of writing of this article.)

[51]B.T. Romanov, *Belorusskij sbornik*, vyp.IV, Vitebski, 1891, p. 163.

[52]N.I. Kostomarov, *Pamjatniki starinnoj russkoj literatury i pr.*, vyp.II, 1860, p. 417.

[53]Romanov, op. cit., IV, p. 163.

[54]Smirnov, op. cit., p. 186.

[55]Kostomarov, *Leg.*, p. 189.

Is the Legend of Oedipus a Folktale?

Alexander H. Krappe

The question of whether the story of Oedipus is or is not a genuine folktale is a legitimate one. Alexander H. Krappe (1894–1947), well-schooled in the international, comparative approach to folk narrative, argues that it is not, suggesting that although individual elements may have come from oral tradition, the tale as a whole is a conscious literary creation. Therefore, the apparently independent Oedipus stories do not, in Krappe's view, constitute bonafide variants of a tale type but are rather derivatives of a literary original. Krappe's approach exemplifies a point of view all too common in departments of literature whereby orally transmitted texts are assumed to be degenerate forms of written precursors. For an appreciation of Krappe, a prolific writer of more than six hundred books, articles and reviews, see Anne C. Burson, "Alexander Haggerty Krappe and His Science of Comparative Folklore," Journal of the Folklore Institute, *19 (1982), 167–195. See also Edith Smith Krappe and Anne C. Burson, "A Bibliography of Works by Alexander Haggerty Krappe,"* Journal of the Folklore Institute, *19 (1982), 197–214.*

Antti Aarne, the great Finnish folklorist, in compiling his *Tale Type Index*,[1] included a number of themes which are not folktales (märchen) in the commonly accepted sense of the word. Since the purpose of an index and of a bibliography is, above all, to orient researchers, one cannot blame him: better give too much than not

Reprinted from *Neuphilologische Mitteilungen*, 34 (1933), 11–22. We are indebted to folklorist Lee Benzinger for translating this essay from French into English.

enough. What is more serious is that, perhaps basing his opinion on this *Index*, the Swedish scholar Martin P. Nilsson felt obliged to refute the "mythic" theory of Carl Robert, noting that the Oedipus "myth," far from having religious ritual origins, is nothing but a folktale of the kind which is still told by European peasants.[2] It will therefore be useful to examine this legend from the folkloristic point of view, in order to determine if it is really a folktale having a legitimate place in Aarne's *Index*.

Let us make this clear: a folktale is a narrative composed of a series of "motifs" arranged in a more or less fixed and logical manner. Each one of them has a considerable number of oral variants independent of one another, and independent also of the written historical variants. For example, the *Tale of Polyphemus* is a true folktale because we know of more than a hundred oral variants of it, independent of the Homeric episode, and derived from an archetype older than the *Odyssey*. The Oedipus legend is composed of several elements of which the first is more than a simple motif: it is in itself a true folktale, that of the "Enfant fatal."

> An oracle predicts that a child to be born will kill his father
> (grandfather, uncle) or will dethrone him. In order to prevent
> the fulfillment of this prediction, the child is abandoned. But
> the prophecy comes true all the same.

This is the well-known legend of Cyrus, a real folktale.[3] The Oedipus legend is more complicated: the oracle announces that the "Enfant fatal" will not only kill his father, but that he will wed his mother, thus adding incest to murder. After having unwittingly killed his father, old Laius, Oedipus arrives in his native city. He conquers the Sphinx, who, in the lost archetype, did not amuse herself by posing riddles but was content to eat the citizens in the manner of folktale dragons.[4] As a reward, the queen of the city, who is his mother, offers him her hand, and he marries her. Many years later (in the archetype, probably soon after the wedding[5]) the spouses discover the horrible secret. Neither he nor his mother survive for long after this revelation.

This classic legend is not altogether isolated. At least several other tales, ancient as well as medieval, have been likened to it. If they are real variants of this theme and independent variants, only then will one be able to consider the Oedipus legend a true folktale. First, there is the legend of Telephus and Auge, subject of a lost drama by Sophocles, the *Mysoi*, but of which the compiler Hyginus has preserved the peripeteia:[6]

> The argonaut Idas wages war against King Teuthras of Mysia, host of the beautiful Auge, in order to deprive him of his kingdom. He would have succeeded in this enterprise if the young Telephus, illegitimate son of Auge, had not come at the last moment looking for his mother. Victorious, he receives the offer of Auge's hand from the grateful king. Refusing to enter into any marriage, she menaces Telephus with a sword when a large serpent, sent by his father Heracles, emerges. The mother and son recognize one another and return together to Arcadia, their native land. It should be added that Telephus had also been abandoned after a sinister prediction that he would kill his uncles; a prophecy which comes true.

One can see that this is a variant of the "Enfant fatal" theme but without the incest. If the tale of Telephus and Auge were to be classified, I would say that it belongs to the genre of "recognitiones," a much cultivated genre during the Greek decline, and later in the comedies of the Italian Renaissance. It is certainly neither myth nor folktale.

This tale was extremely popular in Persia. The following episode has been taken from the *Schah Nameh* by Firdousi:[7]

> The beautiful Humaï gives birth to a posthumous son whom she orders placed in a box with gold brocade and several precious stones and thrown into the Euphrates. The child is found and reared by humble people. But his royal blood soon makes itself known: He becomes a valiant knight. Having learned that his foster parents are not his real parents, he takes leave of them and sets out to join the army sent by Humaï against the king of Rûm. A mysterious voice tells the commanding officer that the young Dârâb (that is the name of the hero) is the king of Iran. He distinguishes himself in this war. Upon the return of the army, Humaï recognizes him as her son and names him her successor.

It is true that in this tale there is not so much as the shadow of incest: There is no question of a marriage of Humaï with her son.

This should not deceive us as to the true character of this episode. Humaï is a widow; Dârâb distinguishes himself in a war; without a doubt, there was originally a reward, and this reward was naturally the hand of the queen. If the existing tale says nothing of all that, it is the fault of Firdousi, who had very good reasons to suppress these things. It is known that he wrote under the noses of the Muslim imams who were wary of the ancient legends of Mazdaist Persia. It so happened that what the new masters abhorred the most were the "incestuous" marriages which were tolerated, or even advocated by the religion of Zarathustra.

That this interpretation is correct, and that Firdousi knew more about it than he wanted to admit, is revealed in a European variant, the curious legend attached to the name of Pope Gregory I:[8]

> The hero is the son of an incestuous union of brother and sister. Abandoned in a barrel which is thrown into the sea, he is found by fishermen and reared by one of them under the surveillance of an abbot. After finding out that he is a foundling, he leaves to take up arms. He arrives at his mother's castle (his father is dead), which is besieged by a knight who is trying to obtain her hand. Our hero defeats the besiegers. The vassals force the woman to marry him as a reward for his services. That is how he becomes his mother's husband. Some time later, she discovers the horrible secret through certain tablets containing the story of his origin. She had put them into the barrel with the child, and the good abbot had given them to him upon his departure. She warns [or informs] her husband of their destiny. Believing himself to be hopelessly doomed by this double incest, he imposes upon himself the most harsh penance, chained to a rock in the middle of the ocean. After seventeen years spent in that way, a miracle announces the end of his suffering: He is elected pope. His mother becomes a nun.

The mere reading of this summary is enough to convince one that it has so little in common with the Oedipus legend that one cannot even say, with E. Littré,[9] that it is a pale reflection of it. This is why the reviser of Aarne's *Index*, Stith Thompson, rightly considers it a type separate from the classic tale.[10] All one can say is that both contain incest, a son marrying his mother without knowing it. But the Christian legend has improved upon the horror of the classic tale by adding a second incest, which was unknown in antiquity. On the other hand, the legend of Saint Gregory contains nothing of the prediction, nothing of the murder, nothing of the Sphinx, nothing of the voluntary death of the sinners. To tell the truth, it gives the impression of being a variant of the Persian legend of Humaï and Dârâb, with the difference that the incest in it is consummated. All the rest is pious drivel invented by the monks.

The same can be said of the legend of Saint Alban.[11] Since the most ancient versions of the legend do not mention it[12], there is no reason to doubt the secondary character of these imaginings. Here are its most important peripeteiai:

> The hero is born of an incestuous union between an emperor and his daughter. The child is abandoned on the highway of a foreign country (Hungary). After many perils, he finds himself at last at the court of the king of Hungary who adopts him as his son and leaves him the throne. The emperor, without suspecting anything, offers him the hand of his daughter. This is how he comes to marry the one who is at the same time his mother and his sister. The secret is discovered through the rings and the coat of arms which the baby had been given before he was abandoned. The two spouses separate in order to lead lives of penance and piety until their deaths.

There is no doubt that this legend is even more remote from that of Oedipus than the preceding one.

On the other hand, here, finally, is one which doubtless belongs to the same type as the ancient myth: the famous legend of Judas:[13]

> There was in Jerusalem a man, Ruben Simeon, whose wife, Cybore, learned in a dream that she was to give birth to an "Enfant fatal." He was put into a box which was immediately abandoned to the waves of the sea. He was found and reared by a queen. Soon afterwards, she gave birth to a son. The foundling, who was none other than Judas, developed a grudge against his foster brother and ended by killing him, after which he embarked for Jerusalem. There, he entered the service of the governor, Pontius Pilate, who one fine day sent him to steal some apples from a neighbor's orchard. The latter was none other than Judas' real father. As he objected to the intrusion of the thief, Judas killed him without ado. Pilate, in order to show his gratitude, had him marry the wife of the victim, who, of course, was Judas' mother. The secret was discovered through

the confession of the wife to her husband of what she had done to her son. Filled with remorse, Judas left Cybore and joined the disciples of Christ. The rest of this somber story is well known.

Looking at this legend, one is struck by its similarities with the Oedipus myth: the sinister prediction, the means of getting rid of the child,[14] the murder of the father by the unknown son, the incestuous marriage. It contains it all. If the Sphinx is missing, it is apparently because it was not needed. Judas is nothing less than a hero. But it goes without saying that the legend of Judas, for these very reasons, has no independent value. It is a Christian and scholarly legend, traced upon the model of the ancient myth.[15]

A Russian tale, which is equally striking, attached itself to the name of Andrew of Crete, one of the heads of the orthodox church in the seventh century:[16]

> One day, a merchant of Crete heard the conversation of two doves predicting the birth of a son named Andrew, who would kill his father, marry his mother, and violate 300 nuns. The merchant ordered the child to be killed. But the mother had him baptized Andrew, had his body opened and attached to a board which she ordered thrown into the sea. The board was recovered by a nun who gave the child to her abbess. This is how Andrew came to be raised in the convent. Grown to maturity, he seduced the 300 nuns including the abbess, was expelled from the monastery, and entered into the service of his own father who had him guard his vineyard. In order to test his new servant, he entered his vineyard at night, was taken for a thief, and killed by his son. After confessing to his mistress what he had just done, he was chosen by her to take the place of her husband. The scar he had on his stomach revealed his identity. Horrified, he fled and received absolution after a long penance similar to that of Gregory. He ended by becoming the successor of the holy bishop who had imposed it.

This Russian text is clearly based upon a Yugoslavian model. What reconciles it to the classic myth is the prediction (through the birds' divination), the mutilation of the "Enfant fatal," the manner in which he is abandoned, the murder of the father by his son, the incestuous marriage, and the discovery of his identity through a scar.[17] The clerical character of the tale makes it clear that, once again, we are dealing with a scholarly or semi-scholarly version of an ancient myth. The same is true of the other extant Slavic and Finnish texts on this theme.[18]

From the existence of this legend among the southern Slavs, some enthusiasts have concluded that it is a question of an "Aryan" myth surviving among the Slavs as well as among the ancient Greeks.[19] One could not imagine a more fanciful theory. It is, on the contrary, certain that we are dealing with relatively recent medieval borrowings from the Byzantines by the Slavs established in these regions.[20] In addition, they are not popular borrowings; the hand of the Christian clergy is so clearly implicated that one cannot doubt the scholarly or semi-scholarly character of these fictions. Neither can one conclude anything from the fact that these texts approach the primitive version of the Oedipus myth, since they tell that the child is abandoned to the waves of the sea and that the incestuous marriage remains sterile, as was the case in the ancient "Oedipodeia."[21] The fact is that the floating casket theme is one of the most widespread and popular.[22] It is therefore highly probable that it presented itself independently to the various narrators. As to the incestuous marriage, one can understand that the revisors, in order to bring their tale to the well-known edifying end, considered it wise to suppress the theme of Oedipus' sons. There remains the motif of the wound inflicted on the baby. But who cannot see that this does not serve any other purpose than to bring about the denouement? Physical marks, scars for example, are such banal occurrences in plots whose subject is the recognition of long-separated close relatives, (think of Odysseus' scar!) that the motif doubtless presented itself to more than one tale teller. What is true of the Slavic texts, is equally true of modern Greek texts: They are all derived, more or less directly, from the classic texts.[23] There is nothing to be drawn from them. One must therefore declare that modern European folklore is of no help to us in resolving the problem.

It remains for us to discover a very curious legend collected in our day in Burma. Here it is:[24]

> The six successive husbands of Queen Kin Saw U are each in turn killed by a dragon. By one of the unfortunate kings, she has a son, Pauk Tyaing, lost in the forest as a child, then reared

by strangers. His foster parents inculcate in him three maxims: In order to attain what you wish for, travel! In order to obtain wisdom, inform yourself by asking questions! In order to live a long time, be prudent! Following the first of these maxims, he arrives at the paternal kingdom (without knowing it), where he is offered the crown. Remembering the second maxim, he asks what happened to his predecessors. Then he accepts the offer and marries the queen. Faithful to the third maxim, he keeps himself from falling asleep on his wedding night. When the dragon comes, he kills it with his sword.

The queen asks him a riddle (it is not known why), menacing him with death if he cannot solve it. Knowing the language of animals, he learns the answer to it from a crow. The queen gives birth to twins, born blind as a result of the dragon's exhalations. They are put onto a raft which floats downstream. They end by regaining their sight and by founding the city of Prome.

Regardless of what one thinks of this legend, it is certainly not of Burmese origin. It is, first of all, a famous tale of Persian or Sanskrit origin, incorporated into the *Book of Tobit.* Another tale, that of the incestuous marriage from which twin sons are born, came along and attached itself to it. Therefore, there cannot remain the slightest doubt about the fact that it is a variant of the classic Oedipus myth which emigrated to India. Here is the proof: (1) The riddle posed by the queen to her husband lacks any motivation. It is obviously the Sphinx's riddle clumsily transposed. (2) The twin sons are obviously Eteocles and Polyneices, no doubt originally twin brothers.[25] Far from being an independent folkloristic variant of our theme, this Indian tale is only a derivation of the Greek legend, without any value whatsoever for our investigation.

Let us return now to the principal problem: Is the Oedipus legend a folktale? The facts reviewed here allow only a negative answer to this question. The ancient myth is composed of two themes, that of the "Enfant fatal" and that of the separation, followed by the reunion of a mother and her son. The two are found to lead isolated existences, the first, for example, in the legend of Cyrus, the second in that of Dârâb and Humaï. No one mentions the incestuous marriage of a mother with her son. In the second one, it is true, there is a danger that the incest takes place, but a noteworthy fact is that it is always in order to prevent the incest that the recognition (recognitio) takes place, often through a veritable "Deus ex machina." The first of the two themes is a true folktale; the second is not. It is rather what is called a "novelette theme" [or "short story theme"] of the kind very common in the work of Boccaccio and of his successors. A fusion of a folktale with such a theme, with the incest added for good measure, does not at all have the feel of folk art. Rather, it gives the impression of a work of art consciously devised by a professional storyteller. It is the product of a great civilization, of an individualistic art knowingly making use of all the means at its disposal. The primitive, rudimentary, collective art of the folktales has nothing to do with it.

The folktale of the "Enfant fatal" and the short story about the recognition of separated relatives have little in common. One must therefore ask oneself why the idea of fusing them occurred. The problem is not difficult. The short story [or novelette] requires the separation of the parents and their son. The stories of the Greek decline and of the Italian Renaissance used, as means toward this goal, sea adventures, tempests, and pirates. Antiquity preferred to add to the interest of the story by motivating the separation through a sinister oracle and the vain precautions which are taken to prevent its fulfillment. The fusion of the two themes was therefore primarily exterior. That this was so, is proved sufficiently well in the tale of Telephus and Auge. There, the hero does not kill his father, as in the Oedipus legend, but his uncles, characters who play no role whatsoever in the rest of the story. Thus, the fusion of the "Enfant fatal" theme with the other is far from being organic. As a result, the story of Telephus and Auge gives the impression of being a first, rather clumsy, draft of this combination of tales. The legend of Oedipus is the logical and perfect culmination of this development.

Besides these considerations, we have ascertained that there is no folktale corresponding to the peripeteia of the ancient legend, except for some derived scholarly or semi-scholarly versions and secondary derivations of the ancient theme. It is unlikely that an ancient popular tale, had it existed, would have disappeared completely or have been suppressed by the scholarly and semi-scholarly versions. This would, at any rate, be a unique event.

All this destroys, in effect, Martin P. Nilsson's thesis. Does this mean that we must adhere to that of Carl Robert? I do not think so. Nilsson's objections regarding this "religious ritual" theory are only too well justified. But I don't know what should prevent us from seeing in this "myth," from the beginning, what it clearly was at a later period: a work of art, the creation of a master tale teller or, if one prefers, of a group of master tale tellers. Homer was certainly not the first in ancient Hellenic civilization.

NOTES

[1]A. Aarne, *Verzeichnis der Märchentypen*, Helsingfors, 1910, no. 931.

[2]*Gött. gel. Anz.*, 1922, p. 36 and following.

[3]*Revue des études grecques*, XLIII, 153–59.

[4]Carl Robert, *Oidipus*, Berlin, 1919, I, 49; D. Comparetti, *Edipo e la mitologia comparata*, Pisa, 1867, p. 28.

[5]Robert, op. cit., I, 62 and following.

[6]Hyg. *fab.* 100; cp. the *Lexikon* of Roscher, V, 277 and following.

[7]*The Sháhnama of Firdausí*, tr. A.G. Warner and E. Warner, London, 1905–15, V, 294 and following.

[8]L. Constans, *La Légende d'Oedipe*, Paris 1881, p. 111 and following; Carl Voretzsch, *Altfranzösische Literatur*, Halle, 1925, p. 109; J.E. Wells, *A Manual of the Writings in Middle English*, New Haven, 1916, p. 172.

[9]*Histoire de la langue française*, Paris, 1863, II, 172.

[10]He gives it the number 933, unfortunately, without adding any bibliographies. For the same reason, I agree with M. Sparnaay (*Verschmelzung legendarischer und weltlicher Motive in der Poesie des Mittelalters*, Groningen, 1922, p. 53) against M.G. Ehrismann (*Anzeiger f. dtsch. Altertum*, XLIII, 64), in reducing to its minimum the influences of the classic myth on this medieval legend.

[11]R. Köhler, *Kleinere Schriften*, II, 184; Littré, op. cit., II, 254.

[12]W. Meyer, in *Abh. d. kgl. Ges. d. Wiss. zu Göttingen*, N.F., VIII (1904), p. 1 and following.

[13]Constans, p. 95 and foll.; Creizenach, in the *Beiträge* by Paul and Braun, II (1875), p. 177–207; A. Graf, *Miti, leggende e superstizioni del medio evo*, Turin, 1892–93, I, 282 and foll.; F. Guillén Robles, *Leyendas moriscas*, Madrid, 1885–86, I 34 & foll.; Paul Lehmann, in *Studi Medievali*, II, 310, & foll.; P.F. Baum, "The Medieval Legend of Judas Iscariot," in *Publications of the Modern Language Association*, XXXI (1916), p. 481 & foll.; R. Foulché-Delbosc, "La Légende de Judas Iscariote," in *Revue Hispanique*, XXXVI (1916), p. 135 & foll.

[14]It is known that, according to a sufficiently old tradition, young Oedipus is gotten rid of by being thrown into the sea; see E. Bethe, *Thebanische Heldenlieder*, Leipzig, 1891, p. 67. Carl Robert, I, 79, leaves undecided the question of whether this version is the oldest.

[15]This is also the very healthy conclusion of an American scholar; see M.B. Ogle, in *Transactions and Proceedings of the American Philological Association*, LIX, 200.

[16]Victor Diederichs, in *Russische Revue*, XVII (1880), p. 131 & foll.

[17]In the primitive version of the Oedipus myth, the wife-mother of the hero recognizes him by the scars on his feet, the result of wounds inflicted on him when he was a baby; see Robert, I, 62 and following.

[18]They can be found in Sir James G. Frazer's book, *Apollodorus, The Library*, London, 1921, II, 370 and following. See also Constans, p. 106 and foll.

[19]*Archiv. f. slav. Phil.*, XI (1888), p. 322.

[20]There are even some who purloined the Latin texts of the Saint Gregory legend, for example the Serbian song in Talvj, *Volkslieder der Serben*, Halle-Leipzig, 1835, I, 139, cited by M. Bethe, op. cit., p. 67, who is not even aware of it!

[21]Bethe, p. 164; Constans, p. 36.

[22]Constans, p. 103, and the bibliography given in my book *Balor with the Evil Eye*, New York, 1927, p. 12, n. 43.

[23]B. Schmidt, *Griechische Märchen, Sagen und Volkslieder*, Leipzig, 1877, p. 248; Constans, p. 104 and following.

[24]R. Grant Brown, *Folk-Lore*, XXXII (1921), p. 93 and foll.

[25]Robert, II, 104. Aeschylus, it appears, was always aware of this major fact; at least this is a natural conclusion of the expression "Kings from the same seeds" used by him. (Sept. 804).

On the Oedipus Myth

Georgios A. Megas

In 1950, Georgios Megas (1893-1976), Professor of Folklore at the University of Athens, challenged the findings of Alexander Krappe with respect to the possible folktale sources of the Oedipus story. By assembling oral texts collected in different regions of Greece and by referring to additional oral texts from other parts of Europe including texts ignored by Krappe, Megas attempted to argue that these modern tales are independent of written tradition. For Megas, written texts do not produce oral tales. Rather oral tales may find their way into written tradition. For an idea of Professor Megas's contributions to folklore, see Richard M. Dorson's "Foreword" to Georgios A. Megas, Folktales of Greece *(Chicago, 1970), pp. xlii–xlv.*

Seven years ago, while writing my essay on the legend of Judas in folk tradition, I made no attempt to discuss the Oedipus myth with which Judas has traditionally been compared. I just contented myself with comparing a few elements of the ancient Oedipus tradition preserved by commentators and fabulists obviously derived from the myth of Oedipus.[1] Unfortunately, I did not know about A.H. Krappe's essay, "Is the Legend of Oedipus a Folktale?"[2] I recently received from Paris an extensive summary of the essay through my friend D. Petropoulos, and because I find its contents

Reprinted from *Epeteris tou Laographikou Archeiou*, 3 (1941–42) [1951], 196–209. We are greatly indebted to Athina Hobiti DeBusk for undertaking the translation of this essay from modern Greek into English.

133

quite different from my own views, I find it useful to consider his ideas. I will first examine related material and then Krappe's opinion about the ancient myth.

Krappe regards the medieval narratives connected with Judas's name as logical fabrications modelled after the Oedipus myth. He claims the many Slavic tales about Andrew of Crete, etc. are borrowings, relatively new, medieval, or taken from Byzantium. With respect to the Pope Gregory I and the St. Alban narratives where the subject of incestuous marriage is brought up twice and there is no mention of a prophecy, or the Sphinx or suicide of the sinner, Krappe contends these stories have so very little in common with the Oedipus legend that one cannot even say with E. Littré that it is only a pale reflection.[3] Even the stories that are told by the people as actual folktales and that have been made known to us through L. Constans' writings[4] are considered by Krappe to be, like the Judas and Andrew of Crete narratives, merely logical or semi-logical fabrications imitating the ancient myth.

To the tales the summaries of which I noted above, I have to add a Ukrainian one, republished by J. Frazer,[5] which in all its action resembles a Finnish one but which in its main points has been influenced by the Russian version of the Andrew of Crete story.[6] I should also add here two Romanian[7] and four Hungarian[8] tales which are listed in the Romanian and Hungarian tale type indices under Oedipus tales. For the Romanian ones, the indication given is: "The exposed son marries the widowed mother." For the Hungarian ones, "The characteristic points of their type are very poor." However the original collections in which these tales were published I was unable to see.[9]

Among the Greek tales of the type belongs a variant which comes from Epirus, and it is written in the semi-peasant dialect.[10] I cite it here, translated word by word as it was rendered by my collaborator in the folklore archives, D. Oeconomides:

Potametes

There was a time and there was not.

Once upon a time, about a hundred years ago, in the end of the world, there lived a man and a woman. They had nine children. After the ninth child, the woman became pregnant again and the days of birth were near.

After the woman had borne the child, the Fates came to order its destiny.

Because the woman had a lot of children, she did not await the new baby with a good heart. So the third night, she did not put a cake, or food, or wine on the table.

Once the Fates came and did not see the table set, they became very angry and began to order upon the child a life full of miseries: his father to die, his nine brothers to die, to be left all alone and miserable, and when his time came to marry and to get his mother for his wife!

When the poor mother heard what the Fates ordered upon her son, she began to tremble the shirt off her body, and she did not sleep until dawn. She thought and thought of what to do! Finally she decided to escape the misfortune.

She got up, took the child, and went down by the river to drown him. But the poor mother was distraught and could not bring herself to throw the child into the river. She left it on the river bank and left. When the unfortunate woman was gone, there came a man passing by. He heard the baby crying, so he picked it up and took it home.

The man came from a different region, and because he found the child by the river, he called him "Potametes."[11]

The child grew up in this man's house until one day he became very strong. When he matured, he asked his father:

"Tell me, why do you call me Potametes?"

In the beginning his father did not want to tell him, but later on because the boy insisted too much "Tell me, tell me," he told him exactly how he found him as a baby left by the river bank.

Unhappy as he could be, the youth did not have any choice. He got up, put a piece of bread in his sack, and left to find his parents.

He reached his father's village, but having been gone since he was a baby, he did not know his origin. He went to an old woman. The woman did not have any children. She asked him, and found that the boy did not have any parents. She tried hard to adopt him and marry him off to a beautiful widow. The old woman told him that the widow was very rich, that she had had nine children and that they all had died, and later on, her husband died too, and she was left all alone. She also told him that no man's foot steps in her house and if he wanted, he could take her for his wife.

By talking and talking, the old woman changed the youth's mind and he married the widow.

Many years went by and the poor widow who had borne him had forgotten the order of the Fates. But after she was married, she questioned the young man about his parents. Potametes sat down and told her everything he knew from the man he was raised by: that many years ago he was left by the river, that a man took him and raised him, and as soon as he grew up, he wanted to know why he had been given such a name.

While Potametes was talking, the poor woman was losing her color and the blood ran cold in her veins. At the end, when the young man stopped talking, she felt very bad and fell down crying! "You are my son."

And so whatever the Fates ordered came true.

The tale, very Greek as it is in its mythological points, has the usual introduction of the tales of destiny with the special Greek tradition. . . . Three days after the child's birth, the Fates came to rule his destiny.[12] However, there are certain differences from the ancient myth: (1) The Fates predict the father's death, but not by parricide. (2) The child is not thrown by the mother into the water but is left on the river bank, and that is how he got his name, a name clearly mythological. (3) The recognition is caused not by the scars on the body but by the telling of the story initiated by the hero's name. Not only by its special features but by the whole plot the tale proves to be completely different from the written tradition.

The other two Greek tales, the Cypriot and the north Epirotic, do not leave any doubt about their true origin. Not only are the characteristic elements of the ancient myth missing, but the main point, turning on the idea of the inevitability of fate's decrees, is embellished with various folkloristic elements with a freedom that can only be found in the living tradition of oral literature. In the Cypriot version, Oedipus is replaced by a girl who first marries her father and then her son. Besides, the son is born in a way that is found only in tales: through the girl's tasting the apple from the tree that was growing on her father's grave, she having killed her father. Of interest also is the way she attracted suitors by placing her picture in the entrance to the palace and the way in which the destiny is revealed by a ghost in the bridal chamber.

In the north Epirotic version, the beginning, with the prophecy of fate and with the child who is thrown into the sea but found and raised by shepherds, is the one known from other tales, too,[13] but later on the tale is mixed with elements taken from the Dragon-Slayer (Perseus and Andromeda). However, the princess whom the hero with the invisible cap saves from the beast that rules the water, and whom he thereafter marries, is his own mother. "While they were playing and jumping, the young man accidentally throws his flute, which hits and kills the king. So the prophecy came true and the young man became the king." In spite of all his efforts to avert the decree of fate, the king met death like Akrisios in the ancient myth, who was hit accidentally by his grandson who in turn married his own mother.[14]

The above tales not only have nothing in common with the texts of the written tradition but they are also independent of one another, as is characteristic of the spiritual fruits produced in oral tradition. Not only in the plot as a whole but also in technique and in style and in individual elements the narratives are generally in accord with the way in which the folk compose and tell their tales. Therefore, they can, in my opinion, be regarded as earlier than all the texts and narratives attached to the name of Judas or to the saints.

Accordingly, I do not agree with my colleague Krappe's findings that "there is no tale with incidents connected with the ancient myth" and that "modern European folk literature does not furnish us with any means for the solution of the problem." At the same time, of course, it is true that there are not as many versions as there are in the case of other myths from ancient times, for instance, the myth of Polyphemus, of which oral variants number over one hundred. But even the very existence of just these three tales from parts of Greece located so far away from one another (Cyprus, Pindus, Epirus)—and as is well known, the systematic gathering of folktale material has not yet been carried out in the whole Greek area—is in itself, I believe, significant. It proves that the occult story was Greek, as well as the Judas-the-traitor narrative from which many Slavic, Western and Coptic variants derive, not to exclude the Legenda Aurea.

Now I come to the investigation of the ancient myth as it was done by Krappe.

"The Oedipus myth," he says, "is composed of several elements of which the first is more than a simple motif. It is rather a true folktale, the tale of the fatal child (l'enfant fatal)," to which the well known tale of Cyrus belongs.[15] The Oedipus myth, which is more complicated, Krappe compares first with the myth of Telephus and Auge, as transmitted by Hyginus (fab. 99–100). In the vulgate of the mythographers, it goes like this: Aleos, the king of Tegea, once learned from an oracle that he was to be killed by his own daughter's son. He made her priestess of Athena, but while Hercules was going through Tegea, he raped the goddess's priestess. Aleos then sent his daughter to Nauplion to either sell her on the other side of the sea or to throw her into the sea. Her child is raised on Mt. Parthenius, where he was born and deserted. As an infant, he was nursed by a deer. Later on he is fed by shepherds, separated from his mother who was saved while coming across Mysia, and adopted by the childless king of Mysia, Teuthras. Telephus—this is the child's name—comes later to the court of his grandfather Aleos. There he arouses the envy of his mother's brothers who are very sarcastic towards him because of his unknown background. Enraged because of this, Telephus kills them all. For punishment, he is sent by the oracle to Mysia in order to be expiated. At that time Idas, son of Aphareos, attempted to dethrone Teuthras. Teuthras promises to give to Telephus his kingdom along with his daughter Auge if he would free him from the danger. Telephus accepted this and he defeated Idas in a battle. After that, the king transfers his reign to Telephus and gives him his daughter for his bride. Auge did not want to marry a mortal, Telephus, and not knowing that he was her son, she tried to kill him in the bridal chamber. At that time by the will of the gods, a huge serpent appeared between them. Auge, frightened, dropped her sword and revealed to Telephus her real intentions. As soon as Telephus heard that, he tried to kill her. Auge then called upon her rapist Hercules through whom Telephus recognized his mother and took her back to their native land.[16]

According to Krappe, in the myth we have a variant of the tale of the fatal child but without incest. In fact, the incest never occurred because the recognition between mother and son took place the first night by means of the appearance of the serpent sent by the gods. But what impresses us about this plot which according to Krappe belongs to the genre of "recognitiones" which was much cultivated during the Greek decline and later on during the years of the Italian Renaissance is that this plot has always existed in this myth. According to Schmid and Stählin, the Telephus story as it was represented in both of Sophocles' tragedies, *Aleadai* and *Mysoi*, which, as it appears, Hyginus followed, has many different and bright colors which were taken from other myths.[17]

The motif which is surely to be found in the original version of the myth is "The Princess and the Kingdom," the reward promised by the king for the hero's services. The element "Princess is actually the hero's mother," just as it takes place in the north Epirotic tale, and the element of imminent incest, constitutes exactly the order of the tale which it is believed nothing can change. Escape through rationalism or moral hesitation has no place here since man's actions are inevitable. Therefore, the transfer of the "recognition" to the same night of the marriage which never took place can be believed only insofar as it is a modification of the initial form of the myth.

But while in the myth of Auge and Telephus Krappe rules out incest, it is found again where we have no hint of it in an episode of the *Schah Nameh* of the Persian Firdousi[18] which many other writers have drawn upon. "The beautiful Humaï bears a son by adultery whom she places in a small trunk filled with materials interwoven with gold and many precious stones. She then throws the trunk into the Euphrates. The child, however, is found and reared by common people. But the child's royal origin is soon discovered. Soon he learns that the people he knew as his parents are not his parents at all. He becomes a great knight and asks the permission of the man and woman who raised him to join the army that Humaï has sent against the Greek king. A mysterious voice reveals to the commander-in-chief that young Dârâb (the hero's name) is the King of Iran. He distinguishes himself in the war. However when the army returns, Humaï recognizes her son and calls him her successor."[19]

About this narrative, Krappe says, "There is no shadow of incest here, but this should not delude us. Humaï is a widow. Dârâb distinguishes himself in the war. There is no doubt that there was originally a reward and the reward of course was the Queen's hand. . . . But Firdousi wrote under the noses of the Moham-

medan imams who greatly mistrusted the ancient legends of Mazdaist Persia."

With this interpretation, Krappe connects the Persian tale with
the story of Pope Gregory I, in which the hero, offspring of an
illegitimate union (brother and sister), married through a brave deed
the princess, his own mother.

Thus Krappe by interpreting the Persian narrative in this manner
uses for definition the second of two themes. For Krappe, the
second theme of the Oedipus myth consists of the separation and
then reunion of a mother and her son. "The first of the two themes is
a true folktale; the second is not. It is rather what is called a
'novelette theme' of the kind very common in the work of Boccaccio
and of his successors. A fusion of a folktale with such a theme, with
the incest added for good measure, does not at all have the feel of
folk art. Rather it gives the impression of a work of art consciously
devised by a professional storyteller." Thus the response Krappe
gives to the question contained in the title of his essay [Is the Legend
of Oedipus a Folktale?] is negative.

I believe that the above does not clearly define the second part of
the ancient myth. The Persian narrative upon which the argument is
based is a poor example. It lacks the necessary evidence and completion, and it appears to have been fundamentally altered. Of course, it
does contain the theme of the child being exposed in water, but the
reason given for this action deviates from the initial form of the
myth: It is not an attempt to change the Fates' decision but is an
action aiming to conceal the illegitimate love affair of the mother.
Thus the recognition at the end has a completely romantic flavor,
with the mother being very happy to see her son again whom shame
had forced her to part with.

How different is the recognition in the Oedipus myth and the
corresponding tales! Here the recognition not only brings together
blood-related persons who have been separated for a long period of
time but also verifies a tragic fact from which the unfortunate
parents attempted to escape. In other words, it helps to recognize
the principal idea of the meaning of the whole narrative: The Fates'
decision is irreversible. This is an idea that is deeply implanted in the
belief system of the people and it has been expressed in many
folktales. The topics differ only because the will of fate is not always

the same for all mortals. For some it is kind and they are the ones who will enjoy riches and happiness in life, and for some it is unkind and they must suffer an early death or a long life full of miseries, and sometimes their fate is disastrous for their parents too. And because of this basic fact, it is understandable why the person who has heard or has been informed of the unfavorable decision of Fate tries so desperately to keep it from being fulfilled.[20] In the Oedipus myth, it is not enough to recognize that the main motif is the "fatal" child, but we should determine its connection with the other elements of the tale, whether for instance they are irrelevant to it or whether they are combined with it in a coherent mythological plot.

I believe there is no doubt that the whole narrative of Oedipus has one main point: the fate was bestowed upon him at birth. In a desperate attempt to thwart the Fates, the child's parents throw him into the water. However, in fulfillment of the prophecy, the child is saved and the following episodes occur: the meeting with Laius, the conquering of the dreadful monster, the Sphinx, and the kingdom along with the queen as the reward. The vain attempt of individuals to escape the fulfillment of prophecy is proved by the recognition of the scars on their bodies and it is a most common element in all the folktales.

Thus the Oedipus myth, like any tale, consists of several motifs which follow a definite pattern and utilize the technique of a folktale which gives completion and unity to the whole myth.

It is therefore a collective unity, a complete tale of the fatal child which differs from other such tales only by what was ordered for him by Fate (patricide and incest) and it is rightly placed by Antti Aarne in the *Types of the Folktale*.[21] And also it is an ancient tale of the kind with parallels found in modern Greek folktales.

Now we should seek the reason that gave the myth such an unheard-of-subject (the heinous patricide and the revealed incest with the mother).

I will mention an odd myth about the descent of the Kalangs, an indigenous tribe in Java. In the story, a woman who is the daughter of a sow marries (without her knowledge) her son. The son kills a dog which is actually his father—he is not aware of his relationship with the dog. In one variation of the myth, the woman bears twin sons by the dog, and later on she marries them both without realizing her relationship to them. At the end she recognizes one of her sons by the scar of a wound which she had inflicted upon his head with a wooden spoon.

According to the Javanese such incestuous relations are not at all uncommon for the Kalangs: Mother and son often live together as husband and wife, and the Kalangs believe that riches and happiness spring from such marriages.[22]

In the first place we have to go along with Frazer that such myths about the descent of alien races of the Indonesian Archipelago are not based on actual facts, but rather they express the racial hatred and the contempt of those who made them up. Frazer in general does not go along with the opinion of those who believe that Oedipus is only one example among many others that derived from an old custom of incestuous relations which some researchers supposed to have existed in an early period in the evolution of society.[23] However, it is only right to recognize that within these narratives stands as a base the ethical perception of people familiar with family ties, and from this perception derive all the myths and folktales about atrocities committed against sacred family ties.[24]

Therefore, in the Oedipus myth as well as the Telephus myth, we have before us one of the elements which, as Martin Nilsson explains in *Gött. gelehrt. Anzeiger* 1922, p. 38,

> relate to the established ways and customs of the people and may be called *ethical elements* so long as we do not add to the expression anything of philosophical ethics. However, all these are an expression of the first glimmering of ideas about the demands of ethics . . . A people like the Greeks, with a strict patriarchal family, were concerned with voluntary or involuntary crimes committed against its principles of morality. Thus follows a whole cycle of well-known subjects (motifs) in Greek myth: marriage with the mother (Oedipus); marriage with the daughter (Thyestes–Pelopia, Oeneus–Gorge), which characteristically appears as not being the cause of the same kind of abomination; the murder of children by their own father or mother; strife between father and son and between brothers; and finally the problem of the revenge for the murder when the murderer is of the same family (Orestes, Alkmeon) . . . If the Oedipus myth . . . contained only the first two elements (the conquering of the monster, here the Sphinx, and the customary folkloristic reward, here the princess and half of the kingdom), it

would be called a tale of fortune (*Glücksmärchen*) of the most
common kind. Only the combination with one of the ethical
elements establishes what it really is and creates its horrible
grandeur. The queen whom Oedipus won along with the
kingdom was his own mother.

And finally the great researcher of Greek mythology and religion
commented, "There is an agreement between my conceptions and
Krappe's, because he too derives only the initial element (*das Aus-
gangsmotiv*), l'enfant fatal, from the folktale."[25]

As is well known, these ethical elements, which others, like my
ever-to-be-remembered teacher Arthur Hübner, place under eth-
nology, constitute only one type of the elements that constitute tales
(ethnological, mythological, magical, ethical, and dream elements).[26]
Therefore, as I have already said, I find that in its combination with
one of the ethical or ethnographical elements the narrative attached
to the name of Oedipus has been greatly enriched in content but has
not at all lost its deeper meaning, the meaning precisely which
forms the foundation on which rests the general type of stories
about the inevitability of fate's decrees; and that in this very form
the ancient myth has preserved intact its authentic folkloristic
character.

NOTES

[1]See above p. 19. [Megas's essay on the legend of Judas in folk tradition
appeared in the same volume where the present essay was published. See *Epeteris tou
Laographikou Archeiou*, 3 (1941–1942) [1951], 3–32, with a summary in French on
p. 219. Ed. Note.]

[2]*Neuphilologische Mitteilungen*, 34 (1933), 11–22.

[3]E. Littré, *Histoire de la langue française*, Paris, 1863, II, 172.

[4]L. Constans, *La légende d'Oedipe*, Paris, 1881, pp. 104–111.

[5]J. Frazer, *Apollodorus, The Library*, London, 1921, Vol. II, p. 372ff.

[6]These main points are: the episode concerning the patricide (the father's
entrance into the garden at night to assure the guard's vigilance), the murder because
of ignorance, recognition by the scars on the stomach, and the long period of
repentance and expiation of the hero. For further clarification, I must add here a
summary of the Russian narrative attached to the name of Andrew, archbishop of
Crete, sixth century: One day, a merchant from Crete overheard the conversation of
two pigeons that spoke of the birth of a son called Andrew who would kill his father,

marry his mother, and rape three hundred nuns. The merchant ordered the child killed, but the mother had the baby baptized and named Andrew. She stabbed him a few times in the stomach, tied him on a board, and threw him into the sea. The board was found by a nun who gave the baby to her mother superior. So Andrew was raised in a convent. When he became a man, he raped three hundred nuns including the mother superior. He was then sent away from the convent. He was engaged to work for his father who ordered him to watch over his vineyard. In order to check up on the new servant, the father went to the vineyard at night, where he was caught as a thief and killed by his son. When Andrew confessed to his mistress what had happened, she offered him her husband's position. The scar on his stomach revealed his identity. Filled with horror, he left and later earned forgiveness after a long period of repentance, similar to that of Pope Gregory I. Finally he succeeded the holy bishop who had prescribed the penitence and assumed his throne.

[7]A. Schullerus, *Verzeichnis der rumänischen Märchen und Märchenvarianten*, FFC 78, Helsinki, 1928. Type 931.

[8]Hans Honti, *Verzeichnis der publizierten ungarischen Volksmärchen*, FFC 81, Helsinki, 1928. Type 931.

[9]The Spanish variation of the tale is contained in Ralph S. Boggs, *Index of Spanish Folktales*, FFC 90, Helsinki, 1930, Type 931*A: A deer asks a hunter, "Why are you chasing me, killer of your parents?" The hunter, horrified, leaves his land and marries in a very distant state. His parents search for him and finally reach his house while he is away. His wife lets them sleep in her bed. The next morning, before dawn, her husband returns while his wife is at the liturgy, and finding two strange people in her bed, kills them. His wife returns and tells him that his parents are sleeping in her bed. He falls dead.

[10]Pericle Papahagi, *Basme Aromâne*, Bucharest, 1905, p. 360, #110. Schullerus included this tale along with the remaining Kutsovlahika tales contained in the Romanian tale type index but other than the language, there is no other connection between Koutsovlahon and Romanians. Concerning the Greek descent of Koutsov-lahon, see And. Keramopolullon, Τί εἶναι οἱ Κουτσόβλαχοι; 1939, and Οἱ Ἕλληνες καὶ οἱ βόρειοι γείτονες 1945, pp. 185–197.

[11]Potametes means literally "River Child."

[12]See the Greek variants of the tale about the individual who married the daughter of a person who learned about the decision of the Fates and tried in vain to prevent it from happening. *Laographia*, 1, pp. 92–100, 115–119, and 2, pp. 575–590, and for foreign versions along with the related observation about their Greek origin, see N.G. Polites, 1, pp. 107–115. See also Aarne-Thompson, *The Types of the Folktale*, FFC 74, Type 930, and A. Aarne, *Der reiche Mann und sein Schwiegersohn*, FFC 23, Hamina, 1916.

[13]The parricide prophecy which was noted as an introduction in the Cypriot tale (p. 17 [see footnote 1]) also appears in the Epirotic version, tale number 32 in Hahn, and in the unpublished Tenian tale in the Folklore Archives, #1390, p. 39ff.

[14]This tale was recorded in Lamboro in northern Epirus by Apostoles G. Panagiotedes from the mouths of Albanian-speaking Greek women. Because of its astonishing resemblance to the Perseus myth, Hahn had expressed in *Albanes. Studien*, p. 164, suspicion of the authenticity of this tale, but he later changed his mind

in *Griech. u. albanes. Märchen,* 11, p. 310, because he says "It does not contain any element that is not found in other tales in our collection."

[15]Herodotus, I, 107–122. About this, see A.H. Krappe, "Le mythe de la naissance de Cyrus," *Revue des études grecques,* 43:153–159 where there are bibliographical references.

[16]In a variant of the myth reported by Ekateros, mother and child are exposed in a chest at sea and the chest floated into Teuthrania. See F. Jacoby, *Fr. Gr. Hist.,* I, p. 19 and p. 326, fr. 29; C. Robert, *Heldensage,* pp. 1138–1144, 1146, 1153. Schmid-Stählin, *Geschichte der griech. Literatur,* Part I, Vol. 2, München, 1934, p. 424ff.

[17]See Schmid-Stählin, p. 425. The points taken from other myths are: oracle predicting the danger from the son (Laius); dismissal of the pregnant daughter; admired breeding of exposed child; murder of the uncles (Meleagros myth); the son searching for the mother; marriage of the son with his mother; the subject of the savior; the recognition in a moment of great danger (Kresphontes-Merope). See p. 90, note 9.

[18]*The Shahnama of Firdousi,* tr. A.G. Warner and E. Warner, London, 1905–15, V, 294ff.

[19]I have given Krappe's summary.

[20]For these subjects, see Stith Thompson, *Motif-Index of Folk-Literature,* FFC 116, Helsinki, 1935. Motifs M300–399, Prophecies: M 300, Favorable prophecies; M 340, Unfavorable prophecies; M 370, Vain attempts to escape fulfillment of prophecy. See also M 343, Parricide prophecy. In spite of all attempts to thwart the fates the child kills his father; M 344, Mother-incest prophecy. In spite of all precautions the youth marries his mother; with bibliographical references. I. Th. Kakrides, Τὸ παραμῦθι Μελέαγρου [The Tale of Meleagros] in *Laographia,* 10, 487, and the note by St. Kyriakides, 11, p. 271.

[21]Antti Aarne, *Verzeichnis der Märchentypen,* FFC 3, Helsinki, 1910. See the translation and expansion of this work by Stith Thompson, *The Types of the Folktale,* FFC 74, Helsinki, 1928; type 931, Oedipus: As foretold by the prophecy, the hero kills his father and marries his mother.

[22]J. Frazer, *Apollodorus,* II, p. 373ff. for a version of type 931 that Thompson also mentions, found, too, on p. 275 of De Vries, *Typen-Register der Indonesische Fabels en Sprookjes: Volksverhalen uit Oost-Indië,* II, No. 238, which at the time of this writing I was unable to see.

[23]J. Frazer, see p. 375ff.

[24]However unheard of and strange it may be for the Greek people, the love relationship of a father-in-law and his daughter-in-law is so common for the Russian people that it is almost considered a social law known by the name *snochatsestvo,* as is pointed out by N.G. Polites in the myths that explain the common riddle: Brother of one father and son of my wife, *Laographia,* 2, p. 360, and p. 372. A tale from the Folklore Archives, #140, p. 233ff: When the peddler learned "that he had had as a wife his son's wife, his gall practically burst from the grief, and he decided to divorce her and let her go home with Yago (her son) and they both supported her (father and son) and they sent her everything she needed. And those two withdrew and stayed in one house, and they never got married again and all three lived a monkish life until their death."

25M. Nilsson, *Geschichte der griech. Religion*, I, München, 1941, p. 23, n. 1. The essay of H.J. Rose, *Modern Methods in Classical Mythology*, where the writer initially sees historical elements in Oedipus, I was unable to see, and it was only from his book, *A Handbook of Greek Mythology*, 3rd ed., London, 1945, p. 188, that I discovered the evidence supporting my views.

26A. Thimme, *Das Märchen* (Handbücher zur Volkskunde 2) Leipzig, 1909, p. 32ff; Fr. Panzer in *Deutsche Volkskunde*, ed. J. Meier, Berlin und Leipzig, 1926, p. 251ff. St. Kyriakides, Ἑλλην. Λαογραφία. Athens, 1922, p. 273ff.

The Sphinx in the Oedipus Legend

Lowell Edmunds

The relationship between folklore and classical literary texts is of interest to classicists as well as folklorists. Professor Lowell Edmunds of the Classics Department at Johns Hopkins University has been concerned with this problem with special reference to Oedipus. In this essay, he re-defines tale type 931 on the basis of an examination of more than seventy medieval and modern versions. Also from this unique vantage point, he is able to illuminate the place of the riddle in the classical Oedipus story. In addition, he shows that the curious figure of the Sphinx, which does not occur in any oral texts, is a secondary elaboration.

For Professor Edmunds' other investigations of Oedipus, see "Oedipus in the Middle Ages," Antike und Abendland, *25 (1976), 140-155; "The Oedipus Myth and Sacred Kingship,"* The Comparative Civilizations Review, *No. 3, Issued as Vol. 8, no. 3 of the* Comparative Civilizations Bulletin *(1979), 1-12; "The Cults and the Legend of Oedipus,"* Harvard Studies in Classical Philology, *85 (1981), 221-238;* Oedipus: Ancient Myth; Medieval and Modern Analogues, *(in press).*

Introduction

The main purpose of this essay is to show that the Sphinx is a secondary element in the Oedipus legend, added at some point in the

Revised and reprinted from *Beiträge zur klassischen Philologie*, Heft 127 (Konigstein/Ts., 1981) pp. 1–39.

development of the legend in order to motivate the hero's marriage to his mother. This proposition is directly opposed to the widespread view, set out in section 1 below, that the Oedipus legend originated from the folktale of the hero who wins a bride by slaying a monster. Two folktales of this sort (quoted in section 2), which also contain riddles, illustrate not the prototype of the Oedipus legend but only the function of riddle-solving, viz., to win the bride. Thus these two folktales show that the riddle-solving in the ancient legend is an over-determination of the motif of monster-slaying, which by itself might have been, and presumably was in earlier versions, sufficient to motivate the marriage. But neither riddle-solving nor monster-slaying is original in the Oedipus legend: the Sphinx can be shown to be very probably a secondary addition (section 3). Furthermore, the reason for this addition is clear: once the parricide was brought into close relation with Delphi, there was nothing in the narrative that would necessarily have led the hero to Thebes. This observation leads to speculation concerning an earlier form of the parricide (section 4). Not only is the Sphinx secondary in the narrative (section 3), but her riddle seems to bear no necessary relation to any detail of the legend (section 5). It is not clear why it must be this riddle and not some other. Although the prevailing folkloristic position on the origin of the Oedipus legend is thus shown to be untenable, one sort of folkloristic analysis, i.e., the definition of the story-pattern, should not be abandoned. The Oedipus legend does have a typical story-pattern, and it is that of kingship myths (section 7). Those who saw a resemblance of Oedipus to Zeus (section 6) were not mistaken. As an instantiation of this story-pattern, the Oedipus legend adapts such motifs as mutilation (discussed in section 7) and monster-slaying without perfectly integrating them into the narrative. In both of these cases, over-determination is involved. Mutilation is an over-determination of the exposure of the child, and riddle-solving is an over-determination of monster-slaying.

For reasons that will become clearer, it has been convenient for me to speak of three kinds of narrative as distinguishable from one another, and these are myth, hero legend and folktale. To justify these distinctions would, of course, require a separate discussion, which is unnecessary here in any case, since the distinctions are more expository than hermeneutical. Writing in English, I have used "legend," which to German ears suggests a saint's life, and not "saga," which Anglophones tend to apply to Icelandic and Norse stories.

1. The Oedipus Legend and Folklore

Folklore has often been used to explain the origins of the Oedipus legend. One can distinguish between a stricter and a looser position. Not the first but perhaps the most dogmatic statement of the stricter folkloristic position occurs in M.P. Nilsson's review of Carl Robert's *Oidipus* (1915).[1] Robert had argued that Oedipus was a hypostatized *Jahresgott* who was the object of a cult at Eteonos, a town near Thebes. "The hero from Eteonos comes to Mount Phix [cf. Hes. *Theog.* 325], kills the monster dwelling there, . . . and becomes the savior of the land. This is the oldest form of the legend. . . ."[2] Nilsson rejected the notion of Oedipus as *Jahresgott* and, reverting without acknowledgement to a thesis originally propounded by Domenico Comparetti in another form,[3] argued that the Oedipus legend is fundamentally a folktale. It is the story of the hero who wins the princess by performing a brave deed. Nilsson did not find any difficulty in the crimes of the hero but postulated an ethical recasting of the folktale in response to the advent of a patriarchal order of society. The hero of the folktale becomes the arch-criminal who commits the crimes that strike at the heart of patriarchy. This notion of the Oedipus legend as a folktale recast by vast historical change, like a landscape reshaped by a glacier, was left by Nilsson as a mere assertion. It was to be argued, however, with all the wit and learning of Vladimir Propp.[4]

The looser folkloristic position has been maintained again and again in encyclopedias and standard works. L.W. Daly, in the article on Oedipus in Pauly-Wissowa,[5] thought it most probable that Oedipus was originally a *Märchenheros*, and Albin Lesky, in the article on the Sphinx in the same encyclopedia, stated, with reference to Wilamowitz and Nilsson, that the Oedipus legend rested on *altes Märchengut*.[6] The inclusion of the Oedipus story in *The Types of the Folktale* probably supported a general sense that the Oedipus legend belonged originally to folklore,[7] even though the Oedipus folktale (Type 931) was clearly distinguished from the folktale of the dragon-slayer (Type 300), and a problem was thus created for anyone who wished to maintain the folktale origin of the Oedipus legend. Did the legend originate from Type 931 or from Type 300? If from the latter, was the former not a folktale in antiquity but only a later derivative from the ancient legend? The problem remains undiscussed, and the looser folkloristic position continues to be asserted. For example, G.S. Kirk has written in *The Nature of Greek Myths* that Oedipus' exposure by his parents, his rescue by a shepherd, and his winning the kingship of Thebes by solving the riddle are "folktale elements" and "the most traditional elements."[8]

The assumption underlying both Nilsson's and Propp's and also the looser folkloristic position was stated by Ludwig Laistner in the second volume of *Das Rätsel der Sphinx* (1889): That which is earliest in literary history may be later, in the history of myth, than modern transcriptions of folk tradition.[9] In other words, folktales collected in modern times may preserve variants of myths or legends older than the oldest literary versions. Thus from our knowledge of modern folklore we can perceive a more primitive form of the Oedipus legend than the one known to us primarily through Attic tragedy.

Besides Propp, the only scholar who, working on this assumption, studied a collection of folktales of the specifically Oedipus-type (Type 931) as distinguished from folktales of the dragon-slayer who wins the princess, was Georgios Megas.[10] Whereas Propp used the folktales to discover something about the early history of mankind, Megas' interest was specifically folkloristic. He wanted to show, first of all, contrary to A.H. Krappe, that the story of Oedipus did exist as an authentic folktale. In this, Megas certainly succeeded. Megas also argued that "many elements in the folktales agree absolutely with elements of the ancient tradition which are not included in the vulgate [i.e. the standard versions of the Oedipus legend, those of Sophocles and Euripides] but which are preserved in other sources, in scholiasts and mythographers, and clearly go back to an older, popular form of the Oedipus myth."[11] An example of such an element is the exposure of the child not on a mountain but in a chest or the like set adrift on the sea. Although Megas' articles were a valuable corrective to Krappe, his conclusions brought nothing new. Like Nilsson and like Propp, he believed that there was an "original" nucleus, the king's daughter and the kingdom as the hero's reward, which was elaborated into the Oedipus folktale and the Oedipus legend, and, like Comparetti, he believed that the narrative was shaped by a fundamental idea, i.e., fate.

But if Megas' work had become known, it would at least have had the desirable effect of causing scholars who posit a folktale origin of the Oedipus legend to distinguish between a folktale of a specifically Oedipus-type, which bears a close resemblance to the ancient legend, and another type of folktale, which would have required drastic alteration in order to become the Oedipus legend. Oddly enough, the latter type, that of the dragon-slayer (Type 300), is the one that continues to be spoken of as the nucleus of the Oedipus legend, as by Kirk. It is worthwhile, then, to examine a pair of modern folktales of this type, in order to see what insight into the ancient legend they provide.

2. The Sphinx and Two Modern Folktales

The usefulness of two modern folktales for the understanding of a fragment of Theodectes has long been recognized.[12] Each of these two folktales contains a similar chain of three riddles. The last riddle in the chain is the famous riddle of the Sphinx, and the penultimate resembles a riddle, presumably the Sphinx', in a fragment of the *Oedipus* of Theodectes (4N[2]). Because of the similarity of these tales to the Oedipus legend, it has been concluded that, in a version of the ancient legend now lost, the Sphinx posed not one but three riddles. If the assumption of the folkloristic position is granted, then the modern folktales shed light on a fragment of Greek tragedy which would be somewhat puzzling otherwise.

But these two folktales also illustrate the story-pattern of the young hero who wins a bride by performing a difficult task, the story-pattern that is held to be the earliest form of the Oedipus legend. For this reason, it is worth quoting and examining these two folktales. One of them was collected by Bernhard Schmidt in Arákhova, Greece:

> There was once a queen down by Thebes who sat on a cliff and set three riddles for all who passed by. She announced that she would let the one who could solve the riddles pass by without holding anything against him, indeed that she was ready to

take him as her husband, but she would eat the one who could not solve them. Many passed by, but no one could solve the riddles. Then a young prince heard of this queen, and, since she was said to be of great beauty, he decided to go to the cliff on which she sat, in the hope of winning her hand. His father tried to hold him back, but the son would not obey him and set out in the direction of that queen. When she caught sight of the new-comer, she said to him, "Oh, you poor fellow! You are such a handsome young man and you want to plunge into ruin? Go back to your father! Already so many have passed by here, but no one has yet been able to solve the riddles. Will *you* be able to?" The young man answered, "Don't worry about that! I hope to solve them." Then she told him the first riddle. This goes: "What is the thing that consumes whatever it begets? It begets its children and consumes them again." Then he answered: "Oh, Madame Queen, that is very easy to solve. That is the sea. This eats its own children, since the waves originate from the sea and fall back in the sea." Then said the queen: "That's right. Now I shall submit to you the second riddle." This goes: "Which is the thing that looks white and black and never grows old?" "Oh," said the young man, "this one is not difficult, either. It is time. This appears black and white, since it is nothing other than day and night; this also never grows old, since it has been since the beginning of the world and will be until the world's end." "Correct," said the queen. "But now I shall submit to you the third riddle, which you will not be able to solve." "We shall see," answered the prince. "Just tell it to me." Now she told him the third riddle, which goes thus: "What is the thing that, at the beginning, goes on four legs, then on two and finally on three?" Then he said, "This is the easiest one of all. That is man. When he is small and begins to move, he crawls on all fours. When he is bigger, he goes on his two legs, and when he reaches old-age and can no longer hold himself upright without support, he takes a staff to help him and thus now goes on three legs."[13]

The other folktale was collected in Gascogne by Jean-Francois Bladé. The following is a summary:

An orphan, handsome and extremely intelligent, lives alone in the village of Crastes. On the side of the mountain [the Pyrenees] lives a Great Beast with a human head, which guards a cave full of gold. She has promised half her gold to the one who can answer three questions. One hundred persons have already tried and failed and have been eaten alive. The young man falls in love with the daughter of the seigneur but cannot marry her unless he has a fortune. He resolves to try the Great Beast. First, he consults the Archbishop of Auch, who tells him that he cannot fail; also that the Great Beast will also first impose three impossible tasks, which he must disregard. Having answered the three questions, the Archbishop says, you must take half the gold and return immediately if you feel that you can do no more. But, if you can, stay and pose three questions to the Great Beast. If she cannot answer, kill her with this gold knife.

Brushing aside the tasks, the young man answers the Great Beast's riddles. First: "It goes faster than birds, faster than the wind, faster than a gleam of light." Answer: the eye. Second: "The brother is white, the sister black. Each morning, the brother kills the sister. Each evening, the sister kills the brother. Yet they never die." Answer: Day and night. Third: "At daybreak, he crawls like snakes and worms. At midday, he walks on two feet, like the birds. He goes on three legs at sunset." Answer: Man. The young man then poses three questions [not riddles] to the Great Beast; he kills her upon her failure to answer. As the blood is spurting out, she says, "Drink my blood. Suck my eyes and brain. Thus you will become as brave and strong as Samson . . . Tear out my heart. Take it to your mistress and have her eat it raw on the night of your marriage. In this way, she will bear seven children, three boys and four girls. The boys will be brave and strong like you. The girls will be as beautiful as day. They will understand what the birds sing. When they are of age, they will marry kings." The young man did as the Great Beast commanded, and so it turned out.[14]

The relation of these two folktales to the ancient Oedipus legend can be analyzed as follows:

	Modern Greek	French	Oedipus legend
Hero's goal	To win the queen	To get gold, as condition of marriage	Marriage the result not the goal (Soph. *OC* 539–41; cf. *OT* 383–4)
Riddler	Queen	Great Beast (female with human head)	Sphinx (female with human head)

	Modern Greek	French	Oedipus legend
Riddler's habitat	Cliff	Mountain cave	A high place[15]
Conditions	Answer or die	Answer or die	Answer or die
Riddles	(a) What eats what it bears? (The sea)	(a) Fastest thing? (The eye)	(a) *No riddle attested.*
	(b) White and black and never ages? (Time, consisting of day and night)	(b) White brother and black sister kill each other? (Day and night)	(b) Siblings, of which the first begets the second, and the second begets the first? (Night and day) (Theodectes frag. 4N²)
	(c) What goes on four legs, then two, then three? (Man)	(c) Crawls at daybreak, walks at midday, goes on three legs at sunset? (Man)	(c) Riddle of the Sphinx.[16] (Man)

What, then, do the modern folktales show about the ancient legend? In particular, do they show that Oedipus' encounter with the Sphinx is the nucleus of the legend? These folktales belong to the well-established category of the riddle-tale (*Rätselerzählung*), which Mathilde Hain describes thus: "Die Rätselaufgabe und ihre Lösung bildet den Höhepunkt einer Handlungsreihe und bestimmt das Schicksal des Helden."[17] But in the Oedipus legend, the solving of the riddle is not the highpoint of the action, nor does it determine Oedipus' fate any more than does the parricide. It might still be argued that the riddle-tale was primary and was expanded into the legend as we know it, but it can be shown that not only the riddle of the Sphinx but the Sphinx motif as a whole is secondary in the legend. The two modern folktales do not represent the earliest form of the legend and may even be a derivation from the ancient legend. Hain, in fact, speaks of the Sphinx as the "prototype" of the riddle-tale.[18]

But the two folktales do show something about the ancient legend. Taken with other folktales in the sub-category of the riddle-tale to which they belong, namely, the *Braut-Werbe Rätsel*, they show that the result of the riddle-solving in the ancient Oedipus legend is really its purpose: to win the bride. Furthermore, in the folktales of this sub-category, the riddle is set by the queen or by her father.[19] In the ancient legend, the riddle has been transferred from the queen to the monster, and thus represents an over-determination of the monster-slaying motif. Either monster-slaying by itself or riddle-solving by itself is sufficient to win the bride, but in the Oedipus legend monster and riddler are conflated and the hero simultaneously achieves two feats. Paradoxically, the modern French folktale (riddling beast) is closer than the modern Greek (riddling queen) to the ancient Greek legend.

3. The Sphinx as Secondary in the Oedipus Legend

Although the story of the dragon-slayer is usually held to be the nucleus of the Oedipus legend, the episode of the Sphinx may be secondary in the development of the legend. There are two different arguments to support this suggestion. The first concerns the awkwardness of the Sphinx's position in the plot of the legend. Where did the Sphinx come from? In the notorious Peisander scholium (*FGrH* 16F10 = schol. Eur. *Phoen.* 1760), Hera sent the Sphinx as a punishment for Laius' rape of Chrysippus. It is uncertain whether this account of the Sphinx goes back to epic or is based on a lost tragedy of Euripides.[20] In any case, the mythographical tradition was tortured by the question of the Sphinx's entry into the legend. Although Apollodorus also says that Hera sent the Sphinx (3.5.8; cf. Dio Chrys. *Or.* 11.8), this motivation of the monster's appearance was hardly canonical. We hear that she was sent by Dionysus (schol. Hes. *Theog* 326; schol. Eur. *Phoen.* 1031=Eur. *Antig.* frag. 178N[2]), by Hades (Eur. *Phoen.* 810-11), and by Ares (hypoth. Eur. *Phoen.*); that she was the daughter of Laius (schol. Eur. *Phoen.* 26=Lysimachus *FGrH* 382F4; Paus. 9.26.3); that she was born out of the blood of Laius.[21] The complexity of the tradition concerning the Sphinx' origin reflects not only the normal and expected variation of the sources for a legend but also an uncertainty about her very raison d'être in the legend.

When did the Sphinx commence her predations? In *Oedipus the King*, Sophocles has left the matter unclear. Kamerbeek remarks: "The difficulty is that nowhere in the course of the play is there any connection explicitly stated, or implied, either between the Sphinx' appearance and Laius' deed [the rape of Chrysippus] . . . or between its appearance and Laius' journey. . . . We do not know whether the Sphinx is supposed to have made her unwelcome appearance before or after Laius' departure, before or after his death; the odds are in favor of the latter."[22] In Aeschylus' lost *Laius*, it is possible that the Sphinx appeared before Laius' death, as Robert suggests.[23] In the fragments of Euripides' *Oedipus* which have been discovered since the time of Robert, the Sphinx seems to have appeared shortly before the death of Laius.[24] As Robert said, the Sphinx was the gravest problem in the logic of the narrative, one that the poets never solved.[25]

The second argument for regarding the Sphinx as secondary in the Oedipus legend is based on the study of modern folktales of the Oedipus-type.[26] My definition of the type differs considerably from Thompson's, which, apparently based on the ancient legend, is misleading and incomplete as a definition of the Oedipus folktale. In the following list, Thompson's motifs are italicized to distinguish them from my additions.

> *M 343 Parricide prophecy*[27]
> *M 344 Mother-incest prophecy*
> Dream or vision concerning unborn son
> Incest of parents as reason for exposure
> Mutilation (cf. Thompson H 56.2, M 375.3)
> *M 371.2 Exposure of child to prevent fulfillment of*
> *parricide prophecy*
> *K 512 Compassionate executioner*
> Nursing by an animal (cf. Thompson S 352)
> *R 131 Exposed infant reared at strange king's court*
> (*Joseph, Oedipus*)
> Precocity (cf. Thompson T 614, T 615.1)
> Conflict with foster-brother(s) or other children
> Departure from foster-home
> Act of valor (cf. Thompson A 531)
> *N 323 Parricide prophecy unwittingly fulfilled*
> *I 412 Mother-son incest*

> Discovery of crimes
> Further crimes
> Conclusion:
>> Hero commits suicide
>> Mother dies or commits suicide or is killed
>>> or
>> Penance of hero and of mother
>> Exaltation of hero

Not all of the Oedipus folktales—in fact, very few—contain all of these motifs. As for monster-slaying, which would come under the heading "Act of valor," I have found in Oedipus folktales only a single example of this motif as a qualification for marriage. It occurs in a Turkish folktale, "The Sultan's Son," and the monster is not the Sphinx but a savage wolf.[28] This wolf may, in fact, represent a variant of the ancient Oedipus legend, since Corinna says that Oedipus killed the Teumesian fox (frag. 19(672), Page), but the corpus of Oedipus-type folktales overwhelmingly supports the view that in the basic story-pattern the Sphinx is secondary. It is not even necessary to assume that these folktales represent an earlier form of the legend. It is enough that they provide a rather substantial quantity of comparative evidence that clearly shows that the Sphinx is not integral to the plot of the Oedipus story, which easily finds other ways to motivate the marriage of son and mother.[29]

4. The Function of the Sphinx in the Oedipus Legend

But in the Oedipus legend it was just this function of the motif, namely, bride-winning, that caused the Sphinx to be inserted into the narrative. In the ancient legend as we have it, the hero's killing of his father would not necessarily have led to his marriage with his mother. Oedipus kills Laius at a crossroads outside of Thebes, either on his way to Delphi (Eur. *Phoen.* 35-8; Diod. Sic. 4.64.2; Apollod. 3.5.4; Hyg. *Fab.* 67; Myth. Vat. 2.230) or on his way from Delphi (Soph. *OT* 785-7; Apollod. 3.5.7; hypoth. Eur. *Phoen.*). (In most of these sources, Laius is on his way to Delphi.) In the received form of the ancient legend, it is only the killing of the Sphinx that brings Oedipus into relation with Thebes. Parricide by itself would not have this result. The motif of monster-slaying has thus been added to motivate the marriage, and bride-winning is the typical function of this motif in folklore, as in one of the tales quoted above.

Why was there no link between the parricide and the incestuous marriage? The answer to this question lies in the close connection of the parricide with Delphi. Both father and son are on their way to or from Delphi; and each is consulting the oracle about the other (for Laius' reason for consulting the oracle: Eur: *Phoen.* 35-8; hypoth. Eur. *Phoen.*; Diod. Sic. 4.64.2; cf. Soph. *OT* 114). This connection of the parricide with Delphi obviously postdates the importance of Delphi as the oracular center of Greece; but the Oedipus legend must predate Delphi's importance.[30] Therefore the received form of the parricide is likely to be a modification of some earlier form. Perhaps the original form of the parricide had more to do with the Erinyes (cf. Pind. *Ol.* 2.41); Aeschylus in his *Oedipus* located the parricide at Potniai (frag. 173N[2]) where the Erinyes were worshipped.[31] The modification of the legend which brought the parricide closer to Delpi also drew it too far from Thebes and thus it was necessary to add the Sphinx in order to motivate the hero's marriage to the widowed queen of Thebes.

If the received form of the legend represents a changed locale of the parricide, does it also represent an altered manner? It is natural to turn to Oedipus folktales to see if they shed any light on this problem. Of the two main categories of folktales which may be cognate with the ancient legend, one is completely unheroic in characters, action and ambience.[32] The hero kills his father in an orchard or a garden. The hero may be either a trespasser in, or the guard of, the place, depending upon the future that is in store for him, further villainy or redemption. Of the folktales in this category, there is only one that has a martial character, and the parricide takes place in a battle in a chicken coop.[33] In the other main category, the hero returns to his native land, defeats an invading army, and then marries the widowed queen, his mother.[34] His father has died or has gone off on a journey years before. In these tales, parricide is therefore missing. The hero, after the discovery of his crime and after severe penance (often he is chained to a rock for years), becomes Pope or a saint. The similarity of the denouement to that of Sophocles' *Oedipus at Colonus* has not escaped notice.[35]

If parricide was once a part of such tales, it would have taken place in battle. The hero would not have defeated an invading army but would have been its leader, and it would have been his own father who opposed the invading army. There are a few tales, possibly related to Aarne-Thompson Type 933, which have a parricide of this sort. One of these is the story of Nimrud in the "Romance of 'Antar."[36] Nimrud is the leader of an army and kills his father Kana'an in battle. The Zulu tale of Usikulumi provides another example of parricide in a military engagement though the narrator does not say in so many words that Usikulumi killed his own father.[37] Finally, there is a Russian tale in which the hero kills his father on a crusade.[38]

In the evidence for the ancient Oedipus legend there is only a single hint of parricide committed in battle and that is the verb ἐξεναρίζω (*Od.* 11.273), which occurs in a summary of Oedipus' life. For obvious reasons, this very usually, in the *Iliad*, refers to the killing of an enemy on the battlefield, but it can be used of other killings (*Il.* 7.146, 16.573; Hes. *Theog.* 289). If at *Od.* 11.273, it means that Oedipus killed Laius in battle, then the Byzantine tradition perhaps represents a preservation of this form of parricide. The Byzantine chroniclers, cited above apropos of the rationalized Sphinx, tell that a certain number of Thebans proclaimed Oedipus king in gratitude for his killing the Sphinx. Laius raised an army to oppose Oedipus and his supporters and was killed—although the chroniclers do not say by whom—in the ensuing battle.

5. The Riddle of the Sphinx

Whatever the original form of the parricide, the received form, for reasons already given, must be a secondary modification. This modification brought with it the introduction of the monster-slaying as a way of motivating the marriage. As vase paintings show, Oedipus once killed the Sphinx with a sword or a spear;[39] there was no riddle to solve; the Sphinx simply attacked her victims. The riddling of the Sphinx is secondary to the Sphinx' forthright destruction of her victims. Although it is relatively clear why the Sphinx herself enters the legend, it is not clear why the motif of monster-slaying is thus over-determined by the addition of riddle-solving. The Oedipus legend provides another example of over-determination in the mutilation of the hero's feet; exposure alone ought to have been enough to dispose of him (cf. schol. Eur. *Phoen.* 26). This example can be explained if, as I have argued elsewhere, the original reason for the name "Oedipus" was lost, so that an etiology for "Swollen Foot" had to be supplied.[40] But what is the reason for the riddle-slaying, which by itself was sufficient to motivate the marriage?

It is natural to look for an answer to this question in the riddle itself. Even though this riddle is found everywhere in the world and presumably had no original connection with the Sphinx,[41] and even though the Sphinx, in one variant of the legend, apparently posed other riddles in addition to the single famous one, the possibility remains that the riddle to which the answer is "man" possesses some special significance in the Oedipus legend. The parechesis at Soph. *OT* 397 even suggests that it was the deformity of Oedipus' feet that gave him the clue to the answer; and there was a tradition that Oedipus gave the answer by pointing to himself.[42] But these are the only indications of a connection between the riddle and particular details of the legend. Usually, the riddle-solving is regarded as indicative of a trait of Oedipus, his intelligence, and, in the fifth century, as vase paintings well attest, the encounter with the riddling Sphinx was the favorite episode in Oedipus' life.[43] In Sophocles' *Oedipus the King*, Oedipus is admired by his people for his high intelligence, shown in solving the riddle (33–6, 52–3, 510, 1197–1203), though the priest believes that he had divine aid (37–9), and in the confrontation of Oedipus and Teiresias, the former vaunts his intelligence, which prevailed where Teiresias was helpless (especially 390–8). Oedipus' self-estimation has been accepted by modern interpreters of the tragedy. In a well-known essay, E.R. Dodds says: "To me personally Oedipus is a kind of symbol of human intelligence which cannot rest until it has solved all the riddles."[44]

Although in *Oedipus the King* Oedipus is engulfed in a larger ignorance of Apollo's plan for him, a point that Sophocles first puts in the mouth of Teiresias (376–7), it is Oedipus' remarkable intelligence that enabled him to solve the riddle. In short, in the tragedy, he solved the riddle because he was intelligent. But it has already been stated that the riddle is secondary in the history of the legend— indeed, the riddle is tertiary, because the Sphinx herself is secondary; and there is nothing else in the legend that would characterize

Oedipus as intelligent. Therefore, in the legend, as distinguished from the tragedy based on the legend, Oedipus became intelligent because he solved the riddle. Whatever other reasons there were for the addition of the Sphinx' riddling to the legend, this motif served to characterize Oedipus as a man of intelligence, and this characterization had special significance in the Athens of Sophocles' day.[45]

If the intelligence of Oedipus is the result of the riddle-solving and not vice versa, this intelligence can hardly explain the overdetermination of the monster-slaying motif. Furthermore, in stories of the *Brautwerbe-Rätsel* there is usually a link between the content of the riddle and the content of the story but no such link is to be found in the Oedipus legend, unless it is the feet of Oedipus.[46] The riddling of the Sphinx in the Oedipus legend remains a riddle, and the discrepancy between the Sphinx as monster and the Sphinx as riddler, already felt in antiquity (Plut. *Mor.* 988A), persists.

To sum up the results of the discussion to this point: the motif of monster-slaying is secondary in the Oedipus legend and is not the most traditional element. Furthermore, the riddling of the Sphinx is secondary to her forthright destruction of her victims. The Oedipus legend is not, therefore, fundamentally the story of the hero who wins a bride by killing a monster. The folktales from Arákhova and Gascogne illustrate not the original form of the legend but only the original function of the riddle-solving motif, viz., to enable the hero to win a bride. It was the definition, as it were, of this motif by such tales that made the motif available for adaptation to the Oedipus legend. The fundamental story-pattern of the Oedipus legend remains to be specified. It can be specified, and the assumption of the folkloristic approach, that the Oedipus legend is a traditional tale with a definable story-pattern, will be pursued.

6. The Myth-ritual Approach

But the main alternative to the folkloristic approach can also make a contribution. This alternative, if the solar-lunar school is disregarded,[47] is the myth-ritual approach. The doxography of the myth-ritual interpretation of the Oedipus legend can be briefly stated. In 1893, in the first edition of his history of Greece, Eduard Meyer pointed to the resemblance of Oedipus to Zeus, in particular, Zeus the consort of earth goddesses.[48] Not many years later, Meyer's suggestion won a sort of official acceptance when Otto Höfer, in the article on Oedipus in the Roscher lexicon, asked: "Ist Oidipus vielleicht eine Hypostase des Zeus χθόνιος?"[49] Around the same time, Otto Gruppe suggested that Oedipus was a forgotten cult-name of Hephaestus.[50] And then, in 1915, came the *Jahresgott* from Eteonos. Although Oedipus-Zeus appeared once again in the magisterial *Zeus* of A.B. Cook (1925),[51] here ended this particular identification. In the second edition of his work (1928), probably because of Robert, Meyer abandoned his earlier view, and spoke of "echt boeotische Kulte und Mythen" as the basis of the Theban cycle of legends, including the Oedipus legend.[52]

Although none of these identifications of the original Oedipus can be accepted, the fundamental notion that there was an Oedipus independent of the legend about Oedipus is sound. The evidence for the cults of Oedipus, taken with certain details of the epic and tragic tradition of Oedipus, points to important aspects of the hero of which the legend does not really take account. The association of Oedipus with Demeter and with the Erinyes is an example. Demeter plays no part in the legend, and, although the Erinyes are mentioned again and again apropos of Oedipus and his sons, they have no proper role in the legend, either. In studying such associations and in attempting to reconstruct the figure of the Oedipus which lies behind the hero of epic and tragedy, it seems best to abandon the old question of the priority of the cult or legend; but it is still possible to see that there was an Oedipus independent of, whether or not prior to, the legend.[53] As I have already suggested, the narrative accommodated him by providing an etiology for his name, and this is why the exposure motif is over-determined by the mutilation of the feet. It will still be necessary, however to explain why the mutilation took this particular form and why it was attached to the motif of exposure.

7. The Story-pattern of the Oedipus Legend

Turning again to the folkloristic interpretation of the legend, one sort of folktale, that of the hero who wins a bride by slaying a monster, has been rejected as the nucleus of the Oedipus legend, but it is correct to think of this legend as having a typical story-pattern. I believe that Meyer, Höfer, and Cook saw part of the truth when they connected Oedipus with Zeus; but the connection lies not in the nature of Oedipus, the hero of the legend, but in the story-pattern itself. The similarities in the story-pattern of the Oedipus legend, other Greek hero-legends, and the myth of Zeus were clearly defined by S. Luria in an article that was unfortunately published in an obscure Italian *Festschrift*.[54] The story-pattern concerns the preparation for and attainment of kingship. It is unnecessary to go beyond the comparative evidence of Greek legend and myth to see that kingship is what the story is about.[55] Oedipus is, after all, a king, even if his kingship is now the most forgotten aspect of the legend. Kingship counts for nothing in the interpretations of the Oedipus legend by Freud and Lévi-Strauss.[56]

If Luria's demonstration is accepted, the kingship of Oedipus can now be set in a larger comparative context, because of the undoubted relation of the myth of Zeus to other, Near Eastern myths of divine kingship.[57] Indeed, in this larger context, the Oedipus legend appears as a cognate, and not a derivative, of the myth of Zeus. One of these Near Eastern myths, which concerns the city of Dunnu, suggests the sort of narrative to which the Oedipus legend may be related.[58] In the dynastic struggles of this city, parricide and incest occur in successive generations. (The causal connection of the exposure motif to incest is found in a Hittite myth, the text of which is dated to the fifteenth or sixteenth century B.C.)[59]

The relation of the Oedipus legend to the myth of divine kingship may help to explain the mutilation of Oedipus' feet. This element in the legend is, I have suggested, an over-determination of the exposure motif, the reason for which was etiological, i.e., to account for the name "Oedipus." But why was this particular motif chosen for the etiological over-determination, and why was the injury to Oedipus' feet the result of mutilation and not, say, an accident, as in the case of Lycurgus (Hyg. *Fab.* 123; Serv. *Aen.* 3.14)? In his comparative study, "The 'Kingship in Heaven' Theme," C. Scott Littleton refers to "the inevitable act of mutilation" in myths of the divine king.[60] One well known form of mutilation is castration. Both Kronos and the Phoenician El castrated their fathers.[61] The Hittite Kumarbi bit off and swallowed the genitals of his brother, Anu.[62] Mutilation may also, however, affect the feet of the victim. The monster Ullikumi, the son and champion of Kumarbi, is placed on the shoulder of an Atlas-like giant, from whom Ea, the champion of the Storm-god, Kumarbi's rival, prepares to remove him by cutting or sawing under his feet.[63] Zeus also undergoes a mutilation like Ullikumi's. Apollodorus gives the following account of Zeus' battle with Typhon:

> Zeus pelted Typhon at a distance with an adamantine sickle and as he fled pursued him closely as far as Mount Casius, which overhangs Syria. There, seeing the monster sore wounded, he grappled with him. But Typhon twined about him and gripped him in his coils, and wresting the sickle from him severed the sinews of his hands and feet, and lifting him on his shoulders carried him through the sea to Cilicia and deposited him on arrival in the Corycian cave.[64]

Zeus, who like Ullikumi was consigned to Earth for his upbringing and who grew with preternatural speed, also has his feet cut from under him, as it were. In all of these examples, the perpetrator of the mutilation is attempting either to secure the dynastic succession for himself or to prevent usurpation. Laius' mutilation of Oedipus' feet is of the same sort. Mutilation is logically attached to the exposure motif, since the intent of the exposure is to prevent the son's violent usurpation of his father's place, and, for the same reason, the mutilation must be deliberate, not accidental.

Laius' mutilation of Oedipus' feet can, then, be regarded as the reflex in heroic legend of the mutilation motif that is usual in myths of the divine king. Perhaps the Oedipus legend contains another such reflex in the deceitful distribution of the parts of a sacrificial victim by Oedipus' sons, which may be a recasting of the banquet at Mecone (*Thebaid* frag. 3 Allen; Hes. *Theog.* 535ff.). To return to the Sphinx, Oedipus' slaying of this monster is perfectly consistent with the kingship myth, in which monster-slaying is usually one of the deeds by which the future king qualifies himself for kingship.[65] In the myth of Zeus, the monster is, of course, Typhon. The Sphinx was readily available to the Oedipus legend because she was a well-known local monster (Hes. *Theog.* 326). Oedipus' slaying of the Sphinx can, then, be regarded as another reflex in heroic legend of a motif appropriate to the myth of the divine king. It is a motif which occurs, to be sure, in several Greek hero legends, which, Luria has shown, typically culminate in kingship.[66]

8. Conclusion

Although the background of the kingship myth helps to explain the motifs of mutilation and monster-slaying, it could not be argued that the Oedipus legend is in origin a kingship myth any more than it could be argued that the Oedipus legend is in origin a folktale. It happens that we have good examples of a shared story-pattern in the form of myths, an heroic legend, and folktales. The first two, the myths and the heroic legend, are attested for antiquity. Whether or not the same story-pattern existed in the form of a folktale in antiquity is not certain. Such a detail in the ancient evidence as the taunting of the hero by his age-mates provides a tantalizing suggestion that it did. In Sophocles' *Oedipus Tyrannus*, this detail occupies only a few lines (775ff.) and might seem incidental. In folktales, however, the hero's conflict with his foster-brothers or age-mates is a regular motif (cf. the list of motifs given above in section 3), which leads to the hero's departure from his foster-home, and Propp may be right that the lines in Sophocles are the pale reflection of a motif that was more pronounced in ancient folktale versions of the story-pattern, as, for example, in the story of Cyrus (Hdt. I.114ff.), where the motif is fully developed.[67] It is also possible, however, that this motif was developed in the *Oedipodeia* or in some lost Oedipus tragedy, in which case one would conclude that the motif was already traditional in the legend.

The taunting of the hero by his age-mates is not, however, the only basis on which one might argue the existence of a popular, oral Oedipus folktale in antiquity. I believe, and have elsewhere argued,[68] that there did exist such a folktale, amongst the others that the Greeks certainly told,[69] and that the modern folktales of Types 931 and 933 or combinations thereof are the descendants or cognates of this ancient folktale. The modern folktales, then, present us with evidence for an ancient popular tradition that ran parallel, so to speak, to the ancient literary tradition; and, if this is the case, one must exercise caution both in applying these folktales to study of the ancient literary embodiments of the legend and to speculation on the origin of the legend.

In fact, one cannot really find an original form of the legend; one can only point to its story-pattern. The Sphinx, more than any other element in the legend, prompts dubiety concerning the possibility of some original version from which later, different versions could have been derived. The Sphinx, i.e., the motif of the monster-slaying, is absent from Oedipus folktales, with a single exception, and yet this motif is regular in the kingship myths which are based on the very same story-pattern as the folktales. The conclusion to be drawn from this observation concerning kingship myths and Oedipus folktales is that the Sphinx is not integral to the story-pattern as such but is an element, i.e., monster-slaying is an element, that typifies one sort of instantiation of the story-pattern. In short, monster-slaying is one of the feats of the future king. Since one sort of instantiation of the story-pattern has thus defined the function of the motif, another sort can take it over, and this, I believe, is the reason for the Sphinx's presence in the Oedipus legend. That she is a secondary addition to the legend is apparent.

The question might arise how a story-pattern which gave rise to myths of the divine king and to the Oedipus legend and which seems to be specifically the story-pattern of kingship could also have given rise to a type of folktale. Surely, one might think, the concerns of the folktale are quite different. On the contrary, the medieval and modern folktales simply transpose kingship into papacy or saint-hood. It is still the story of the hero destined for the greatest honor in his society. These folktales also, however, present the negative form of the hero. He may be the greatest criminal, Judas, the betrayer of Christ,[70] or Nimrud, the enemy of God.

What is new in each instantiation of the story-pattern is the hero himself. As I have suggested, the very name "Oedipus" created a difficulty for the ancient legend and required an etiology, and there are certain matters that seem to remain extraneous, for example, Oedipus' association with Demeter and the Erinyes. The story-pattern has not accommodated everything the hero brought with him. Although the hero is the new element in each successive version and can cause the narrative to make adjustments, ultimately the story-pattern makes the hero and not vice versa. The solving of the riddle created the intelligence of Oedipus at some point in the de-velopment of the legend. Thereafter, the intelligence of the hero was a given, and had to be provided for in the narrative. In the Oedipus legend, it seems that the typical confrontation of king and seer—one can compare Agamemnon and Calchas or Pentheus and

Teiresias—became a locus in which this relatively new trait of the hero was expressed.

But in the history of the legend, the intelligence of the hero reacted upon the motif of riddle-solving and caused this motif to assume greater and greater importance, as the character-trait of intelligence came to be felt as the source of Oedipus' achievement. Already in the fifth century, as vase paintings and Sophocles' *Oedipus Tyrannus* show, this episode had become the favorite. In the twentieth century, Oedipus' encounter with the Sphinx is climactic in Hofmannsthal's *Oidipus und die Sphinx*, the first play in an intended trilogy. In Cocteau's *La machine infernale*, the encounter absorbs an entire act. In Gide's *Oedipe*, it is not dramatized but has hardly less importance, and likewise in Cocteau's text (in effect an extreme condensation of the Sophoclean tragedy) for Stravinsky's *Oedipus Rex*, Oedipus is the riddle-solver. The emphasis on the Sphinx-episode was anticipated in nineteenth-century philosophy. In Hegel's *Philosophy of History*, at the transition from the Egyptian to the Greek world, Oedipus is the symbol of Greek consciousness,[71] and for Nietzsche, in section 9 of *The Birth of Tragedy*, the solving of the riddle, the parricide and the incestuous marriage form a "mysterious triad of fated deeds."

The Sphinx, who was not worthy of mention in the summary of Oedipus' life in *Odyssey* 11, becomes as important as anything else in the legend.[72] But these are not the only modern versions of the legend. In Freud, the story-pattern is treated quite differently. Parricide and incest are, of course, far more important than the solving of the riddle. For Lévi-Strauss, the narrative as such is relatively meaningless; it is only the separate elements of the narrative, separated and then recombined into binary oppositions, which will lead to an understanding of the legend. The overcoming of the Sphinx is thus reduced to a denial of autochthony—autochtony is a central concern of the legend—and the riddle-solving has practically no significance. In other words, Freud and Lévi-Strauss have given the greatest emphasis to motifs other than the riddle-solving, and, for them, the Sphinx is of minor importance. The history of the Sphinx in the Oedipus legend has thus come full circle. A late-comer to the legend, she provided what was to be for many centuries the most illustrious episode, so that Oedipus is still known amongst both scholars and laiety as the great riddle-solver. And yet in these later times, with the thinkers just named, she begins to fade into the background. Will she fade away, or is she still there near Thebes awaiting future Oedipuses?[73]

NOTES

[1]M.P. Nilsson, "Der Oidipusmythus," *GGA* 184 (1922) 36–46= *Opuscula Selecta*, vol. 1 (Lund, 1951), pp. 335–48; *The Mycenaean Origin of Greek Mythology* (Berkeley, 1932), p. 103.

[2]C. Robert, *Oidipus: Geschichte eines poetischen Stoffs im griechischen Altertum*, vol. 1 (Berlin, 1915), p. 58.

[3]D. Comparetti, *Edipo e la Mitologia Comparata* (Pisa, 1867), pp. 63ff. argues that the Oedipus legend contains three basic folklore formulas: (1) exposure of child to avoid destiny; (2) the hand of the queen is given to the one who performs a brave deed and rids the land of a monster; (3) the riddle-contest. Comparetti believed that, in combining these formulas to form the legend, the Greeks were guided by an *idea morale*, viz., fate.

[4]V. Propp, "Edipo alla Luce del Folclore," in *Edipo alla Luce del Folclore*, ed. C.S. Janovič (Turin, 1975), pp. 85–137, a translation of "Edip v svete fol'klora," *Učenye zapiski Leningradskogo gosudarstvennogo universiteta*, Serija filologičeskich 72 (1944) fasc. 9, pp. 138–75. (A translation is included in this casebook.) The Oedipus narrative arises from the clash of two conflicting social orders, one matrilineal, in which succession to the throne is through the son-in-law, who kills his father-in-law, the old king, and the other patriarchal. The narrative originally concerned regicide by the son-in-law; the motif of parricide enters the narrative when, in changed historical circumstances, the conflictual succession by the son-in-law is ascribed to what ought to be the non-conflictual succession by the son. As the son-in-law becomes the son and the father-in-law the father, the princess becomes the hero's mother, though, in Propp's view, I think she should be his sister.

[5]L.W. Daly, "Oedipus," in *RE* suppl. vol. 7 (1940), cols. 769–86 at 786.

[6]A. Lesky, "Sphinx," in *RE*, 2nd series, 6th half vol. (1929), cols. 1703–1726 at 1708.

[7]A. Aarne and S. Thompson, *The Types of the Folktale*, 2nd rev. (FFC 184: Helsinki, 1964) Type 931. In Thompson's view, however, the Oedipus legend (or myth, in his terms) did not derive from a folktale, but vice versa: "One famous story from Greek drama keeps being repeated as an oral tale, the myth of Oedipus," *The Folktale* (New York, 1946), p. 141. He adds, however: "The fact that it is still told as a traditional story testifies to the close affinity of this old myth with real folk tradition."

[8]G.S. Kirk, *The Nature of Greek Myths* (Penguin Books, 1974), p. 165; cf. p. 24.

[9]L. Laistner, *Das Rätsel der Sphinx*, vol. 2 (Berlin, 1889), p. 378.

[10]G. Megas, "Ho Ioudas eis tas Paradoseis tou Laou," *Epeteris tou Laographikou Archeiou* 3(1941–2) 3–32 (French summary, p. 219); "Ho peri Oidipodos Mythos" in

the same volume, pp. 196–209 (French summary, pp. 222–3). The first of these articles was written in 1943, the second in 1950. The volume was not published until 1951. (A translation of the latter article is included in this casebook.) I am grateful to Mrs. Margaret M. Thorne for helping me to understand these articles. The article by Krappe which Megas challenged was: "La légende d'Oedipe êst-elle un conte bleu?" *Neuphilologische Mitteilungen* 43 (1933) 11–29. (A translation of Krappe's article is included in this casebook.)

[11]The first of the articles just cited, pp. 19–20.

[12]G. Hüsing, *Kraaspa im Schlangenleibe und andere Nachträge zur iranische Überlieferung* (Mythologische Bibliothek IV, 2: Leipzig, 1911), p. 20; W. Schultz, *Rätsel aus dem hellenischen Kulturkreise*, Part 2 (Leipzig, 1912), pp. 64–9; id., "Rätsel," in *RE* 2nd series, 1st half vol. (1914) col. 92; A. Lesky, "Sphinx," in *RE* (n.6 above), col. 1722.

[13]B. Schmidt, *Griechische Märchen, Sagen und Volkslieder* (Leipzig, 1877), pp. 143–4.

[14]J.F. Bladé, *Contes populaires de la Gascogne*, vol. 1 (Paris, 1886), pp. 3–14.

[15]Eur. *Phoen.* 806 (a mountain); Paus. 9.26.2 (a mountain); Myth. Vat. 2.230 (a mountain); schol. Hes. *Theog.* 326 (Mt. Phicium, named after her); Apollod. 3.5.8 (acropolis of Thebes); schol. Ov. *Ib.* 378 (a steep cliff); schol. Stat. *Theb.* 1.66 (a steep cliff).

[16]Athen. 10.456B (citing Asclepiades *FGrH* 12F7b); *AP* 14.64; Tz. Lyc. 7; Apollod. 3.5.8; D.S. 4.64.3–4; schol. Eur. *Phoen.* 50; hypoth. Eur. *Phoen.*; schol. Hom. *Od.* 11.271; hypoth. Aesch. *Sept.*; Myth. Vat. 2.230. The riddle seems to have been quoted in hexameters in Eur. *Oed.* frag. 83.22–25 Austin.

[17]M. Hain, *Rätsel* (Sammlung Metzler 53: Stuttgart, 1966), pp. 36–42.

[18]Hain, op. cit., p. 37.

[19]See Schultz, op cit. (n. 12), cols. 69–70. Cf. in this casebook the riddle in the story of Pauk Tyaing in the article by R. Grant Brown.

[20]On this problem, see E.L. de Kock, "The Peisandros Scholium—Its Sources, Unity and Relationship to Euripides' *Chrysippos*," *Acta Classica* 3 (1960) 15–37.

[21]Alfred Koerte, "Literarische Texte mit Ausschluss der christlichen," *Archiv für Papyrosforschung und verwandte Gebiete* 11 (1935), no. 806 (p. 259).

[22]J.C. Kamerbeek, *The Plays of Sophocles: Part IV: The Oedipus Tyrannus* (Leiden 1967), p. 53 (on line 127).

[23]Robert, *Oidipus* (n. 2 above), p. 281.

[24]On these fragments, see E.G. Turner, in *The Oxyrhyncus Papyri*, Part 27 (London 1962), no. 2459 (pp. 81–6); Hugh Lloyd-Jones, in *Gnomon* 35 (1963) 446; J. Vaio, "The New Fragments of Euripides' *Oedipus*," *GRBS* 5 (1964) 43–55; J. Dingel, "Der Sohn des Polybus und die Sphinx," *MH* 27(1970) 90–6.

[25]Robert, *Oidipus* (n.2 above), p. 58. Palaephatus, the fourth-century rationalizer, explained that the Sphinx was the jilted Amazon wife of Cadmus. She retired to Mt. Phikion with many of her fellow-citizens and from there made war on Cadmus. Ambush was her mode of warfare, and, explains Palaephatus, the Cadmeans call an ambush an "ainigma." Cadmus promised a reward, and Oedipus, a Corinthian, came and "discovered the ainigma" and killed the Sphinx (Palaephat. 4; cf. Phanodemus *FGrH*325F5bis). Pausanias has a slightly different version: the Sphinx was a robber-woman whom Oedipus defeated with a Corinthian army (Paus. 9.26.2; cf. schol. Hes.

Theog. 326). In the Byzantine tradition, Oedipus destroys her after pretending that he and his companions want to join her band (Tz. on Lyc. 7; Joh. Antioch. *FHG* 4 frag.8; Malalas 2 0 61; Cedren P 25 C). From the time, then, of Palaephatus, the Sphinx represented an inconsistency in the legend which needed to be adjusted. J. Fontenrose, Python: *A Study of Delphic Myth and Its Origins* (Berkeley and Los Angeles, 1949), p. 310 combines Palaephatus, Pausanias and hypoth. Eur. *Phoen.* (Ares sent Sphinx against Thebans to get revenge for the killing of his son, the dragon, by Cadmus), and suggests that the Sphinx is the typical female counterpart of the dragon in the combat myth.

²⁶Type 931 in Aarne-Thompson (n.7 above).

²⁷M 343 etc. in the list of motifs refer to S. Thompson, *Motif-Index of Folk-Literature*, 2nd ed., 6 vols. (Bloomington, Ind. 1955-1958).

²⁸TK1 in Appendix 1 in the original publication of this article (see headnote). I want to stress the uniqueness of this tale amongst tales of the Oedipus-type: for example, only in this tale does a plague occur.

²⁹There are seventy-five Oedipus folktales in my collection (forthcoming as *Oedipus: Ancient Myth; Medieval and Modern Analogues*).

³⁰See N.W. Parke and D.E.W. Wormell, *The Delphic Oracle*² (1956), vol. 1, p. 300: "The legend of Oedipus which originated in a folktale without much local reference was ultimately modified, so that all the features were adjusted to the part played by Delphi. Hence the divergent accounts which placed the scene of Laius' murder at random were superseded by the version which made Laius perish on the Cloven Way between Delphi and Thebes."

³¹References for worship of Erinyes at Potniai: see E. Wüst, "Erinyes," in *RE* suppl. vol. 8, cols. 91, 130-1.

³²For a description of these two categories, see L. Edmunds, "Oedipus in the Middle Ages," *Antike und Abendland* 22 (1976) 140-155 at 149-154.

³³FI14 in Appendix 1 in the original publication of this article (see headnote).

³⁴Aarne-Thompson Type 933. See H. Oesterley, *Gesta Romanorum* (Berlin, 1872), cap. 81 (pp. 399-409). English translation: C. Swan, *Gesta Romanorum: or, Entertaining Moral Stories, etc.*, rev. and corr. W. Hooper (London, 1877) Tale LXXXI (pp. 141-54).

³⁵G. Zuntz, "Ödipus und Gregorius," *Antike und Abendland* 4 (1954) 191-203. Repr. in *Hartmann von Aue*, ed. H. Kuhn and C. Chormeau (Wege der Forschung CCCLIV: Darmstadt, 1973), pp. 87-107 and in *Sophokles*, ed. H. Diller (Wege der Forschung XCV: Darmstadt, 1967), pp. 348-69.

³⁶AR1 in Appendix 1 in the original publication of this article (see headnote).

³⁷ZL1 in Appendix 1 (cf. n.36).

³⁸RS1 in Appendix 1 (cf. n.36).

³⁹Boston lecythus: Hetty Goldman, "Two Unpublished Oedipus Vases in the Boston Museum of Fine Arts," *AJA* 15 (1911) 378-385; Robert, *Oidipus* (n.2 above), vol. 1, p. 49, Abb 14; H. Walter, "Sphingen," *Antike und Abendland* 9 (1960) 63-72, Taf. XI, Abb. 33; U. Hausmann, "Oidipus und die Sphinx," *Jahrbuch der staatlichen Kunstsammlungen in Baden-Württemberg* 9 (1972) 7-36 at 9-10 and photo. 1 (p. 7). Thebes cantharus: R. Lullies, "Die Lesende Sphinx," in *Neue Beiträge zur klassischen Altertumswissenschaft: Festschrift zum 60. Gebürtstag von Bernhard Schweitzer*, ed. R. Lullies (Stuttgart, 1954), p. 144 and Taf. 29, 2. Capua amphora:

Hausmann, op. cit., pp. 10–11 (with photograph). Gems: A. Furtwängler, *Die Antike Gemmen: Geschichte der Steinschneidekunst im klassischen Altertum* (Berlin, 1900), vol. 1, Taf. 24, nos. 21–22. But the forthcoming study of the Sphinx in Greek art by J.-M. Moret argues convincingly that none of the vase paintings I have cited is good evidence: The first is a modern forgery and the others do not represent Oedipus. It was too late, when Dr. Moret communicated his findings to me, to change the text of my article.

[40]"The Cults and the Legend of Oedipus," *HSCP* 85 (1981) 221–238.

[41]For references, see Apollodorus, *The Library*, trans. J.G. Frazer, vol. 1 (Cambridge, Mass., and London, 1921), p. 347; A. Aarne, *Vergleichende Rätselforschungen*, II (FFC 27: Helsinki, 1919), p. 11. J. de Vries, *Die Märchen von klugen Rätsellösern* (FFC 73: Helsinki, 1928) does not discuss the Sphinx or the riddle.

[42]References in *Enciclopedia dell' Arte Antica*, vol. 3, p. 218, *e.* under "E. davanti alla Sfinge." (All of these references are to reliefs and gems.)

[43]See the list of Oedipus vase paintings in F. Brommer, *Vasenlisten zur griechischen Heldensage*[3] (Marburg, 1973), pp. 482–3; also *ARV*,[2] vol. 3, p. 1729.

[44]E.R. Dodds, "On Misunderstanding the *Oedipus Rex*," *Greece and Rome*, 2nd series, 13 (1966), 37–49 at 48.

[45]See B.M.W. Knox, *Oedipus at Thebes* (New Haven, 1957).

[46]Lesky, op cit. (n.6 above) col. 1717 doubts such a link.

[47]Main representative of solar-lunar interpretation: Michel Bréal, *Le mythe d'Oedipe* (Paris, 1863). Bréal was followed by G.W. Cox, *The Mythology of the Aryan Nations*, (London, 1882), pp. 313–17, and by M. Margani, *Il Mito di Edipo* (Syracusa, 1917). For a summary of the solar-lunar interpretation, see the last note in the selection from Frazer included in this casebook.

[48]E. Meyer, *Geschichte des Altertums*, vol. 2 (Stuttgart, 1893), pp. 101–3.

[49]O. Höfer, "Oidipus," in *Ausführliches Lexikon der griechischen und römischen Mythologie*. ed. W.H. Roscher, vol. 3 (Leipzig, 1897–1909), col. 743.

[50]O. Gruppe, *Griechische Mythologie und Religionsgeschichte*, vol. 1 (Munich, 1906), pp. 503–5.

[51]A.B. Cook, *Zeus: A Study in Ancient Religion*, vol. 2, part 2 (Cambridge, 1925), p. 1154.

[52]E. Meyer, *Geschichte des Altertums*,[2] vol. 2 (Stuttgart and Berlin, 1928). pp. 256–7.

[53]As I have argued in the article cited above (n.40).

[54]S. Luria, "ΤΟΝ ΣΟΤ ΤΙΟΝ ΦΡΙΞΟΝ (Die Oidipus-sage und Verwandtes)," in *Raccolta di Scritti in Onore di Felice Ramorino* (Publicazioni della Università Cattolica del Sacro Cuore, 4th series: Scienze Filologiche, vol. 7, 1927), pp. 289–314.

[55]For a statement of the case based on comparative anthropological evidence, see L. Edmunds, "The Oedipus Myth and African Sacred Kingship," *Comparative Civilizations Review*, no. 3 (1979) (issued as *Comparative Civilizations Bulletin*, vol. 8, no. 3) 1–12.

[56]The first interpretation of the legend, apropos of what was later called the Oedipus complex, in *The Interpretation of Dreams* (1900), pp. 261–4 in *The Standard Edition of the Complete Psychological Works of Sigmund Freud*, ed. J. Strachey (London, 1966–), vol. 4. (A passage from this part of *The Interpretation of Dreams* is included in this casebook.) The canonical account of the Oedipus complex, with

reference to the legend, in *Introductory Lectures on Psycho-Analysis* (1916–17), in *The Standard Edition*, vol. 16, pp. 329–338. C. Lévi-Strauss, "The Structural Study of Myth," *Journal of American Folklore*, 68 (1955) 428–44= *Structural Anthropology* (Anchor Books, 1967), pp. 202–28 (with slight modifications).

[57]See Hesiod, *Theogony*, ed. M.L. West (Oxford, 1966), pp. 18–31.

[58]For the Dunnu myth, see W.F. Albright, *Yaweh and the Gods of Canaan* (London, 1968), pp. 81–2 and W.G. Lambert and Peter Walcot, "A New Babylonian Theogony and Hesiod," *Kadmos* 4 (1965) 64–72. The myth is also discussed in Littleton (n.60).

[59]H. Otten, *Eine althethische Erzählung um die Stadt Zalpha* (Studien zu den Bogazköy-Texten 17: Wiesbaden, 1973).

[60]C. Scott Littleton, "The 'Kingship in Heaven' Theme," in *Myth and Law Among the Indo-Europeans,* ed. Jaan Puhvel (Berkeley and Los Angeles, 1970), pp. 83–121.

[61]Kronos: Hes. *Theog.* 162, 175, 180. El: Eusebius, *Praeparatio Evangelica,* 36d7ff.

[62]"Kingship in Heaven," trans. A. Goetz, in *Ancient Near Eastern Texts Relating to the Old testament,*[3] ed. J.B. Pritchard (Princeton, 1969), p. 120. The progress of comparative mythology in this area has been rapid, it seems. F. Dirlmeier, in the first edition of his *Der Mythos von König Oedipus* (1948), could explain the similarities between Boeotian and Near Eastern mythology only on the basis of a vague, aboriginal, non-Indo-European, non-Semitic Mediterranean substrate population. In the second edition (1964), he took account of the Kumarbi myth but none of the other comparative material studied by Littleton. Walter Pötscher, "Die Oidipus-Gestalt," *Eranos* 71 (1973) 12–44 looked to Near Eastern mother-son myths for the origin of the Oedipus legend.

[63]H.G. Güterbock, *The Song of Ullikummi*, (New Haven, 1952), p. 47.

[64]Apollodorus, *The Library* 1.6.3. Trans. by J.G. Frazer, op. cit. (n. 41 above). On this myth in relation to the Hittite myth of Illuyankas, see W. Burkert, *Structure and History in Greek Mythology and Ritual* (Berkeley, 1979), pp. 7–9.

[65]Cf. Littleton, op. cit. (n. 60), pp. 120–121.

[66]Although Luria, op. cit. (n. 54), does not discuss dragonslaying as an aspect of these legends.

[67]Propp, op. cit. (n. 4), pp. 121–23.

[68]In the introduction to the collection of folktales mentioned above (n. 29).

[69]See Johannes Bolte, *Zeugnisse zur Geschichte der Märchen* (Folklore Fellows Communications 39: Helsinki 1921), p. 1–14.

[70]For discussion, see the place cited in n. 32 above.

[71]*Vorlesungen über die Philosophie der Weltgeschichte*, ed. G. Lasson, vol. 2 (Leipzig, 1921), pp. 510–11.

[72]And not only in literature and interpretation. Mario Praz, *The Romantic Agony* (New York 1968), pp. 295–296 writes as follows concerning the painter Gustave Moreau: "Moreau sought the theme of satanic beauty in primitive mythology and treated it in his pictures of the so-called 'Sphinx' series; this began with the painting which was the success of the 1864 Salon, in which the cruel beast with the face of an imperious woman plants her claws on the breast of the languid youth Oedipus, and ended with the water-colour exhibited in 1886 at the Goupil Galleries,

Le Sphinx vainqueur, in which the Sphinx reigns supreme over a promontory bristling with bleeding corpses. . . ."

[73]The revision of parts of this essay was prompted by conversations with Professor William Hansen and by the forthcoming review of the original monograph (see headnote) by Dr. C. Callanan for *Fabula*, which he kindly sent me in advance of publication.

Freud on Oedipus

Sigmund Freud

Nearly everyone has heard of the Oedipus Complex, but relatively few have bothered to read the original passages where Sigmund Freud (1856–1939) first articulated his still-provocative theory. These passages are well worth reading. For one thing, Freud was a great literary stylist. The force and eloquence of his insights survive translation from the original German. For another, given the taboo nature of his delineation of the family romance, and the fact that it took approximately twenty-five hundred years from the appearance of Sophocles' Oedipus *to appreciate the psychological significance of the plot, one should not take Freud's contribution for granted. Whether one agrees with the Freudian reading of Oedipus or not, one's assessment should be based upon Freud's own words rather than a secondary source's excessive praise or dismissal of his ideas.*

Freud himself had a lifelong interest in folklore. His analysis of traditional jokes and of folktales containing dreams reflects this interest. See his Wit and Its Relation to the Unconscious *or his joint work with D.E. Oppenheim,* Dreams in Folklore (*New York, 1958*). *For a convenient entrée into the still-proliferating psychoanalytic literature on Oedipus, all of which was ultimately stimulated by Freud's revolutionary reading of Sophocles' tragedy, see Lowell Edmunds and Richard Ingber, "Psychoanalytical Writings on the*

Reprinted from Sigmund Freud, *The Interpretation of Dreams* (1900) in *The Basic Writings of Sigmund Freud*, Translated and Edited by A.A. Brill, M.D. (New York: Random House, 1938), pp. 306–309, by permission of Gioia Bernheim and Edmund R. Brill, owners of 1938 copyright; and copyright © renewed in 1965.

Oedipus Legend: A Bibliography," American Imago, *34 (1977),*
374–386.

According to my already extensive experience, parents play a
leading part in the infantile psychology of all persons who subsequently become psychoneurotics. Falling in love with one parent
and hating the other forms part of the permanent stock of the
psychic impulses which arise in early childhood, and are of such
importance as the material of the subsequent neurosis. But I do not
believe that psychoneurotics are to be sharply distinguished in this
respect from other persons who remain normal—that is, I do not
believe that they are capable of creating something absolutely new
and peculiar to themselves. It is far more probable—and this is
confirmed by incidental observations of normal children—that in
their amorous or hostile attitude toward their parents, psychoneurotics do no more than reveal to us, by magnification, something
that occurs less markedly and intensively in the minds of the majority
of children. Antiquity has furnished us with legendary matter which
corroborates this belief, and the profound and universal validity of
the old legends is explicable only by an equally universal validity
of the above-mentioned hypothesis of infantile psychology.

I am referring to the legend of King Oedipus and the *Oedipus
Rex* of Sophocles. Oedipus, the son of Laius, king of Thebes, and
Jocasta, is exposed as a suckling, because an oracle had informed
the father that his son, who was still unborn, would be his murderer.
He is rescued, and grows up as a king's son at a foreign court, until,
being uncertain of his origin, he, too, consults the oracle, and is
warned to avoid his native place, for he is destined to become the
murderer of his father and the husband of his mother. On the road
leading away from his supposed home he meets King Laius, and in a
sudden quarrel strikes him dead. He comes to Thebes, where he
solves the riddle of the Sphinx, who is barring the way to the city,
whereupon he is elected king by the grateful Thebans, and is rewarded with the hand of Jocasta. He reigns for many years in peace
and honour, and begets two sons and two daughters upon his
unknown mother, until at last a plague breaks out—which causes
the Thebans to consult the oracle anew. Here Sophocles' tragedy
begins. The messengers bring the reply that the plague will stop as

soon as the murderer of Laius is driven from the country. But where
is he?

> Where shall be found,
> Faint, and hard to be known, the trace of the ancient guilt?

The action of the play consists simply in the disclosure, approached step by step and artistically delayed (and comparable to
the work of a psychoanalysis) that Oedipus himself is the murderer
of Laius, and that he is the son of the murdered man and Jocasta.
Shocked by the abominable crime which he has unwittingly committed, Oedipus blinds himself, and departs from his native city.
The prophecy of the oracle has been fulfilled.

The *Oedipus Rex* is a tragedy of fate; its tragic effect depends on
the conflict between the all-powerful will of the gods and the vain
efforts of human beings threatened with disaster; resignation to the
divine will, and the perception of one's own impotence is the lesson
which the deeply moved spectator is supposed to learn from the
tragedy. Modern authors have therefore sought to achieve a similar
tragic effect by expressing the same conflict in stories of their own
invention. But the playgoers have looked on unmoved at the un-
availing efforts of guiltless men to avert the fulfilment of curse or
oracle; the modern tragedies of destiny have failed of their effect.

If the *Oedipus Rex* is capable of moving a modern reader or
playgoer no less powerfully than it moved the contemporary Greeks,
the only possible explanation is that the effect of the Greek tragedy
does not depend upon the conflict between fate and human will, but
upon the peculiar nature of the material by which this conflict is
revealed. There must be a voice within us which is prepared to
acknowledge the compelling power of fate in the *Oedipus*, while we
are able to condemn the situations occurring in *Die Ahnfrau* or
other tragedies of fate as arbitrary inventions. And there actually is
a motive in the story of King Oedipus which explains the verdict of
this inner voice. His fate moves us only because it might have been
our own, because the oracle laid upon us before our birth the very
curse which rested upon him. It may be that we were all destined to
direct our first sexual impulses toward our mothers, and our first
impulses of hatred and violence toward our fathers; our dreams
convince us that we were. King Oedipus, who slew his father Laius
and wedded his mother Jocasta, is nothing more or less than a

wish-fulfilment—the fulfilment of the wish of our childhood. But we, more fortunate than he, in so far as we have not become psychoneurotics, have since our childhood succeeded in withdrawing our sexual impulses from our mothers, and in forgetting our jealousy of our fathers. We recoil from the person for whom this primitive wish of our childhood has been fulfilled with all the force of the repression which these wishes have undergone in our minds since childhood. As the poet brings the guilt of Oedipus to light by his investigation, he forces us to become aware of our own inner selves, in which the same impulses are still extant, even though they are suppressed. The antithesis with which the chorus departs:

> . . . Behold, this is Oedipus,
> Who unravelled the great riddle, and was first in power,
> Whose fortune all the townsmen praised and envied;
> See in what dread adversity he sank!

This admonition touches us and our own pride, us who since the years of our childhood have grown so wise and so powerful in our own estimation. Like Oedipus, we live in ignorance of the desires that offend morality, the desires that nature has forced upon us and after their unveiling we may well prefer to avert our gaze from the scenes of our childhood.[1]

In the very text of Sophocles' tragedy there is an unmistakable reference to the fact that the Oedipus legend had its source in dream-material of immemorial antiquity, the content of which was the painful disturbance of the child's relations to its parents caused by the first impulses of sexuality. Jocasta comforts Oedipus—who is not yet enlightened, but is troubled by the recollection of the oracle—by an allusion to a dream which is often dreamed, though it cannot, in her opinion, mean anything:

> For many a man hath seen himself in dreams
> His mother's mate, but he who gives no heed
> To suchlike matters bears the easier life.

The dream of having sexual intercourse with one's mother was as common then as it is to-day with many people, who tell it with indignation and astonishment. As may well be imagined, it is the key to the tragedy and the complement to the dream of the death of the father. The Oedipus fable is the reaction of fantasy to these two typical dreams, and just as such a dream, when occurring to an adult, is experienced with feelings of aversion, so the content of the fable must include terror and self-chastisement. The form which it subsequently assumed was the result of an uncomprehending secondary elaboration of the material, which sought to make it serve a theological intention. The attempt to reconcile divine omnipotence with human responsibility must, of course, fail with this material as with any other.

NOTES

[1]None of the discoveries of psychoanalytical research has evoked such embittered contradiction, such furious opposition, and also such entertaining acrobatics of criticism, as this indication of the incestuous impulses of childhood which survive in the unconscious. An attempt has even been made recently, in defiance of all experience, to assign only a "symbolic" significance to incest. Ferenczi has given an ingenious reinterpretation of the Oedipus myth, based on a passage in one of Schopenhauer's letters, in *Imago*, i, 1912. The "Oedipus complex," which was first alluded to here in *The Interpretation of Dreams*, has through further study of the subject, acquired an unexpected significance for the understanding of human history and the evolution of religion and morality. See *Totem und Taboo*.

Oedipus and Erichthonius:
Some Observations of Paradigmatic
and Syntagmatic Order

John Peradotto

One of the important trends in the analysis of folktale and myth is structuralism. The term "structuralism" includes a wide variety of methods ranging from Propp's Morphology of the Folktale, *in which the sequential or syntagmatic structure of Russian fairy tales is delineated, to Lévi-Strauss's analysis of the Greek Oedipus story, in which he seeks to extrapolate what he considers to be the underlying paradigmatic structure of the narrative. Lévi-Straussian paradigms tend to be binary oppositions, and as with most anthropologists analyzing folk narrative, the meaning of narrative structure inevitably turns out to be kinship relations.*

Since Lévi-Strauss declined to allow us to reprint his original essay of 1955 on the grounds that his "so-called analysis of the Oedipus myth has given rise to innumerable misunderstandings," we have elected to include one of the studies inspired by the Lévi-Strauss methodology. In this paper by classicist John Peradotto, the reader will find a lucid account of the critical distinction between syntagmatic and paradigmatic structuralism as well as an insightful re-analysis of Oedipus à la Lévi-Strauss.

Reprinted from *Arethusa*, 10 (1977), 85–101.

*For other examples of Lévi-Strauss's analysis of myth, see his
brilliant essay, "The Story of Asdiwal," in Edmund Leach, ed.,* The
Structural Study of Myth and Totemism (*London, 1967*), *pp.
1-47, and his four-volume* Introduction to a Science of Mythology: I.
The Raw and the Cooked (*New York, 1969*); II. *From Honey to
Ashes* (*New York, 1973*); III. *The Origin of Table Manners* (*New
York, 1978*); IV. *The Naked Man* (*New York, 1981*). *For an over-
view of the different structural approaches to folk narrative, see
Alan Dundes, "Structuralism and Folklore,"* Studia Fennica, 20
(*1976*), *75-93. For a useful survey, see Bengt Holbek, "Formal and
Structural Studies of Oral Narratives: A Bibliography,"* Unifol,
Arsbetetning 1977 (*Copenhagen, 1978*), *pp. 149-194. For other
critiques of Lévi-Strauss's analysis of Oedipus, see Michael P.
Carroll, "Lévi-Strauss on the Oedipus Myth: A Reconsideration,"*
American Anthropologist, 80 (*1978*), *805-814; and Dorothy Willner,
"The Oedipus Complex, Antigone, and Electra: The Woman as
Hero and Victim,"* American Anthropologist, 84 (*1982*), *58-78.*

The term "structuralism" covers a surprisingly wide variety of
approaches and analytic models. Only to the uninformed can it be
reduced to the work of a single school, or of a single man. When it is
so reduced, that man is Claude Lévi-Strauss. Not without reason,
for perhaps no one has done more to bring structuralism to the
attention of the scholarly world, and even to popular audiences. But
the method, now so widely diversified, was derived from linguistics,
and when we return to that starting-point, it becomes clear that, in a
certain sense later to be qualified, Lévi-Strauss has taken only half
the method to the analysis of narrative. In the present essay I should
like to return to these linguistic roots of structural narrative analysis
to explicate what is unquestionably its most important aspect: the
distinction between paradigmatic and syntagmatic order, for it is
basically only one of these that Lévi-Strauss employs, that is, analysis of paradigmatic order. I shall then try to present a concrete
example of myth analyzed the other way, that is, syntagmatically,
cautioning the reader—especially the classicist—to expect no more
than a tentative, introductory, exploratory essay.

The opposition between paradigm and syntagm is basic to modern structural linguistics.[1] Indeed, to insist that "linguistic units have

no validity independently of their paradigmatic and syntagmatic relations with other units"[2] has been called the defining characteristic of structural linguistics. Both paradigm and syntagm are presupposed in any product, conscious or unconscious, of systematic thought. A linguistic unit sustains a paradigmatic relationship with all other units that could be conceivably substituted for it in the same context. It sustains a syntagmatic relationship with all other units that occur with it and constitute its context, that is, units that may precede, follow, include it, or be included within it. Paradigms constitute a substitutional set. In linguistic activity, elements are selected from such sets and combined in a restricted linear context in which their interrelationship is syntagmatic. Paradigms are united in a virtual set *in absentia*; by definition, they never occur together. Syntagms are united *in praesentia*; they occur together in an actual series or chain.[3] In the following schema, each vertical column represents a paradigmatic set:

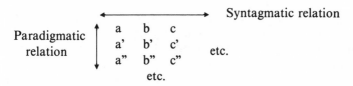

A language event occurs when one unit is selected from each of these vertical columns to form a syntagmatic chain (e.g.: abc, ab'c", a"b'c', a"b"c", etc.). This abstract description can be clarified by some examples. At the phonological level in English,[4] because it can occur in the context /-et/, the expression element /b/ stands in paradigmatic relationship with /g/, /j/, /l/,·/m/, /n/, etc., and in syntagmatic relationship with /e/ and /t/. Schematically:

$$
\begin{array}{ll}
/\text{b}/ & \\
/\text{g}/ & \\
/\text{j}/ & \\
/\text{l}/ & /\text{-et}/ \\
/\text{m}/ & \\
/\text{n}/ & \\
/\text{p}/ & \\
\text{etc.} &
\end{array}
$$

At the word level consider the context *the . . . of a dog*. The word *bark* belongs to a paradigmatic set containing such other words as *tail, paw, head, habits, fur, gait*, etc.; it has syntagmatic relations with *the, of, a*, and *dog*. Schematically:

	tail	
	paw	
	head	
the	habits	of a dog
	fur	
	gait	
	etc.	

These examples are taken from speech, but paradigm and syntagm are no less operative in other signifying systems or types of communication. One such nonlinguistic signifying system is the selection, preparation, and consumption of food.[5] The rules for the actual juxtaposition, both sequential and spatial, of food-units in the meal are syntagmatic; the sets of permissible servings at various stages in the meal are paradigmatic. One such paradigmatic set in this system would be, for example, that of appetizers, comprising such possible choices as soup, hors d'oeuvres, fruit, fruit juice, etc. The relation of any one of these to the entrée and the dessert (themselves paradigmatic, substitutional sets) is syntagmatic. In what might be called the "garment system,"[6] a paradigm would be a "set of pieces, parts or details which cannot be worn at the same time on the same part of the body, and whose variation corresponds to a change in the meaning of the clothing."[7] A syntagmatic relationship results from "juxtaposition in the same type of dress of different elements: skirt, blouse, jacket."[8] The combinatory rules here are often as restrictive as those of grammar: it would be "ungrammatical" to wear a silk top hat with gingham.

The essence of the syntagm is association by *juxtaposition*, whether temporal or spatial. The essence of the paradigm is association by any sensed *similarity* (as, for example, in language: grammatical likeness, semantic affiliation, or mere phonetic similarity [rhyme]). If I say "ball" and you respond "bat," or "game," or "chain," or "socket," you have made a syntagmatic association; if you respond "sphere," or "testicle," or "cube," or "fall," you have made a paradigmatic association. And if you compulsively make only one of these kinds of association and cannot effect the other, you are afflicted with one of the two distinct types of aphasia.[9] Indeed, one might even characterize scholars as paradigmatic or syntagmatic, depending on whether they delight more in cataloguing and classifying or in syllogistic reasoning and narrative!

A final general observation to be made is that syntagmatic relationships are not necessarily *sequential*. That is to say, some elements of a structure may be identified or defined by their relative positions in sequence, but not all. "Sequence," M.A.K. Halliday says, "is at a lower degree of abstraction than order and is one possible formal exponent of it."[10] In language, for example, word-sequence in the sentence is in some cases more restrictive (as in English), in other cases less so (as in Greek and Latin). In the food-system, or so-called "culinary code" most familiar in Western culture, the syntagmatic relation between entrée and dessert is rigidly sequential; that between the elements within the entrée—"joint" (flesh), "staple" (cereal), and "adjunct" (vegetable)—is not sequential. It is obvious how large a role sequence plays in the syntagms at the phonological level in most languages (e.g.: "eat" as opposed to "tea," and "lie" as opposed to "isle"), and how small a role it plays in the syntagms of the garment-system.

Returning now to the subject of mythic narrative analysis, we see that Lévi-Strauss describes patterns which allegedly underlie the text as it is given, and that these patterns are usually reducible to an *a priori* principle of binary opposition. These patterns have little at all in common with the *sequential* structure. Rather the basic narrative units or "mythemes" are extracted from the chronological (or "diachronic") order as it stands and are re-grouped according to their logical, conceptual, or, as he puts it, "synchronic" interrelations.[11] This type of organization has been called paradigmatic, borrowing from the notion of paradigm in linguistics.[12] But long before Lévi-Strauss applied himself to the study of narrative, the Russian formalist, Vladimir Propp published a study of Russian folktales (1928)[13] in which a distinctly different type of analysis—still structural—was emphasized. In this type, the structure or formal organization of a text is described without diverging from the linear, chronological sequence of basic narrative units or my-themes. Thus if a tale is constituted out of a series of events A to Z, the structure of the tale is delineated in terms of this same sequence.

Borrowing from the notion of syntax in linguistic analysis, this type
has been called syntagmatic structural analysis. These two types of
analysis, as Alan Dundes points out, possess contrasting character-
istics, appealing to quite different scholarly predispositions: "Generally speaking, the syntagmatic approach tends to be both empiri-
cal and inductive, and its resultant analyses can be replicated. In
contrast, paradigmatic analyses are speculative and deductive, and
they are not as easily replicated."[14]

Now there is a clear correspondence between Lévi-Strauss'
exclusively paradigmatic analysis of narrative and the subject matter
to which he addresses himself. In the Amerindian narratives which
appear in *Mythologiques*,[15] chronology and genealogy are for the
most part negligible or non-existent, both within each tale, and in
the relation of tale to tale. They positively invite paradigmatic
analysis, and promise little yield to syntagmatic analysis. By contrast, in Greek (and for that matter Judaeo-Christian) myth, genealogical preoccupations are prominent, together with rigid temporal
priority and posteriority, and irreversible time. More important,
prophecy, than which there is probably no more critical element in
Greek myth, establishes irreversible sequential and causal continuity
—teleology—*as an element of structure*.[16] By contrast, in all 813 of
the Amerindian tales studied by Lévi-Strauss, there is not a single
prophecy!

Lévi-Strauss has been criticized by Edmund Leach[17] and Paul
Ricoeur[18] for so obstinately resisting the analysis of Greek and
Judaeo-Christian myths following his use of the Oedipus myth as a
methodological model. In response, he has argued that in the Greek
and Judaeo-Christian materials intellectual operations (e.g., that of
Biblical compilers and redactors) have worked in conflict with the
randomized nonintellectual operations of the ancient structures,
thus making them undecipherable. There is, of course, more to it
than that. His Rousseauvian prejudice in favor of the primitive, of
"cold" cultures defined by equilibrium more than by change and
history, his corresponding disavowal of "hot" or historically-defined
cultures, especially Western culture, and of the very notions of
history and progress—all this suggests a disavowal of the syntagmatic as such, especially of the sequentially syntagmatic. The clos-
ing pages of *L'Homme nu* (*Mythologiques IV*) declare that myth
and the study of myth represent a liberation from the enslavement

of time. Be that as it may, it remains to be proved that chronological sequence—one form of syntagmatic structure—is insignificant in the analysis of Greek (and Judaeo-Christian) myth.

In what follows, I propose to demonstrate how the message which, through exclusively paradigmatic analysis, Lévi-Strauss discovers underlying the manifest content of the Oedipus myth is found in the *syntagmatic* structure of another myth—that of Erichthonius, a message which in this latter form lies a good deal closer to consciousness, and to the manifest content of the narrative. Before examining the Erichthonius myth, we should review in its essentials Lévi-Strauss' interpretation of the Oedipus myth, always bearing in mind, of course, that he intended[19] it as a methodological model rather than as a conclusive and preferable alternative to other interpretations. His four-column skeletal scheme has been reproduced and explained with sufficient frequency to justify concise summary here. All but eleven basic units have been extracted from the chronological chain of the narrative and arranged in columns according to their generic similarities: *over-valuation of kinship* in column I, *under-valuation of kinship* in column II, *denial of man's autochthonous origin* in column III, and *assertion of man's autochthonous origin* in column IV.[20]

I	II	III	IV
Cadmus seeks lost sister Europa.			
		Cadmus kills the dragon.	
	Spartoi kill one another.		
	Oedipus kills Laius.	Oedipus kills the Sphinx.	Labdacus = "lame."
Oedipus marries mother Jocasta.			Laius = "left-sided."
	Eteocles kills Polyneices.		Oedipus = "swollen-foot."
Antigone buries Polyneices.			

Logically, column IV is the opposite of column III just as column II is the opposite of column I:

$$I : II :: III : IV$$

Lévi-Strauss sees this as an attempt to overcome a cultural dilemma: experience shows that man is the product of bisexual union; but the primal pair would inevitably be related as brother and sister, making all their offspring incestuous products. To escape such an unacceptable conclusion, autochthony—birth from *one*—is posited, but at the cost of experience. "The myth," to quote Lévi-Strauss,[21]

> has to do with the inability for a culture which holds the belief that mankind is autochthonous, to find a satisfactory transition between this theory and the knowledge that human beings are actually born from the union of man and woman. Although the problem obviously cannot be solved, the Oedipus myth provides a kind of logical tool which relates the original problem—born from one or born from two?—to the derivative problem—born from different or born from same?

And further:

> The inability to connect two kinds of relationships is overcome (or rather replaced) by the assertion that the contradictory relationships are identical inasmuch as they are both self-contradictory in a similar way.

Parenthetically, what continues to scandalize me about this early explanation is that Lévi-Strauss failed to articulate a latent characteristic of his Oedipus model, a characteristic which would give it increased analytical elegance. And this is all the more strange in that he adverts explicitly to this characteristic in describing the Pueblo trickster-myths in the very same essay. This characteristic is the tendency to replace two unmediatable oppositions by two equivalent or analogous terms which admit a third one as a mediator.[22] Lévi-Strauss sees this process at work in the tendency of North American myth to assign the trickster's mediating role to either coyote or raven. He schematizes the structure of such tales as follows:

INITIAL PAIR	FIRST TRIAD	SECOND TRIAD
Life	Agriculture	Herbivorous Animals
	Hunting	*Carrion-eaters* (*Raven, Coyote*)
Death	Warfare	Beasts of Prey

The movement from two unmediatable opposites (as above, Life and Death) to analogous opposites permitting mediation (Agriculture and Warfare) is the process called *transformation,* whose product is a four-part homology: Life : Agriculture :: Death : Warfare. Hunting represents a preliminary mediation inasmuch as it is like agriculture in being life-sustaining food-gathering, and like warfare in that it involves killing. Dissatisfaction with the fact that hunting still involves killing engenders another transformation, the goal of which is a new pair of opposites analogous to agriculture and hunting, and capable of mediating them: Agriculture : Herbivorous Animals :: Hunting : Predatory Animals. The new opposites admit carrion-eaters as mediation, in that, like predators, they eat dead animals, but like herbivores, do not kill them.

Now, so far as I know, no one has pointed out that this mode of mythic problem-solving is precisely what we have in the four-term homology of Lévi-Strauss' Oedipus model: columns III and IV are related to one another as *contradictories* (without possible mediation); but columns I and II are logical *contraries* between which mediation (i.e., *proper* valuation of kinship) is possible:

(IV) Assertion of Autochthony   (I) Over-valuation of kinship

                                 Proper valuation of kinship

(III) Denial of Autochthony   (II) Under-valuation of kinship

Thus, the problem of autochthony vs. bisexual union (columns III and IV) is resolved by making it equivalent to the potentially mediatable opposition between under-valuation and over-valuation of kinship relations (columns I and II). Of course, from the standpoint of strict Aristotelian logic, this kind of resolution amounts to a fallacy: equating contradictories with contraries.[23]

Returning to the main line of our argument, it is important to observe, as Lévi-Strauss himself emphasizes, that in the Oedipus myth the initial problem—assertion vs. denial of autochthony—is not fully conscious on the surface of the narrative. But when we turn to the myth of Erichthonius and the beginnings of the Athenian people, we are from the outset *consciously* concerned with origins and the problem of autochthony. The inevitably discontinuous and unreproductive character of autochthony is evident in the manifest content of the genealogy[24]: three false starts—Cecrops, Cranaus, Amphictyon—each (necessarily) autochthonous, the whole series showing progressively diminished reproductivity: from Cecrops, with three daughters and a son who dies young and without issue, to Cranaus, with three daughters and no sons, to his rebellious son-in-law Amphictyon, who is expelled altogether without issue. He is expelled by Erichthonius, with whom begins an uninterrupted line of continuity down to "historical" times. What makes Erichthonius different from his unsuccessful autochthonous predecessors? The answer lies in the story of his birth—one of the most often repeated and best attested myths in the corpus—here presented in version of Apollodorus (3.14.6):

> Some say that this Erichthonius was a son of Hephaestus and Atthis, daughter of Cranaus, and some that he was a son of Hephaestus and Athena, as follows: Athena came to Hephaestus wishing to have some armor fashioned. Hephaestus, who had been abandoned by Aphrodite, fell into a sudden passion for Athena, and began to pursue her; but she fled. When with a great deal of effort he closed on her (he was lame, remember), he made an attempt at intercourse. But she was chaste and a virgin, and would not submit. He ejaculated on her thigh. In disgust, she wiped the semen away with wool and threw it on the ground. She fled away, and as the semen fell into the earth, Erichthonius was born. Him Athena raised unknown to the other gods, wishing to make him immortal. And having put

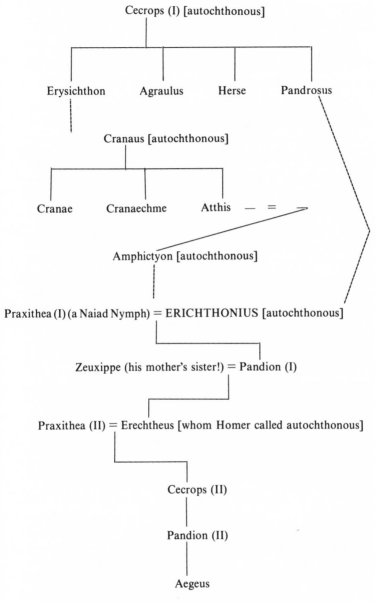

(*Athena entrusts the infant Erichthonius to Pandrosus.)

him in a chest, she committed it to Pandrosus, daughter of
Cecrops, forbidding her to open it. But the sisters of Pandrosus
opened the chest in their curiosity, and beheld a snake coiled
about the infant. As some would have it, they were killed by
the snake; others say that Athena's anger drove them insane,
and they threw themselves from the Acropolis. Erichthonius
was raised by Athena herself in the sacred precinct. He expelled
Amphictyon, became king of Athens, set up the wooden image
of Athena on the Acropolis, instituted the Panathenaeic festival,
and married Praxithea, a Naiad nymph, by whom he had a son
Pandion.

What more could one ask for in a contradiction-mediating
figure? Erichthonius not only resolves the old autochthony contradiction by being at one and the same time autochthonous *and*
product of a bisexual transaction, he also permits his Athenian heirs
to claim that they are offspring of Earth, of Hephaestus, whose cult
was so strong among them, and even of Athena, and this without
any damage to her virginity. Beyond what immediately meets the
eye, there is a measure of elegant logical "overkill" bound on making
the solution really air-tight: Hephaestus bears the telltale lameness
of the autochthonous, but more important for our original dilemma,
he is born from *one*, as Athena is born from *one*,[25] in the one case,
male from unaided female, in the other, female from unaided male,
and it is out of their explicit *difference*, their remaining apart (*eris*)
that *Eri*-chthonius is paradoxically born. The cleansing wool (*erion*)
is there to dramatize the original disjunction (*eris*) all the more.[26]

I would further suggest that the detail wherein Athena entrusts
the infant Erichthonius to Pandrosus, daughter of Cecrops, could
be a device for bridging the prior discontinuities, for establishing
continuity with the chronologically prior but otherwise unproductive
Cecrops, bypassing the wholly irredeemable Cranaus and Amphictyon. The variant that makes Erichthonius son of Hephaestus and
Atthis, daughter of Cranaus, seems a similar, though weaker attempt to establish continuity with the chronologically prior family
of Cranaus, just as another variant, the marriage of Cranaus' daughter Atthis to Amphictyon seems like an attempt (obviously unsuccessful) to fill the vertical gap in filiation with a horizontal affinal
relation.

There is another noteworthy observation on the syntagmatic
order here, although it is not evident in the selective genealogical

table. There is progressive *increase* in reproductivity after Erichthonius answering to the progressive decline in reproductivity from Cecrops through Amphictyon: Erichthonius has *one* son; that son, Pandion I, has *two* sons [+ two daughters]; his heir to the throne, Erechtheus, has *three* sons [+ four daughters]; the second Cecrops momentarily reverses the trend with *one* son, but that one, Pandion II, has *four* sons, which brings us down to Aegeus, where the problem of reproductivity re-asserts itself, but that is another story.

This sequence obviously cries out for further analysis, especially concerning the function of wives and daughters, the repetition of proper names in successive generations, the astounding, unparalleled marriage of Pandion I to his mother's sister, but the main point has been made: what Lévi-Strauss extracts with much difficulty from the Oedipus myth by the use of aprioristic and deductive categories is easily visible in the syntagmatic structure of the Attic myth, is more available to consciousness, and is replicated with far less "subjective" selectivity among the manifest narrative units. In the study of Greek mythic materials, clearly neither paradigmatic nor syntagmatic analysis must be neglected.

However, it would be intellectually hazardous not to scrutinize more closely Lévi-Strauss' dismissal of syntagmatic order. In Saussure, there is not only a clear bias for the paradigmatic relationship, but the first steps toward the logical reduction of syntagmatic to paradigmatic order are taken, a reduction on which Jacques Derrida is considered to have put the finishing touches. The syntagmatic dimension reduces to the paradigmatic in the sense that a given syntagmatic chain has significance only in terms of its *absent,* alternative substitutes, just as in the case of paradigms. In other words, the interrelation of units within a syntagmatic series or chain is able to signify because it differs from other possible series or chains, with which the series actually used forms a substitutional or paradigmatic set.[27] Consider the following example:

	hunting a dog
He saw Fido	a hunting dog
	a dog hunting

That the arrangement of "a hunting dog" conveys the syntagmatic relation of *attribution* depends on the potential sequential re-arrangement of those words to convey different syntagmatic relations (e.g., *predication* in "a dog hunting"); all of these potential re-arrangements constitute a substitutional paradigmatic set.

Lévi-Strauss' relative disinterest in syntagmatic (or "diachronic") order, therefore, already has its precedent in linguistic theory. His procedure is analogous to the study of a linguistic system. "In both cases," as Jonathan Culler[28] puts it, "one compares syntagmatic sequences in order to construct paradigmatic classes and examines those classes so as to determine the pertinent oppositions between members of each paradigm." In *Le Cru et le cuit* (*Mythologiques I*) Lévi-Strauss argues that a single syntagmatic chain is meaningless from the analyst's point of view; there are but two procedures for overcoming the difficulty:[29]

> One consists in dividing the syntagmatic sequence into super-posable segments, and in proving that they constitute variations on one and the same theme [*his procedure in the Oedipus essay*]. The other procedure, which is complementary to the first, consists in superposing a syntagmatic sequence in its totality—in other words, a complete myth—on other myths or segments of myths. It follows, then, that on both occasions we are replacing a syntagmatic sequence by a paradigmatic sequence. . . . Two syntagmatic sequences, or fragments of the same sequence, which, considered in isolation, contain no definite meaning, acquire a meaning simply from the fact that they are polar opposites.

It has become fashionable to discount Lévi-Strauss' Oedipus essay, or at least to point out the presumed embarrassing discrepancy between the method advocated and employed there and the one found in *Mythologiques*. In point of fact, the early essay proves to be the only method applicable to a kind of narrative, like Greek and Judaeo-Christian, which Lévi-Strauss would call debased myth—something closer to the novel than to "genuine" myth of the Amerindian variety, a kind described in the following terms in *L'Origine des manières de table*:[30]

> [Their] structural content is dispersed. For the vigorous trans-formations of genuine myths we now find feeble ones substituted. . . . The sociological, astronomical and anatomical codes whose functioning we hitherto observed out in the open now pass beneath the surface; and the structure sinks into seriality. This degradation begins when oppositions turn into

> mere reduplications: episodes succeeding each other in time, but all formed in the same pattern. It is complete when reduplication itself takes the place of structure. The form of a form, reduplication receives the dying breath of structure itself. Having nothing more, or so little, left to say, myth now survives by repeating itself.

The Oedipus myth is just such a product in Lévi-Strauss' calculation. For that reason, he insisted on extracting bundles of identical units—repeated units, and ranging them against one another in a four-term homology. However, *transformation*, that methodological concept so critical to *Mythologiques*, does not figure in the Oedipus analysis, for none appear in the debased myth that this narrative typifies. In fact, his explication of the Pueblo trickster myths in the very same essay with the Oedipus interpretation proceeds almost as if the methodological ground-rules at the outset of the essay had been utterly abandoned. "The Structural Study of Myth" turns out to be anything but a methodological model which just happens to use the Oedipus myth because everyone knows it; rather, the material restricts the method. Whatever Lévi-Strauss' original intentions may have been, the essay appears to apply only to the study of "debased," time-bound, serialized myth, the narrative of what Lévi-Strauss would call "hot" cultures. His scholarship, curiously enough, turns out to be as "synchronic" as the relations he purports to discover in his Amerindian data. The Oedipus interpretation, which at first sight seems so ill-suited as an introduction to the method employed in *Mythologiques*, is perfectly consonant with his observations on "debased" myth published thirteen years later in *L'Origine des manières de table*. In a sense, the local discrepancy forces us to view his work, as he himself views Amerindian myth, simultaneously as a whole, "synchronically."

My own reading of the Erichthonius story, at first sight syntagmatic, is reducible to a paradigmatic relation. It implies other possible sequential orders against which the Erichthonius sequence— with diminishing procreativity and absolute discontinuity between "generations" up to Erichthonius, and continuity and increasing procreativity after him—forces upon us the limitations of any theory of autochthony. Taking the other approach advocated by Lévi-Strauss, i.e., that of dividing the syntagmatic chain into segments shown to constitute variations on a single theme, forces us to range the birth of Erichthonius against the cases of Cecrops, Cranaus, and Amphictyon, which constitute a single paradigmatic set, and to abstract its distinction from them as the solution to the original problem. Is this a case of "debased" myth? Its narrative situations are not cases of simple repetition. Rather, it is repetition with a significant enough difference to draw attention to itself. Furthermore, although the syntagmatic chain is reducible to a paradigmatic relationship, the meaning of the myth still lies on the syntagmatic level, not in the logical relationship between the actual and the potential sequences. The meaning is validated by its absent alternatives, by its *difference* from them. Sequence, or, more abstractly, syntagmatic order still proves to be critically important in the analysis of at least a certain kind of myth.

NOTES

[1]These appear to be the most generally accepted terms for the concepts under discussion. See John Lyons, *Introduction to Theoretical Linguistics* (Cambridge 1968) 70–81, 428–429. But different terminology will be encountered in certain key authors. Ferdinand de Saussure: *"association"* and *"syntagm"* (*Cours de linguistique générale,* ed. Charles Bally and Albert Sechehaye [1910 rpt. Paris 1960] 170ff.); Hjelmslev: *"correlations"* and *"relations"* (*Prolegomena to a Theory of Language,* trans. F.J. Whitfield [Madison, Wis. 1961] 38–39, 65–66); Jakobson: *"similarities"* and *"contiguities"* (or as processes, *"selection"* and *"combination"*), but more often, especially in his extension of the opposition to nonlinguistic languages, *"metaphor"* and *"metonym"* ("Two Aspects of Language and Two Types of Aphasic Disturbances" in R. Jakobson and M. Halle, *Fundamentals of Language* [The Hague 1956] 55–82); A. Martinet: *"oppositions"* and *"contrasts"* (*Elements of General Linguistics,* trans. Elizabeth Palmer [Chicago 1964] 36); Roland Barthes: *"system"* and *"syntagm"* (*Elements of Semiology* [printed together with *Writing Degree Zero*] trans. Annette Lavers and Colin Smith [Boston 1970] 58–88). Most of the present discussion of paradigm and syntagm is reproduced from my "*Odyssey* 8.564–571: Verisimilitude, Narrative Analysis, and Bricolage," *Texas Studies in Literature and Language* 15.5 (1974) 803–832, esp. 818–821.

[2]John Lyons (above, note 1) 74–75.

[3]Saussure (above, note 1) 17: "Le rapport syntagmatique est *in praesentia*: il repose sur deux ou plusieurs termes également présents dans une série effective. Au contraire le rapport associatif unit des termes *in absentia* dans une série mnémonique virtuelle."

[4]This example is taken from Lyons (above, note 1) 73–74.

[5]See Claude Lévi-Strauss, *The Raw and the Cooked,* trans. J. and D. Weight-

man (New York 1969), or, for a simpler introduction to the so-called "Culinary Triangle," *Partisan Review* 33 (1966) 586–595; Michael A.K. Halliday, "Categories of the Theory of Grammar," *Word: Journal of the Linguistic Circle of New York* 17 (1961) 241–291, but esp. 277–280; Mary Douglas, "Deciphering a Meal," *Daedalus* (Winter 1972) 61–81.

⁶See Roland Barthes, *Système de la mode* (Paris 1967).

⁷Barthes (above, note 1) 63.

⁸*Ibid.*

⁹Jakobson, "Two Aspects of Language" (above, note 1).

¹⁰Halliday (above, note 5) 254–255. See also Lyons (above, note 1) 76–78. On sequence in narrative, see Gérard Genette, *Figures III* (Paris 1972) 77–121.

¹¹See his "Structural Study of Myth" in *Structural Anthropology,* trans. Claire Jacobson and Brooke Grundfest Schoepf (Garden City, N.Y. 1967; orig. 1963) 202–228. This is a considerably revised version of the essay which first appeared under the same title in Thomas A. Sebeok (ed.), *Myth: a Symposium* ("Bibliographical and Special Series of the American Folklore Society," vol. 5; Bloomington 1955).

The terms "synchronic" and "diachronic" have been preserved in my analysis for the convenience of those wishing to refer to Lévi-Strauss' essay, even though linguists familiar with these terms in Saussure will be troubled by their misguided application in Lévi-Strauss' usage.

¹²For a brief general discussion of the two types of narrative analysis, paradigmatic and syntagmatic, see Alan Dundes' introduction to the second edition of Vladimir Propp, *Morphology of the Folktale,* trans. Laurence Scott ("Bibliographical and Special Series of the American Folklore Society," vol. 10; Austin and London 1968) xi–xvii.

¹³See note 12, above.

¹⁴Dundes (above, note 12) xii.

¹⁵*Mythologiques I: Le Cru et le cuit* (Paris 1964), translated by J. and D. Weightman, *The Raw and the Cooked* (New York 1969); *Mythologiques II: Du Miel aux cendres* (Paris 1966), translated by J. and D. Weightman, *From Honey to Ashes* (New York 1971); *Mythologiques III: L'Origine des manières de table* (Paris 1968); *Mythologiques IV: L'Homme nu* (Paris 1972). We must, of course, rely on Lévi-Strauss' versions of these tales. It must, however, be questioned whether and to what extent he or his secondary sources have underplayed whatever temporal elements there may be in them.

¹⁶For a description of the type of analysis which might be brought to bear on prophecy-tales, see my "*Odyssey* 8.564–571: Verisimilitude, Narrative Analysis, and Bricolage" (above, note 1).

¹⁷"The Legitimacy of Solomon: Some Structural Aspects of Old Testament History," *European Journal of Sociology* 7 (1966), reprinted in Michael Lane (ed.), *Structuralism: a Reader* (London 1970) 248–292, and in Edmund Leach, *Genesis as Myth and Other Essays* (New York 1970).

¹⁸"Structure et herméneutique," *Esprit* (November 1963) 596–628, reprinted in the author's *Le Conflit des interprétations* (Paris 1969) 31–63, translated in *The Conflict of Interpretations*, ed. Don Ihde (Evanston 1974).

[19]But how closely the result coincided with his stated intentions we shall shortly have cause to question.

[20]Lévi-Strauss argues that the killing of monsters (column III) by men argues to the denial of man's autochthonous origin as follows: "The dragon is a chthonian being which has to be killed in order that mankind be born from the Earth; the Sphinx is a monster unwilling to permit men to live. The last unit reproduces the first one, which has to do with the autochthonous origin of mankind. Since the monsters are overcome by men, we may thus say that the common feature of the third column is *denial of the autochthonous origin of man.*" As for column IV, where all the names suggest difficulty in walking straight or standing upright, he says, "In mythology it is a universal characteristic of men born from the Earth that at the moment they emerge from the depths they either cannot walk or they walk clumsily" (p. 212).

[21]"Structural Analysis of Myth" (above, note 11) 212.

[22]"Structural Analysis of Myth" (above, note 11) 221.

[23]There are many other detailed criticisms which might be leveled at the content of Lévi-Strauss' essay.

[24]The genealogy is constructed out of the version by Apollodorus 3.14.6. For other sources of the myth, see Frazer's Loeb *Apollodorus,* vol. 2, pp. 90–95, and B. Powell, *Athenian Mythology: Erichthonius and the Daughters of Cecrops* (Chicago 1977, orig. 1906).

[25]In telling the story of Erichthonius, Nonnus, *Dionysiaca* 13.175, refers to Athena by the curious expression παρθένος αὐτολόχευτος.

[26]The etymological element is evident in most of the sources (see Frazer [above, note 24] 91), sometimes quite explicitly, as in the following account by Hyginus (*Fab.* 166):

> Neptunus, quod Minervae erat infestus, instigavit Vulcanum Minervam petere in conjugium, qua re impetrata in thalamum cum venisset, Minerva monitu Jovis virginitatem suam armis defendit, interque luctandum ex semine ejus quod in terram decidit natus est puer qui inferiorem partem draconis habuit; quem Erichthonium ideo nominaverunt quod ἔρις Graece certatio dicitur, χθών autem terra dicitur.

[27]On Saussure's bias for the paradigmatic, see Fredric Jameson, *The Prison-House of Language* (Princeton 1972) 36–39, esp. 38: "The syntagmatic dimension . . . looks like a primary phenomenon only when we examine its individual units separately; then they seem to be organized successively in time according to some mode of temporal perception. In reality, however, we never perceive them separately: the 'verb' is always felt to be part of a larger unity, which is the syntagma itself, and which now, since it is no longer a series of units but rather a unity of its own, is reabsorbed into associative [= paradigmatic] thought and understood through its resemblance to other syntagmata."

[28]*Structural Poetics: Structuralism, Linguistics and the Study of Literature* (London 1975) 44.

[29]P. 307 of the English translation.

[30]*L'Origine des manières de table* (above, note 15) 105: Jameson's translation (above, note 27) 72.

Cú-chulainn and the Origin of Totemism

Géza Róheim

*Not all Freudians write with the lucidity of Freud. The writing style
of Géza Róheim (1891–1953), one of the most brilliant Freudian
students of folklore and anthropology, strains the credulity of even
the most sympathetic reader. Immensely learned and well read,
Róheim does not hesitate to freely associate and present his "stream
of consciousness" in a fast-paced elliptical fashion. In this Oedipal
reading of the Irish Cuchulain hero cycle, we find Róheim at his best
or at least at his most typical. He believes he has found evidence
supporting Freud's theory of the primal horde presented in* Totem
and Taboo, *according to which a band of sons united to kill their
father. This theory, intended to explain the origin of totemism and
the incest taboo, is not given much credence by anthropologists. But
Róheim's use of the primal horde theory does not diminish the
success of his fascinating attempt to discover an Oedipal pattern
underlying the celebrated Cuchulain cycle.*

For a more extended treatment of Oedipus stories, see Róheim's
The Gates of the Dream *(New York, 1952), pp. 529–544. For further
discussion of Róheim's many contributions to folklore and anthropology, see Roger Dadoun,* Géza Róheim *(Paris, 1972).*

It has been pointed out by various authors that some of the Irish
geasa and notably the dog taboo of Cú-chulainn are probably

Reprinted from *Man*, 25 (1925), 85–88.

totemic in origin.[1] We fully endorse this view and intend to go even further: we believe that the saga of Cú-chulainn throws some light on the much disputed question of totemic origins.

There is nothing particularly remarkable in the idea that a hero who is frequently called Cu, *i.e.,* dog, should be prohibited from eating dogs' flesh,[2] and it is also quite natural that the broken taboo proves fatal to the hero of the dog clan. What calls for attention is that Cú-chulainn only becomes a dog by killing a dog,[3] much as the manitou[4] or personal totem must be killed in certain North American tribes before it endows mortal man with the faculties belonging to the supernatural animal. Now Freud regards totemism as the form of social organisation that arose out of the repression of the great conflict between fathers and sons for the women in the Cyclopean family;[5] in other words, as co-eval with exogamy, and in the same sense as the latter, an embodiment of the Primal Law. Totemism is a system of defence against the possibility of relapsing into the two crimes of Œdipous: man is not allowed to kill the totem-animal, whom primitive tribes regard as their father, and to mate with women belonging to the same totem, *i.e.,* to commit incest with the mother.[6] According to this view, totemism arises after the violent death of the Jealous Sire out of the feeling of guilt and compunction in the young males of the horde who had done the deed to which they were prompted by their genital impulse. I think it will go far to confirm this theory if we can show that the totemic saga of Cú-chulainn contains more or less veiled traces of the conflict between father and son, of the animal symbol or name originating out of a feeling of guilt for the act of parricide, and of incest committed by the hero.

One of the youthful feats of our hero is to slay the supernatural watch-dog of the smith Cu-lann. He offers to serve in the dog's stead, guarding the smith's stronghold and cattle till he finds another dog of the same breed.[7] It is a typical feature in the life of Aryan heroes that they serve a term of apprenticeship with a smith from whom they usually obtain their terrific weapon.

Gratitude is not one of the outstanding virtues of our heroes, for they frequently kill their benefactor.[8] Now primitive people usually regard smiths as uncanny or supernatural[9] and it is very probable that this quality is derived from the awe felt by the child before the mystery of its own origin, the life-giving sexual act.[10] For primitive mankind all objects are endowed with life and therefore to make a tool is the same thing as "making," *i.e.,* procreating a new human being.[11] This is how the smith becomes a representative of the father, and we find that Tvashtri the smith, killed by Indra, is really the father of the hero-god.[12] In some variants of the Bear's-Son type we find the hero killing a smith, whilst in others he is represented as another Œdipous who deals his father the mortal blow.[13] We shall, therefore, conclude that, mythologically speaking, the smith and his dog are but "Abspaltungen" of the same unconscious idea,[14] and that Cú-chulainn derives his totemic name from the very act of parricide which it serves to hide. The hero becomes a dog when he has killed his father who was a dog.[15] His servitude as the smith's watchdog is not merely the practical settling of a question of property, but, strictly analogous to the term of penance undergone by Greek dragonslayers after their heroic, yet murderous deed.[16] It is an act of expiation, of "subsequent obedience," if Cú-chulainn becomes a dog after having killed a dog.[17]

Anthropologists will have noticed that the Law of the Pack represented by the hypothetical primal state of human society reappears in the case of the King of Nemi who is king as long as he holds his own against the new pretenders to his office. Originally, danger must have threatened the leader of the herd from his own sons, who would be the natural successors to the throne. Some slight trace of the original pre-human state of things perhaps survives in the figure of Conchobhar, Cú-chulainn's uncle, who—although the mightiest warrior on earth—was not suffered to encounter any danger "for the preservation of the king's son,"[18] a curious taboo which becomes comprehensible if we regard his son as Conchobhar's adversary, whom he must inevitably have killed in the combat. In an ingenious paper on the "European Sky God," A.B. Cook shows that some of the taboos which prove so fatal to the "fortissimus heros Scottorum" are really those of the divine king of Tara.[19]

Since the publication of the "Golden Bough" no anthropologist doubts the specific importance of the oak for Aryan divine kings; Cú-chulainn is bred in an oak-house,[20] he kills Roi, Son of the Oak, and mates with Curios' wife Blathnath.[21] This is the natural thing for a King of the Wood of the Nemi type, and our interpretation of the taboo laid upon Conchobhar finds a striking confirmation in the fact that what is feared in him, actually comes to pass in the person of his nephew: the invincible Cú-chulainn fights and kills his own son.[22] There seems reason to suppose that this is not the only case of the father-son combat in the Cú-chulainn cycle, for Lugaid, the man who deals him the death-blow, is the son of Curoi of the Oak, with whose wife Cú-chulainn had intercourse. This is nearly as much as to say that he is Cú-chulainn's own son, and thus it would be quite comprehensible that Cú-chulainn should part with a woman who ought to belong to him and pass her on to Lugaid.[23] The unconscious content of the episode can only be interpreted from the infantile Œdipous-wish: Cú-chulainn handing the princess on to Lugaid, is the father relinquishing his claim to the love of the mother in favour of the son.[24] We guess that the amorous relations of our hero to Blathnath, the wife of Curoi, correspond to the same situation; in other words, Curoi the Oak-man whom he kills, is really the father of Cú-chulainn. For is not the uncouth giant Curoi simply an archaic form of the divine king? Now, Conchobhar of the Ultonians is originally not only the uncle, but also the father of Cú-chulainn, for the divine fatherhood of Lug is only a thin mythical veil to cover the incest of Conchobhar with his sister Dechtire.[25] Born of incest, Cú-chulainn must commit incest, and if we openly find him engaged in mortal combat with his son, we must conclude that this is but the repetition of another battle fought between him and his father.[26]

If we have been right in equating the smith with his hound it will be significant to find that Curoi mac Daire is not only an Oak man, but also the Hound of Roi, Son of the Oak, and that the battle is, therefore, between two heroes of the dog clan.[27] Finally, when Cú-chulainn breaks the dog-taboo and eats his totem animal, he is killed by Lugaid, who is, or might be, his son, at the same time bearing a name suspiciously like that of his father, Lug.[28] The case of the Baja king who is compelled to eat his own totem animal when death at the hand of his son and heir draws near, is a striking parallel that illustrates the final conclusion of our speculations.[29]

We believe that man's primal conflict, the fight of successive generations for the women of the horde, is condensed in the life-history of the famous Ultonian hero, both in its totemic phase (men of the dog totem breaking through the cardinal taboos of totemism) and in the violent succession of the divine king to his father's throne.

NOTES

[1]A. Lang, "Custom and Myth," 1904. 265. G.L. Gomme, "Folk-Lore as an Historical Science," 1908. 286, 287.

[2]E. Hull, "Old Irish Tabus or Geasa." *Folk-Lore*, XII, *49, 50. Cf.* Windisch, "Tain bo Cualnge," 1905. 444, 888.

[3]E. Windisch, "Tain bo Cualnge," 1905. 118.

[4]*Cf.* for the explanation of manitu-killing, Róheim, "Das Selbst": *Imago*, VII. 492.

[5]S. Freud, "Totem and Taboo," 1919. Lang-Atkinson, "Social Origins and Primal Law," 1909.

[6]Freud, *l.c.,* 239.

[7]Windisch: "Tain," 118.

[8]*Cf.* Siegfried and Mime; Grimm, "Deutsche Mythologie," 1875. 315. F. Panzer, "Studien zur germanischen Sagengeschichte II." Siegfried, 1912. 42. In Rome we have the annual expulsion of Mamurius Veturius, the smith-father of the hero-god Mars, by the Salii, who represent the young god himself. L. Preller, "Römische Mythologie," 1838. 296. The Finnish Kullervo, who commits incest with his sister, serves as a slave of the smith Ilmarinen and kills his master's wife. "Kalevala," *Runo,* XXXI–XXXVI.

[9]R. Andree: "Ethnographische Parallelen und Vergleiche," 1878. 153. O. Schrader, "Sprachvergleichung und Urgeschichte," 1906, II, 13. For the type of folk-tale in which the uncanny aspect of the smith survives, *see* Macdougall and Calder, "Folk-Tales and Fairy Lore in Gaelic and English," 1910, 17.

[10]*Cf.* B. Gutmann, "Der Schmied und seine Kunst," *Z.f.E.,* 1912. 83, 87. The Dsagga regard the power which unites blade and shaft, *i.e.* man and woman, as supernatural.

[11]In Egypt the sculptor is "he who causes to live" and to "fashion" is "to give birth." G. Elliot Smith, "The Evolution of the Dragon," 1919. 25.

[12]H. Oldenberg, "Die Religion des Veda," 1894. 234, 235.

[13]F. Panzer, "Studien zur germanischen Sagengeschichte," 1910. $\sqrt{23}$, 39, 52.

[14]*Cf.* A. Nutt, "Aryan Expulsion and Return Formula." *Folk-Lore,* IV, 26. Originally it was the smith who was killed by the hero.

[15]*Cf.* a Transylvanian legend on the struggle between father and son, who both appear as bears. Hermann, "A hegyek kultusza." "Mountain cults." *Erdély,* 1893. 182.

[16]Apollo: Apollodor. III, 3, 2. Kadmos: Schol., Il. II, 494; Ov. Met. IV, 563. Like Cú-chulainn Kadmos is transformed into the animal he has killed. For the totemistic origin of the myth, *see* Frazer, "Dying god," 1911, 70, 84.

[17]*Cf.* Freud, "Totem and Taboo," 238.

[18]Book of Leinster, fac. pp. 106, a, 33–107*b*, 16, quoted by E. Hull, "Old Irish Tabus." *Folk-Lore,* XII, 54.

[19]A.B. Cook, *Folk-Lore,* XVII, 1906. 336.

[20]J. Pokorny, "Der Ursprung der Arthursage," *Mitt. d. Anth. Ges.,* XXXIX, 1909. 113.

[21]A.B. Cook, *l.c.,* 335, 336.

[22]M.A. Potter, Sohrab and Rustem. *Grimm Library,* XIV, 1902. 22–28.

[23]A. Nutt, "Cú-chulainn, the Irish Achilles." *Popular Studies,* No. 8, 1.

[24]Cú-chulainn sucks the blood of the woman he has rescued and therefore cannot marry her. Modern parallels show the same ritual act with the opposite result: as a betrothal or marriage ceremony. (F.C. Conybeare, "A Brittany Marriage Custom." *Folk-Lore,* 1907. 448.) In both cases the explanation is to be sought in the fundamental, though ambivalent, nature of the mother-son relation for love-life; the woman from whom the hero sucks blood (a substitute of milk) represents the mother. The Swanetian knight sprinkles the breast of his lady with salt, and then touches it with his teeth, repeating thrice: "Thou mother, I son." (Singer, "Blood-Kinship." *Folk-Lore,* XIX, 1908. 344.) The hero who obtains her hand may perhaps have been regarded as a reincarnation of Cú-chulainn's father Lug (Lugaid derived from Lug; A.B. Cook, "The European Sky-God." *Folk-Lore,* XVII, 343) and hence the rightful husband of Cú-chulainn's mother.

[25]Cú-chulainn is the son of his maternal uncle Conchobhar, who does violence to his sister Dechtire. At the same time he has a supernatural father in the sun-god Lug, or rather he is Lug himself, *i.e.,* his own father (Nutt: Meyer, "The Voyage of Bran." Grimm's Library VI., Vol. II, 1897. 38–42. For a parallel case *see* ibid, 26, Mongan; *cf.* Pokorny, 1, c. 104). I intend to show, in connection with primitive views on the supernatural origin of children, that the myth arises as a substitute for the repressed incest-wish and both Cú-chulainn and his father Conchobhar are represented as reincarnations of the sun-god Lug. Was it the regular thing for the divine king to be the son of a brother and sister and re-incarnation of the sun? A striking analogy would be the case of the Pharaoh. *Cf.* A. Moret, "Du Caractère réligieux de la Royauté pharaonique," *Annales du Musée Guimet,* XV, 1902. 38.

[26]From a psychoanalytic point of view it is significant that when the smith asks Conchobhar whether he may let the watch-dog loose, the king quite *forgets* Cú-chulainn and answers that all his followers are assembled, thus exposing the young boy to mortal danger (Windisch, "Tain," 122. *Cf.* on forgetting, Freud, "The Psychopathology of Everyday-Life)."

[27]*Cf.* J.A. Macculloch, "The Religion of the Ancient Celts," 1911. 219, following J. Rhys, "Celtic Britain," 1908. 267. He is also called "three dogs" and his son Lugaid, "son of three dogs" (mac tri con, "Annals of Tigernach"), is another divine king and hero and of the dog-clan. In an important variant of the dog-myth the hound of Culan is a reincarnation of Conganchness, who is the brother of Cu-roi, the Hound of Roi. K. Meyer, "The Death Tales of Ulster Heroes." Royal Irish Academy, Todd Lecture Series, Vol. XIV, 1906. Quoted from Nutt's review in *Folk-Lore,* XVIII, 230. I am compelled to content myself with secondhand references as most of the original sources are completely inaccessible here. Budapest (I, VIII, 1924).

[28]He, in his turn, is killed by Conall, a hero whose horse has a dog's head. J. Rhys, "Arthurian Legend," 222.

[29]The totem animals are leopard, hyena, white cock; and the person who compels the king to break his "geasa" and die in consequence, is his own son. L. Frobenius. *Und Afrika sprach,* 1913, III, 181, 182. We have interpreted the smith (whose name our hero inherits after the feat which may be regarded as his totemic initiation) as a representative of the royal father and here Frobenius tells us that the smith is an object of extraordinary veneration and regarded as standing nearest to the king.

The Oedipus Complex in Burma

Melford E. Spiro

Anthropologists are wary of assuming universality, committed as they are to the notion of cultural relativism. Is the Oedipus Complex universal or not? Most anthropologists would say no, perhaps citing Malinowski in his famous debate with Ernest Jones. Malinowski claimed that matrilineal societies (such as the one he studied in the Trobriand Islands) did not have an Oedipus Complex, but rather an avuncular complex. In such matrilineal societies, he argued, it is the mother's brother who possesses the wealth and who disciplines his nephews. In rebuttal, Ernest Jones and Géza Róheim pointed out that a boy's uncle did not constitute a sexual rival for the affections of the boy's mother. That rival was the boy's father. In Malinowski's own published field data, one can find myths in which a boy slays a threatening monster who has a separate identity from the boy's maternal uncle. Spiro's essay on Burmese narratives and family structure is a contribution to this debate. Professor Spiro of the Department of Anthropology of the University of California at San Diego is a specialist in psychological anthropology. His analysis of Oedipus stories in a particular cultural context provides a contrast to those many studies which treat texts without reference to contextual data.

For samples of the cross-cultural debate, see William N. Stephens, The Oedipus Complex: Cross-Cultural Evidence (*Glencoe, 1962*),

Reprinted from the *Journal of Nervous and Mental Disease*, 157 (1973), 389–395.

and Anne Parsons, "Is the Oedipus Complex Universal? The Jones-Malinowski Debate Revisited," in Belief, Magic and Anomie: Essays in Psychological Anthropology *(New York, 1969), pp. 3-66. For a discussion of Oedipus myths collected by but not recognized by Malinowski, see John Ingham, "Malinowski: Epistemology and Oedipus,"* Papers of the Kroeber Anthropological Society, *29 (1963), 1-14. For a more detailed refutation of Malinowski, see Melford E. Spiro,* Oedipus in the Trobriands *(Chicago, 1982).*

Although my research in Burma villages was not specifically oriented to personality dynamics, I could hardly avoid the psychodynamic issues that persistently arose in my studies of folk-religion[1], Buddhism[2] and kinship. In the latter investigation, it became apparent that one of the reasons—there are numerous others—for the Burmese preference for neolocal residence arises from the tensions, hostile and libidinal, that obtain between parents and children. In analyzing these dimensions of parent-child tension, it became apparent that (although the expression has long since become a cliché) they comprise the basic elements of the Oedipus complex. In this short paper, I can do little more than offer a sketch of these dimensions as they are found among parents and adult children.

Although the norms governing the relationship between parents and their adult children stress respect and deference as obligations of children to parents, and affection and assistance as mutual obligations of parents and children, and although these norms are usually expressed in action, it would be naïve to assume that the parent-child relationship in Burma, any more than elsewhere, is unidimensional. Intimate relationships are characterized everywhere by ambivalence, and to stress exclusively the positive dimension of the parent-child relationship—as is true of those anthropologists who attend to cultural ideals alone—not only gives a false picture of that relationship, but it impedes an understanding of the behavior that flows from the ambivalence.

Western writers have often neglected to see the hostility-based tensions in Oriental families either because, impressed by their normative expressions of solidarity, they have tended to sentimentalize them, or because they have confused formal deference patterns with actual sentiment. Viewed psychodynamically, customs of formal deference may not only, however, express respect, but they may also serve as constraints on the expression of hostility and other negative sentiments. Often such customs are as much an index of tension as of respect. That this is so is suggested on the macroscopic level by the acting-out behavior of postwar Japanese youth and the Chinese Red Guards, and on the microscopic level by the tensions revealed by studies of family interaction in a variety of Oriental societies.

In Burma, tensions between parents and children relate, in the first place, to problems of autonomy and independence. This, at least, is how it is articulated on a conscious level in Yeigyi, the village I studied.[3] Negligible in the cross-sex relationships, and submerged in the especially close mother-daughter relationship, this tension is especially prominent, as it is elsewhere in Southeast Asia, in the father-son relationship. The following example, though hardly typical of father-son *behavior*, is illustrative of the potentially explosive tension that is often found below the surface.

When U Htin, a respected village elder, discovered that his (20-year-old) son had stolen food from a village shop, he struck him with the palm of his hand. Furious, his son picked up a knife and, threatening his father, dared him to strike him again. Shaking and (obviously) frightened, U Htin walked away.

Usually under control, and therefore invisible, tensions between father and son only infrequently erupt in such a disruptive and (to the Burmese) shocking form. Nevertheless, so long as the son remains in a subordinate status, the tensions engendered by his struggle for autonomy persist.

Although somewhat less pronounced, the mother-daughter relationship often exhibits similar characteristics. As long as the daughter lives with her, she must remain subordinate to her mother. As one mother put it, she would have no objection to her divorced daughter living with her because, though she is an adult, "I can order my daughter to do whatever I like." This same theme, from the obverse position, was stressed by a young widow who refused to move in with her parents after her husband died. "At times," she said, "they will be good [*i.e.*, they will not try to dominate], but at times they will be bad."

This desire for autonomy is by no means one sided. Parents are just as keen to avoid subordination to their children as the latter are to escape from the domination of their parents. This desire emerges in sharpest relief in the comments of those widows and widowers (and divorcées) who, despite their option of living with their children, have nevertheless chosen to live alone. Their choice is based on the *personal* expectation, reinforced by the *cultural* premise, that living with children (like living with parents) is a source of trouble. Thus, one widow, who lives apart from both a married son and a married daughter, said simply: "It is not easy to live with (married) children. They tell you what to do." Another, with only a married son, said that if she lived with him, he would "try to squeeze money from me." The widowers echo the sentiments of the widows. One, an older man with married sons and a married daughter, said: "If I lived with my children, they would try to govern me." Another said, "If you live with your children, they try to control you."

Parent-child conflict can be explained not only in terms of the Burmese (personality) need for autonomy, but also in terms of Burmese (cultural) values regarding deference and respect. Normatively, the young offer deference and respect (*neia tade*) to their elders, especially to their parents, whether they live with them or not. But since power (*awza*) in the household resides with the one who owns the house and controls the income, the children have the power when their parents live with them, and although they may continue to treat them with formal deference, the parents no longer occupy a superior status. Their position of respect, the Burmese say, is destroyed (*neia matubu*).

If, as I have already noted, parent-child conflict is especially prominent in the relationship between parents and children of the same sex, then it may not only be explained in cultural, but also in social terms. In general, it is the parent of the same sex who is the greater frustrater of the young child. The father is both authoritarian and punitive, and his punishments more frequently fall on the son than the daughter, if only because the son is more frequently in his physical presence and because his chores are assigned by the father rather than the mother. It is natural, then, that dereliction of duty or acts of irresponsibility are punished by the father. Although the mother is less punitive toward the daughter, at least physically, than the father is toward the son, she is nevertheless a frustrating figure. The daughter is inducted into the work force at an earlier age than the son, as is appropriate to the sexual division of labor characteristic of an agricultural economy, in which a great deal of unskilled female work can be turned over to the daughter at a relatively early age. It is the mother, then, who imposes chores on the daughter, who consequently keeps her confined to the family compound (while her brother can wander freely about the village), and who punishes her for lack of attention to her responsibilities. For children of both sexes, then, parents (and especially same-sex parents) are frustrating figures, and the consequent hostility and rage of the Burmese child no more disappear in adulthood than those of other children anywhere else in the world.

But childhood punishment and restraint are not the only social bases for parent-child conflict in adulthood, nor for the special conflict that obtains between same-sex parents and children. The latter conflict, especially, may be explained not only in uniquely Burmese terms, but in more general, panhuman—*viz.*, Oedipal— terms. Our data suggest that part of the parent-child conflict is an expression of normal Oedipal hostility, and that this dimension of the conflict is especially prominent in the son-father relationship.

Since the husband-wife relationship takes precedence over all others, and since the son resents his father's privileged position *vis-à-vis* his mother, this resentment is an especially important basis for the son's hostility. The Burmese psychologist, Sein Tu, emphasizes this process when he writes of the son's "perception of the importance of the father to the mother, and of his prior and more powerful claim to her attention and love." This situation, according to Sein Tu, generates "great aggressiveness" in the son, so that the deference required in interaction with parents (and elders in general) serves as a defense against these aggressive impulses which "have to be kept rigidly in check."[4]

At the adult level, the Oedipal basis for the son's hostility to the father emerges most clearly in the vehemence with which sons attack philandering fathers. In those cases which I know of personally, some sons refused to have anything to do with their fathers when they discovered their infidelities. Others, while not severing their relationship, spoke of their "hatred" for them. The following comment of one son, describing how he felt when he first found out about his father's infidelity, is not atypical. "I really hated him, sometimes I wanted to kill him."

The Oedipal-based father-son hostility is reflected, at the cultural level, in a prominent and widely known myth. That this myth originated in India—the villagers allege that the myth is a *Jataka* tale, although I have been unable to find it in the standard Cowell edition—does not diminish its psychological force in Burma; it has not only been incorporated into Burmese mythology, but its theme is the basis for a pervasive element in Burmese religious art and architecture, and is recounted as well in Burmese literature and classical drama.

As told in Yeigyi, the tale begins with a young princess who was a nymphomaniac. As a young woman, her sex drive was so insatiable that once she was abducted by 500 robbers in the forest, and although each had sexual intercourse with her, she was still not satisfied. Her father, ashamed of his daughter's nymphomania, banished her from the court. While wandering in the jungle, she met a lion, with whom she had intercourse, and since he alone could satisfy her sexually, she married him. Eventually they had two children, a son (who was eventually to become the Buddha) and a daughter. The son, Thihabahu, was ashamed that his father was a lion, and he persuaded his mother and sister to abandon him. They left the jungle while the lion was away, and eventually returned to the court where the princess' father, the king, warmly welcomed them.

In the meantime, the lion, who was filled with grief, set out to find his family. As he wandered through the villages, the people were frightened and asked the king for protection. When the king asked his court whether any would volunteer to hunt down the lion, Thihabahu, realizing that the lion must be his father, volunteered to kill him. So he set out for the jungle, and eventually found his father. Although the latter was overjoyed to see him, the son slew his father with a bow and arrow.

As a reward for slaying the lion, Thihabahu was made king of a new kingdom. However, shortly after ascending the throne he was struck blind and the court physicians were unable to cure him. One day, however, a hermit came to the court and informed Thihabahu that his blindness was retribution for his patricide, and that his sight could only be restored if he would repent of this sin. He told him to construct an image of a lion in honor of his father, and to pay homage to it. Ashamed to be seen doing homage to a lion image, Thihabahu ordered the image to be placed in front of a pagoda where, if he did obeisance to it, people would think that he was really worshipping the pagoda. This done, Thihabahu prostrated himself before the image, and his sight was restored. That is why, the villagers say, a leogryph stands at the entrance of large and important pagodas. (Actually, there are two of them, one at either side of the entrance.) Indeed, this symbol of the slain father is ubiquitous in Burma, the lion image being portrayed graphically, as well as plastically, in a variety of contexts—official documents, formal invitations, dust jackets, and so on.

A more remarkable Oedipal tale, remarkable for reasons which will soon become apparent, was recounted by an American-educated woman from Rangoon. When I asked a group of Rangoonians whether the Oedipus complex was found in Burma, they expressed surprise that I should have asked the question—of course the Oedipus complex is found in Burma!—and they then proceeded to give all kinds of examples. When I then asked if they knew any Oedipal legends or myths, they knew only the Thihabahu myth. However, the above-mentioned woman said she knew yet another, but after thinking a few moments she expressed surprise that she had characterized it as Oedipal. When she recounted the tale, it became apparent that on the manifest level it indeed was not an Oedipal tale, for although the theme was Oedipal, the *dramatis personae* were not. That, however, she had originally offered it as one, suggested that this was what it signified to her at a latent level.

The tale concerns one Maung Ba Cein, a traveler, who came to a certain kingdom and was told that a *naga*, a mythical dragon, had killed the king, taken the queen as his wife, and satisfied his hunger by eating people. After hearing this tale, Maung Ba Cein decided that he would become king. One night he entered the queen's chamber, and placed a banana stalk in the queen's bed, so that, when both were covered with a blanket, it would appear as if the queen were sleeping with a man. Hiding behind the curtain, Maung Ba Cein then waited for the arrival of the *naga*. When he entered the chamber, the *naga*, seeing what he took to be the body of a sleeping man, pierced it with his sword. Just as Maung Ba Cein had planned, the sword stuck in the banana stalk, and, as the *naga* attempted to extricate it, Maung Ba Cein stepped from behind the curtain and slew him. He then took the queen as his wife and he himself became the king.

I would suggest, then, that one of the reasons for the Burmese preference for nuclear family households, and their avoidance, whenever possible, of joint family households, is their desire to avoid the conflict that is found in the parent-child relationship, a conflict which, in large part, reflects normal Oedipal hostility. But the libidinal component of the Oedipal relationship is just as important a reason for this neolocal residence pattern, for, as I have said, the libidinal is as strong as the hostile component. Although Sein Tu, whose research was primarily concerned with male personality, stressed the sexual element in the mother-son relationship only— "The child comes to regard the womenfolk (mother and sister) in the house as dispensers of nurturance and objects of sex desire"[5] —it is just as prominent in the father-daughter relationship.

So that I am not misunderstood, I wish to stress that these libidinal ties between parents and children are normal, and they are weaker in Burma than in many other societies. Thus, to take but one example, the erotic overtones in the parent-child relationship in South Asia are much stronger than in Burma. In India (at least in the urban, upper-middle class, Bengali family) the father-daughter bond is highly eroticized, according to the compelling data of Roy,[6] and importantly influences the daughter's entire life cycle. Although the mother-son relationship is equally eroticized, the son remains with his mother when he marries, and, if I may extrapolate from Roy's data, his strong Oedipal tie to his mother is rarely severed. This is also the case in Ceylon, as Obeyesekere[7] has shown in convincing detail.

That, in Burma, the avoidance of joint family households is motivated, in part, by avoidance of incest temptations is a thesis which the Burmese themselves, the villagers at least, consciously verbalize. Although villagers knew of no cases of parent-child incest, they (unlike most Westerners) acknowledge the presence of libidinal feelings in the parent-child relationship, and the daughter, especially, is trained from a relatively early age to avoid physical intimacy with her father (and brothers). Beginning at about the age of 10, girls are forbidden to sit on their father's lap or to cuddle with him, in order to prevent the arousal of erotic feelings. To act upon such feelings (at any age) would be monstrous, even though no well-conceived grounds for the incest taboo were ever adduced by the villagers. Mother-son incest is prohibited, they contend, because one should not have intercourse "in the same hole from which you were born." Father-daughter incest is even more heinous, so that reasons are neither required nor offered. As the village headman put it, it is so evil, "you shouldn't even think about it."

The enormity of parent-child incest is reflected in its punishment. Today, villagers say, parent-child incest would be punished by a physical beating of the culprits, followed by their banishment from the village (and, if their deed were known, they would be barred from any other village). In traditional Burma, according to Daw Than Ohn (personal communication), the punishment was even more severe. The offenders were forced to eat "like dogs and pigs"—for so they were viewed—following which they were deported from the country. In addition to social punishment, the karmic retribution for incest is rebirth in hell, but only after the male has been reborn as a female, and the female as an animal. (The discrepancy between the respective punishments of males and females is in accordance with Buddhist folk belief in which one can fall only one step at a time in the ladder of existence. Hence, given the Buddhist value hierarchy, males fall to a female, females to an animal, status.)

If insults and accusations can be interpreted as expressions of anger as well as techniques of aggression then the fact that incestuous insults and accusations are viewed by the Burmese to be the gravest of all may be taken as yet another measure of the horror attached to incest. As an urban informant put it, "If someone walks across my property, and I ask him not to do it, he may not take me seriously, no matter how sharply I speak. But if I say, 'Go fuck your mother!,' he knows I'm not joking. He knows I'm really angry, and he gets off."

Some of the more common incestuous insults are: "Fuck your father" (*pei malou*), and "Fuck your mother" (*me-ei lou*). The latter has a variety of embellished variants, such as, "Go back and fuck your mother" (*nint amei nint pyan lou*), or "Fuck your big mother astride" (*nint ameici khwat lou*), in which "big mother" is elliptical for "mother with the big vagina," and to copulate "astride" makes the act that much more offensive.[8] Significantly, there are obvious boundaries that separate permissible from impermissible incestuous insults.

Those recorded above are permissible; to be sure, they express anger and they provoke anger, but I have never observed them to provoke physical aggression. But there is an important difference, for example, between uttering the permissible, "Fuck your mother," and the impermissible, "You are a mother fucker." The rage aroused by the latter has been known to provoke murder. If the accused is so strongly offended and provoked by such an accusation, it is perhaps plausible to infer that it touches a raw nerve, so that (psychodynamically viewed) the intensity of his reaction conceals the intensity of his desire to commit the very deed which the insult accuses him of committing.

Perhaps, too, a similar explanation accounts for the rage aroused by another form of insult, *viz.,* one in which another is alleged to have intercourse with the parent, usually the mother. Thus, "I fuck your mother" (*nint amei nga lou*), or, as embellished, "I stretch and fuck your mother's large cunt" (*nint amei saukpat-ci nga hpyei lou*), or again, "mother giver!" (*i.e.,* you offer your mother to others for fornication), (*me-ei pei*) arouse rage, I would suggest, because (among other reasons) others are fantasied to commit the very act which the victim of the insult is prohibited from committing.

Thus far, then, I have suggested that the avoidance of joint families is motivated, in part, by the conflict between incestuous desires and incest prohibitions. This suggestion is confirmed by the explicit statements of the villagers. Somehow, these desires are not seen as a problem so long as the spouse of the child or both of the child's parents is alive; it is as if the presence of these other dyads serves as a powerful counterinfluence to incestuous desires. When they are present, then, the problem is merely anticipatory, *i.e.,* it might arise should the other spouse die, and parent and child of opposite sex are consequently left alone in the house. It becomes actual, however, in those cases in which a married child, who had been living neolocally, loses his spouse, and the question of coresidence with his widowed parent arises. Here, the evidence is very clear. Although there are cases of mother and son living together, there is only one case—and this, as we shall see, is the exception which truly proves the rule—of father and daughter. That father and daughter do not live together is explicitly related to village notions concerning sex and incest. Father and daughter cannot live alone together, so it is assumed, without being susceptible to either the temptation or the suspicion of incest. The exception noted above consists not of a father-daughter, but of a father-in-law—daughter-in-law, dyad, who are above suspicion because the woman is in her 50s and the man in his 90s.

It should be noted that urban informants typically deny that incestuous feelings or suspicions play a role in the determination of residence or household composition. Nevertheless, I know of one case, a widower and his spinster daughter, in which the father demanded that his daughter-in-law visit them every day. His alleged reason was that his daughter "should not be lonely." But the real reason, according to his granddaughter, was to forestall gossip and suspicion of incest. And suspicion of this kind is easily aroused. In the village, once the daughter has reached puberty, father and daughter will not even remain alone in the same room. This, too, is viewed as a quaint notion by their city cousins, although the latter are shocked by events to which Westerners would pay little or no attention. Thus, some Rangoon friends recounted the shock of a sophisticated Rangoon club when a father and daughter sang a popular duet which described how a couple behaved when the lights went out. The same sophisticated group was even more shocked when a father and daughter danced together at a ball.

To summarize, then, temptations and/or accusations of incest constitute one of the grounds for the avoidance of parent-child (or, at least, father-daughter) households. Why this reason applies more strongly to father and daughter than to mother and son is a question to which, unfortunately, I was not alert when conducting field work.

The ramifications of the Oedipus complex—in the relationships between men and women, in sexual behavior, in marriage patterns, in politics and political factionalism, in attitudes toward authority, and in religion (especially in Buddhist monasticism)—cannot be described here, nor can I describe its childhood antecedents and development. Some of these topics are treated in the references mentioned in the text, as well as in forthcoming publications.

NOTES

[1]Spiro, M.E. *Burmese Supernaturalism: A Study in the Explanation and Reduction of Suffering.* Prentice-Hall, Englewood Cliffs, New Jersey, 1967.

[2]Spiro, M.E. *Buddhism and Society: A Great Tradition and its Burmese Vicissitudes.* Harper & Row, New York, 1970.

[3]Field work in Burma, conducted in 1961 to 1962, was supported by a grant from the National Science Foundation. Subsequent research in the summers of 1969 to 1971, within the Burmese community in Thailand, was supported by a grant from the National Institute of Child Health and Human Development.

[4]Sein Tu. The psychodynamics of Burmese personality. J. Burmese Res. Soc., *47* (1964) pp. 276, 283.

[5]Sein Tu, p. 280.

[6]Roy, Manisha. Ideal and compensatory roles in the life cycle of upper-class Bengali women. Ph.D. dissertation, University of California, San Diego, 1972.

[7]Obeyesekere, Gananth. Pattini and the Mother Goddesses. Unpublished manuscript.

[8]All of these examples, it will be noted, are parent directed. I have never heard any incestuous insults that are child directed such as, "Fuck your son," or "Fuck your daughter." It is my impression that this unidirectionality is characteristic of most societies and although one might speculate on the reasons, I can think of none that is especially compelling.

Why Oedipus Killed Laius:
A Note on the Complementary
Oedipus Complex in Greek Drama

George Devereux

From the essays contained in this casebook, it is easy to see that the vast majority of discussions of Oedipus take the child's point of view as a point of departure. George Devereux, Professor of Ethnopsychiatry at the École des Hautes Études en Sciences Sociales, looks at the classic Greek story in terms of Laius rather than of Oedipus. This perspective brings new insights not only to the Greek account, but by implication it permits a re-evaluation of other Oedipal stories. One could profitably re-read the "Oedipus in Papuan Folklore" selection with special reference to the homosexuality element in the light of Devereux's analysis.

Devereux has written other essays on Oedipus stories. See, for example, "The Oedipal Situation and Its Consequences in the Epics of Ancient India," Samiksa, *5 (1951), 5–13; "Retaliatory Homosexual Triumph over the Father: A Further Contribution to Counter-Oedipal Sources of the Oedipus Complex,"* International Journal of Psycho-Analysis, *41 (1960), 157–161; "Sociopolitical Functions of the Oedipus Myth in Early Greece,"* Psychoanalytic Quarterly, *32 (1963), 205–214; and "The Self-Blinding of Oidipous in Sophokles: Oidipous Tyrannos,"* Journal of Hellenic Studies, *93 (1973), 36–49.*

An earlier version of this paper appeared in *International Journal of Psycho-Analysis,* 34 (1953), 132–141.

Psychoanalytic theory pays exceedingly little attention to certain complexes which, in a very genuine sense, complement the Oedipus complex. Thus, despite occasional references (20) to the tender and even erotic components of what may be called the Laius complex and the Jocasta complex, the sadistic (and homosexual) components of these complexes are, generally speaking, ignored.[1] Yet there exist Greek traditions regarding Laius which suggest that the complementary Oedipus complex, even in its homosexual and sadistic phases, was close enough to the threshold of consciousness to receive at least a mythological expression. Nonetheless even Rank (29), who does discuss these traditions, fails to stress that they provide a specific and "historical," rather than only a general and "paleopsychological," explanation of Laius' behavior towards the infant Oedipus.

This scotomization of the complementary Oedipus complex is probably rooted in the adult's deep-seated need to place *all* responsibility for the Oedipus complex upon the child and to ignore, whenever possible, those parental attitudes which stimulate the infant's Oedipal tendencies. That this deliberate scotoma is rooted in the characteristic authoritarian atmosphere of the nineteenth-century family is suggested by the history of Freud's own thoughts on the etiology of hysteria. At first, Freud accepted as genuine the seduction stories told by his patients. When he discovered that these tales simply expressed fantasies and wishes, he made the necessary revisions in his theory of the etiology of the neuroses. Unfortunately, from that time onward he also began to ignore the genuinely seductive behavior of parents,[2] perhaps because the theory of the Laius and Jocasta complexes was even more egodystonic and culturally objectionable than was the theory of the Oedipus complex which, in a sense, confirmed the nineteenth-century adult's low opinion of children in general.[3] The scotomization of the Laius and Jocasta complexes then led certain later writers to develop an elaborate, and unconvincing, theory of a phylogenetically determined infantile fantasy-life, which predicates that, regardless of how loving the father may be, the infant's instinctually determined and phylogenetically anchored fantasies will cause him to view even his kindly father *primarily* as a monster.

The trend away from the recognition of the seductive behavior of adults, bolstered not only by Freud's prestige, but also by social pressure and by the analyst's own need to scotomize this anxiety-arousing idea, was too strong to be reversed even by the findings of Ferenczi (*20*) and of certain of his students that, presumably by means of the "dialogue of the unconscious," children recognize the real instinctual roots of the tenderness which adults display towards them (*33*).

Yet, it is a matter of common experience that in sexual relations between adults and children—which are far more common than is generally believed—it is usually the adult who takes the initiative. Only in rare instances are the children the actual seducers (*9*).

The great popularity of Sophocles' three Oedipus dramas also supports this interpretation. It is probable that Greek audiences found the play of absorbing interest precisely because they success-fully—though perhaps unconsciously—identified themselves with the problems of the principal characters.[4] Alice Bálint's (*2*) analysis of the irrational and primitive aspects of the mother-child relation-ship also lends plausibility to my inference that the women in Sophocles' audience must have at least unconsciously empathized with Jocasta's problems. By extension, the male audience must likewise have felt a certain (repressed) kinship with Laius who, as I propose to show, was not a mere puppet of Fate, but a psychologi-cally consistent and plausible person, whose character-structure explains his destiny.

The part of the Oedipus myth that concerns Chrysippus is available only in Euripidean and (probably) post-Euripidean ver-sions, which are uncertain and often mutually incompatible. Some philologists even believe that the whole story was invented by Euripides in his lost drama *Chrysippos*. I have not tried to reconcile unreconcilable chronologies, nor did I need to do it, for the latent content of the myth elements that matter in this context is unaffected by the chaotic state of their chronology.

The Character of Laius

Laius' early life vaguely resembles that of Oedipus. King Labdakos of Thebes died when Laius was but a year old. A man named Lykos (Wolf) usurped the throne, and grievously wronged his niece Antiope. Later on Antiope's sons conquered Thebes, slew Lykos, and banished Laius, who only regained his throne after the death of Antiope's sons. At that time Laius was perhaps not yet burdened with a curse, which he had brought on himself through an act of homosexual rape—a curse which eventually culminated in the Oedipus tragedy (*30, 32*).

According to some Greek sources,[5] Laius was the inventor of pederasty. It is not clear whether it was before or after he married Jocasta and fathered Oedipus, that Laius fell violently in love with Chrysippus, son of King Pelops. Instead of decorously courting and winning the handsome youth, he chose to kidnap him during the sacred Nemean games, without seeking to obtain the consent of Pelops which, or so Licht boldly intimates (*26*) would probably have been forthcoming. The enraged Pelops therefore laid upon Laius the curse that his own son should slay him. According to a (perhaps later) version, it is the Delphic oracle which informed Laius of Zeus' decision that Laius' own son would kill him in retribution for the rape of Chrysippus. This curse shows that the Greeks somehow linked Oedipus with Chrysippus—an inference further substantiated by still another version of this myth, according to which Hera was so greatly angered by the rape of Chrysippus that she sent the Sphinx to ravage Thebes, in order to punish the Thebans for having tolerated Laius' homosexual escapade (Scholium to Euripides, *Phoenissae* 1760). The *Oidipodeia* may have been even more specific in linking the fates of Chrysippus and of Oedipus: According to one modern reconstruction of this lost epic, Oedipus was perhaps exposed as a propitiatory sacrifice, in order to appease Hera's wrath over the Chrysippus incident (*30*). In other words, Hera caused Laius to lose not only Chrysippus but also his son Oedipus.[6]

After the imposition of the curse, and especially after the birth of Oedipus, almost nothing further is heard of Chrysippus, until the moment of the fatal encounter between Laius and Oedipus. It is at that point that the scholia to Euripides *Phoenissae* 26 and 66 bring Chrysippus into the plot. They allege that Laius and Oedipus fought each other, because they were rivals for the love of Chrysippus. It is not quite clear whether Oedipus tried to wrest Chrysippus from Laius or vice versa, and it is only implied that Chrysippus was present during the struggle. One source specifies that it was Jocasta, who was present during the fatal combat (Nicolaos of Damascus *fr.* 15, *Fragmenta Historicorum Graecorum*). Be that as it may, some versions of this myth represent this combat as a homosexually motivated encounter (sch. Euripides, *Phoenissae* 60). Chrysippus may have killed himself (sch. E. *Ph.* 1760 and Sir J.G. Frazer at Apollodoros 3.5.5); at any rate he disappears definitely from the Oedipus myth. The overall impression created by these various accounts is that, psychologically at least, Chrysippus is, in a sense, the representative of Oedipus' own passive homosexual character-istics, which were brought into being, or were at least aroused, by Laius' aggressive and homosexual impulses towards his son.

Regardless of whether this "curse" was uttered by Pelops in person or by the Delphic oracle, it made a considerable impression even upon the impulsive Laius. According to various sources he thereafter (self-castratively) had refrained from cohabiting with Jocasta for several years, in order to avoid the risk of procreating a son.[7] However, on a certain occasion, when Laius was either drunk or else unable to resist Jocasta's seductiveness, he succumbed to temptation and procreated a son, even though he well knew what calamities the birth of an heir would entail for him. Thus, after a period of self-restraint, Laius' self-destructive impulsiveness once more got out of hand, only to be followed by another futile (symbol-ically self-castrative) attempt to ward off the consequences of his second hasty sexual act by exposing the infant Oedipus.

Laius appears to have retained throughout life a propensity for impulsive violence, witness his wanton aggression against the way-farer Oedipus, which caused his death, since Oedipus himself had—at least in Sophocles' play—as violent a temper as his father.

This, however, is still not the whole story. Indeed, the best-known version of this incident is that Oedipus and Laius quarrelled over the right to *pass first* over a certain *narrow road*. This incident appears to be a somewhat bowdlerized and symbolic version of the far more explicit accounts of Laius' death, according to which Oedipus and Laius did not quarrel over so symbolic a trifle as the right to pass first over a narrow road. If one—not universally accepted—reconstruction of Praxilla's fragment 6 (Bergk), is correct, not only Laius, but Oedipus too was in love with Chrysippus. The scholium to Euripides *Phoenissae* 60 reports that Oedipus killed Laius in a quarrel over Chrysippus.

In apparent contradiction to this homosexual motive, Rank (*29*)
following apparently Nicolaos of Damascus *fr.* 15 (op. cit.) states
that the combat took place in the presence of Jocasta, who was with
Laius when the provoked Oedipus killed him. Both sch. E. *Ph.* 1760
and Nicolaos of Damascus, *fr.* 15 (op. cit.) state that Oedipus took
the slain Laius' sword and belt. This represents a feminization of
Laius since, in ancient Greece, undoing a woman's belt was a
preliminary to coitus—and perhaps to her submission, for Herakles
had been sent out to capture that Amazon queen's belt (*19*, chap. 6).
Nicolaos also specifies that Oedipus did *not* harm the woman. This
negative specification tends to suggest to me that Nicolaos tries to
negate an earlier tale, in which, after slaying Laius, Oedipus co-
habited at once with his widow. At any rate scholium Euripides
Phoenissae 26 seems to cause Oedipus to cohabit with Jocasta when
the latter comes back to attend to her Lord's corpse. If this inference
is correct, Oedipus did more than kill his father and marry his
mother, in token of his heterosexual maturity. He also turned the
tables on his homosexual father, by castrating (sword) and feminiz-
ing him (belt), as he himself had once been castrated and feminized
(by the piercing of his ankles) by Laius. If this be so, cohabitation
with Jocasta was not only coitus with the mother as a woman, but
also with the mother as the representative of the now-feminized
homosexual paternal ogre.

This inference gives added meaning to Gruppe's opinion (*23*)
that Oedipus originally bested the Sphinx—a Rankian phallic
mother—in physical combat.[8] If this interpretation is correct, then
Oedipus' triumph over the phallic mother—whose phallus, needless
to say, was derived from the father—represents both a heterosexual
and a homosexual victory and gesture of triumph. This meaning of
incest with the phallic mother—i.e., the combination of heterosexual
relations with the mother and of symbolic active homosexual relations with the father (*19*)[9]—is a relatively novel inference.

The important point in all these considerations is the fact that
many Greek sources emphasize primarily the homosexual element
in the causation of Laius' death, and bring in the incest with Jocasta
more or less as an afterthought, e.g., as the link which couples the
tragedy of Laius with the later fate of Oedipus. Cohabitation with
Jocasta should thus be viewed primarily as a symbolically homosexual and only epiphenomenally as a heterosexual act, Oedipus'

true love-hate object being the now feminized homosexual ogre Laius.

Thus, Greek mythology, which, after all, is our sole authority in regard to the problem of King Oedipus, did not derive Oedipus' hostility to Laius from heterosexual, but from homosexual sources. Indeed, Oedipus is not even said to have been particularly fond of his foster-mother, Queen Merope, while practically all accounts of his early life emphasize his devotion to his savior and foster-father, King Polybus, who apparently represented the "good father" in Oedipus' unconscious.

What we do find in Greek accounts is an explanation of Oedipus' aggression against Laius in terms of Laius' character-structure: his propensity for homosexual rape, for unconsidered, injudicious violence and for overbearingness ("hybris").[10] Indeed, Laius is presented to us as a pederastic ogre—as a homosexual rapist, rather than as a seducer—deprived both of his real love-object, Chrysippus, and of the hope of an heir (*25, 30*). After the birth of Oedipus, Laius made himself guilty first of attempted infanticide, and, later on, of an attempt to kill his adult son in the course of a quarrel which the overbearing old man had wantonly started with the wayfarer Oedipus.

Laius' character, as depicted both by Greek mythology and tragedy, is not an attractive one. It corresponds to what clinical psychoanalysis often finds to be the small boy's conception of his father. Indeed, unlike many other tragic figures of Greek drama, Laius is not a good man caught in the toils of fate with "An Appointment in Samarra" with death, but a violator of good manners, which for some Greeks was almost more important than good morals. In brief—and despite Oedipus' possible rivalry with Laius for the love of Chrysippus (scholia to Euripides *Phoenissae* 26 and 60)—Laius' death was not caused primarily by Oedipus' own incestuous impulses, but by Laius' character, which included both "hybris" and a proneness to homosexual and other violence.

Despite the alleged rivalry over Chrysippus, I do not assert that Oedipus himself was not partially motivated also by the violent impulses connected with the normal Oedipus complex. I simply suggest that, according to Greek data, Oedipus' murderous and incestuous wishes were neither purely heterosexual nor truly spontaneous but were elicited by the behavior of his father Laius. In fact,

Oedipus' partly heterosexual attraction to Jocasta may have been motivated also by his desire both to escape and to gratify indirectly his own sado-masochistic and homosexual wishes, which his father's behavior had stimulated. At the same time, Oedipus' marriage to Jocasta may also represent an unconscious attempt at restitution, since he took Laius' place at Jocasta's side,[11] and provided further heirs for the kingdom of Thebes.[12] Conversely, aggressively homosexual paternal attitudes towards the child *may*—in part at least—represent a defence against murderous impulses elicited by the sight of the nursing infant, whose very existence interferes with the formerly close relationship between husband and wife.[13]

My central thesis—that Oedipus' own impulses were stimulated by the behavior of his father—appears at least plausible in the light of the preceding considerations. However, in order to render this thesis worthy of being taken into account in clinical work, it is necessary to examine rather closely the unconscious causes of King Pelops' extreme wrath, and the motives which impelled him to utter *precisely* and *specifically* the rather unusual curse that Laius' son should kill his father.

Pelops, Oedipus and Electra

According to Licht, whose views I do not necessarily accept, Pelops' wrath over the abduction of Chrysippus should be understood as follows: (Pelops) "is not driven to the curse because Laius loved a boy and was intimate with him, consequently not by the unnatural nature of his passion . . . but simply and solely because Laius steals the boy, and abducts him against his father's wish: It is not the perverted direction of the impulse that makes Laius guilty, but the violence employed by him. . . . Laius becomes a curse-laden man in consequence of an offence against conventional form; he thought he might be allowed to abduct the boy, when he could have sued for the beautiful prize freely and openly" (*26*). In other words, Laius is guilty of a breach of manners, rather than of morals, in a context—paedophilia—in which the Greeks manifested that "poetic chivalrousness" which the knights of the feudal period manifested towards women. If so, Laius' behavior towards Chrysippus is "hybris"—

excess and overbearingness—which, in Greek tragedy, often causes a man's downfall.

These considerations only elucidate the conscious causes of Pelops' reaction. On a deeper level the psychological problem of Pelops' wrath has an even more significant connection with the fate of Laius and of Oedipus.

More even than Oedipus himself, Pelops had experienced the potential cruelty of fathers and father figures. He was the son of Tantalus who, from sheer overbearingness, wished to test the omniscience of the Immortals whom he had invited to his feast. He therefore had young Pelops slain and served to the Immortals as the *pièce de résistance* of a banquet. The gods discovered the deed, but not before Demeter, still distressed by Persephone's loss, had "absentmindedly" eaten the dismembered Pelop's shoulder (*16*). At the request of the Immortals, either Rhea (or perhaps Clotho), cast Pelops' remains into a cauldron, from which he re-emerged alive, but with an ivory shoulder. The cannibalistic impulses of Tantalus are further underscored by the fact that his eternal punishment in Hades consisted in being "tantalized" by food and drink, and in his being in constant fear of death. Despite these evil deeds, Greek legends stress that Pelops honoured his deceased father devoutly.

Now, it is hard to understand why Pelops should display such filial piety towards his brutal father. His devotion would be understandable only if, by some twist in his unconscious fantasy-life, Pelops construed this cannibalistic act as a token of love. This startling inference is strikingly confirmed by Pindar's first Olympian Ode, which both Hellenists and the psycho-analyst Bunker (*4*) interpret *primarily* as a bowdlerized version of the original cannibalistic feast. According to Pindar, the gruesome Feast of Tantalus never took place at all; in reality, Poseidon had abducted Pelops, with whom he was in love, and had taken him to the abode of the Immortals, just as Zeus had brought Ganymede to Olympus. On the basis of the contrast between the original myth of the Feast of Tantalus and Pindar's version of Pelops' disappearance, Bunker concludes, perhaps rightly (*4*), that the Feast of Tantalus is a disguised description of initiation ceremonies.

However, Pindar's version is not only a bowdlerization of a cannibalistic myth which originated in ruder days. It enunciates the selfsame theme as the original myth, though in a language and by means of symbols which pertain to a different stage of psychosexual development (*19*). The earlier version tells the story in the language of the oral stage and represents the anxiety-laden and yet pleasurable fantasy-experience of being devoured by the "mother." In Pindar's version the experience pertains to the second phase of the Oedipus complex, and is presented to us as an anxiously erotized submission to a divine homosexual father figure, Poseidon.

When seen in this light, Pelops' filial piety toward his ogre-like father Tantalus is no longer a paradox; it is the one-sided—and highly erotized—expression of the positive component of Pelops' ambivalence towards his father, whose idealized representative is Pelops' divine lover, Poseidon.

Yet Pelops could not have accepted without ambivalence his passive role either in the Feast of Tantalus, or in his abduction by Poseidon, which so startlingly duplicates the abduction of his son Chrysippus by Laius or, better still, his abduction by Zeus himself, as (erroneously) reported by Praxilla (*fr.* 6 Bergk). I must examine therefore also the manner in which Pelops expressed the hostile component of his ambivalence toward Tantalus, by means of a displacement of his hostility from its initial object Tantalus to Pelops' murderous father-in-law, King Oenomaus, ruler of Elis. Oenomaus had a daughter, Hippodameia, of whom it was prophesied that her husband would slay her father.[14] Being cognizant of this prophecy, Oenomaus tried to fend off his daughter's suitors, by proposing to them a chariot race. If the suitors lost, the king was free to slay them, and, until Pelops' arrival had always succeeded in his designs. However, Pelops asked Oenomaus' coachman Myrtilus, son of Hermes, to replace the bronze linch-pin of his master's chariot with a waxen one. To pay for this treachery, he promised that Myrtilus would be permitted to share Hippodameia's favors (*15*).[15] When the king pursued Pelops and Hippodameia, his sabotaged chariot disintegrated and he was killed. Then, in order not to have to pay Myrtilus the promised bribe, Pelops drowned his accomplice.

From the sociological point of view, this peculiar courtship episode is understandable in terms of Sir J.G. Frazer's discussion of the transmission of kingly powers in Alba Longa and his references to Greek myths (except that of Oedipus!) (*21*), from the present king to the king's son-in-law. Hence, in permitting his daughter to marry, the king automatically created a rival for his throne, exactly as Laius provided a future king for Thebes by fathering Oedipus. In this system, in which power was transmitted from mother to daughter, although the exercise of power was delegated to the spouse—a mechanism characteristic of matri*liny*, as distinct from matri*archy*—the same results could be achieved by marrying either the mother or the daughter. Thus, Oedipus married Jocasta, as Pelops married Hippodameia, in order to be elevated to the throne. The fact that Oedipus obtains Jocasta after mortal combat, while Pelops obtains Hippodameia by means of a (murderous) race fits Frazer's view that athletic competitions for the bride were attenuated echoes of earlier mortal combats. The fact that Hippodameia rode in Pelops' chariot is reminiscent of the practice of bride theft and, of course, of the abduction of Chrysippus.

From the psychoanalytic point of view, even if one disregards the obvious symbolism of the chariot-race, the sexual bribe offered to Myrtilus, and the fact that he was killed so that the bribe (*ius primae noctis?*) need not be paid, clearly suggest that—psychologically speaking—King Oenomaus and his unfaithful coachman Myrtilus are one and the same person in the eyes of Pelops and that Oenomaus' murder was oedipally motivated. At the same time Myrtilus is perhaps also a part of Pelops himself, who, after profiting by the treachery, kills his accomplice. These deeds created a blood-guilt which gave rise to the tragedy of Pelops' sons and also to that of Electra.[16]

Indeed, Tantalus seems to have been psychologically reincarnated in Pelops' vicious sons, Atreus and Thyestes. The latter seduced his brother's wife Aerope, and also stole a marvelous golden ram given to Atreus by the gods, in token of sovereignty over Mycenae.[17] Atreus first banished Thyestes, then feigned to be reconciled with him, and set before him a *dish made of the flesh of Thyestes' own children*. When Thyestes realized what he had eaten, he departed, but first cursed his brother Atreus. This curse eventually led to the tragedy of Electra, precisely as that of Pelops led to the tragedy of Oedipus. Indeed, Thyestes soon discovered that he could be avenged on his brother only *by cohabiting with his own daughter, Pelopia* (Apollodoros, *Epitome* 2.14).[18] The son born of this incestuous union, Aegisthus, became the slayer of Agamemnon and the lover of

Clytaemnestra, who was slain by Orestes and Electra—a deed which is the prototypal expression of the Electra complex. These events show that the legend of the Pelopid dynasty is intimately connected with that of the house of Laius. It is therefore sufficient to summarize here only Pelops' connections with the death of Laius.

Pelops—who was practically cannibalized by Demeter on behalf of his father and homosexually raped by the father-figure Poseidon but nonetheless revered his father—slew his father-in-law. This explains precisely why Pelops was so enraged by Chrysippus' abduction, and why he chose to curse Laius in so peculiar a manner.

The chief features of Pelops' conflict may be summarized as follows: (1) Pelops behaves toward Chrysippus as a fond father should behave. In so doing he shows Tantalus how he *should* have treated him, and Poseidon how he should *not* have treated him. (2) Laius' deed enraged Pelops beyond all measure, probably because, in the rape of Chrysippus, Laius acted out one of Pelops' own, most severely repressed, impulses, and, at the same time, reawakened Pelops' own passive homosexual conflicts. (3) The curse which Pelops laid on Laius was clearly rooted in Pelops' own conflicts: Oedipus was to slay his father Laius. This curse reveals the unconscious meaning of Pelops' killing his father-in-law the very day on which he married Hippodameia: It reflects the displacement of his oedipal homosexual hostility from Tantalus and Poseidon to Oenomaus and Myrtilus.

Character and Fate in Greek Drama

The analysis of Laius' character, and of the character and curse of Pelops, casts a great deal of doubt upon the conception of Greek tragedy as an account of man's helplessness in the face of *undeserved* Fate. Laius' death at the hands of Oedipus is not the trigger-event which sets in motion the millstones of the gods. Rather it is a rigidly determined consequence of Laius' own character-structure, just as the nature of the curse laid upon him is an unavoidable consequence of Pelops' passive homosexual conflicts and of his repressed murderous hatred of his father Tantalus, which was displaced to, and then acted out in, the killing of Oenomaus and of Myrtilus. Thus, one must credit Greek poets and dramatists with more psychological acumen than is customary. What they called "Fate" was merely the personification of man's character-structure, and of his need to act out those of his intra-psychic conflicts which determine the course of his life. The rôle which Greek drama assigned to the character-trait "hybris," as a determinant of man's tragic fate, confirms this view, and casts a vivid light upon the psychology of Greek society, in which a character-structure involving hybris was the one least well adapted to social demands.[19] At the same time the need to manifest overbearingness and excess must have been very strong indeed in a society which professed to follow the path of moderation. This subjective need to escape the bounds of moderation explains why the Greek dramatists not only condemned but also admired and pitied those whose hybris brought about their downfall.[20]

Greek drama is, thus, not a tragedy set in motion by a fate external to man, but by man's character-structure and latent conflicts; those whom the gods wish to destroy they first make mad. If one replaces "the gods" with parental figures (with whom the Greeks equated them), this adage confirms my interpretation of the characterological and conflictual sources of Greek tragic destinies. This fact was simply obscured by the Greek's habit of personifying character-structure as "Fate," and also by the tendency of the dramatist to deal with well-known mythical personages, whose background and early history were expected to be familiar to the audience. It is very much to be doubted whether the intelligent Greek attending the representation of Sophocles' main Oedipus drama was unaware of Laius' character and early history, and believed that Laius' death was predetermined by Fate in the literal sense. He probably accepted this thesis simply as a poetically appropriate allegorical reference to Laius' personality, since at that time—and until very recently—explicit "psychologizing" was not felt to be a poetical or even a literary device. The dramatist was therefore compelled to achieve plausibility—both psychological and other—by means which his audience was culturally conditioned to accept as proofs of "literary plausibility."[21] These considerations further justify the psychoanalytic interpretation of nominally non-psychologically formulated narratives and myths.

Concluding Hypotheses

The following remarks, and in particular those which pertain to clinical problems, are admittedly tentative. They are attempts to indicate the location of certain problem-areas in psychoanalytic theory, which deserve to be explored further. Though expressed in simple declarative sentences, they should not be taken as statements of fact, or as time-tested theoretical insights. I use declarative statements solely because I do not wish to encumber my text with monotonous and repetitive warnings that all I say is tentative and in need of further confirmation.

This being said, the material here presented suggests that the following hypotheses stand in need of further study.

(1) *History of Psychoanalysis.* Culturally determined scotomata may be responsible for minimizing the significance of the Laius complex and the Jocasta complex which complement the Oedipus complex.

(2) *Metapsychology.* The Oedipus myth does not support the view that biological and/or phylogenetic factors are *primarily* responsible for the *Oedipus* complex. The notion that the child's psyche is, for *biological* reasons, a "chamber of horrors" is also contradicted by Freud's thesis (*22*) further elaborated by me (*12*), that instincts become luxuriant and monstrous *only as a result of repression.* It may even be necessary to assume that the child's sensitiveness, even to minimal aggression, may be epiphenomenal to its sensitiveness to minimal tokens of love (*11, 3*) since the latter appears to be one of the child's chief psychic homeostatic mechanisms.

(3) *Psychosexual Development.* The Oedipus complex appears to be a consequence of the child's sensitiveness to its parents' sexual and aggressive impulses. Homosexual conflicts appear to play a great rôle in the genesis and development of the Oedipus complex.

(4) *Clinical Implications.* It seems worthwhile to investigate to what extent heterosexual impulses, seemingly directed at the parent of the opposite sex, include and/or disguise also homosexual impulses directed at the parent of the same sex. Genitality seems to mean more than the attainment of heterosexuality pure and simple. In the case of males it seems to require also a shift from a sublimated passive to a sublimated active homosexuality, and, in the case of

women, a shift from sublimated active to sublimated passive homosexuality. It is even possible that "activity" and "passivity" in the sexual sphere may have homosexual rather than heterosexual sources, since these attitudes are closely related to aggression, which belongs to the pre-genital stage of psychosexual development (*19*, chap. 6).

(5) *Applied Psychoanalysis.*

(a) *The Oedipus myth.* The early history of Laius contains data which are fundamental for the understanding of the Oedipus myth. They appear to express the Greeks' insight into the external and realistic sources of the male child's tendency to view his father as a homosexual ogre, and of his desire to exchange rôles with the father also in this respect.

(b) *Greek literature.* A study of the problem of Laius suggests that, especially in Greek drama, "Fate" is actually a personification of character-structure.

(c) *Mythology.* Whenever there exist divergent and even seemingly contradictory versions of a given mythical episode, these variants not only do not contradict each other psychologically, but actually supplement each other, and provide a deeper insight into the latent nuclear meaning of the basic theme, *motif*, or plot-element. For example, the bowdlerized explanation of the causes of the quarrel between Laius and Oedipus not only repeats in a symbolic form (narrow road) the sexual theme alluded to in other sources, but also provides a deeper insight into Laius' character-structure, which is of paramount importance for the understanding of the Oedipus myth.[22] Furthermore, the various unexpurgated versions, some of which highlight the rôle of Jocasta, while others highlight that of Chrysippus, enable one to discover the combined heterosexual and homosexual undercurrent in the male child's struggle against his father and in his love for his mother. As regards the legend of Pelops, the striking contrast between the traditional version of the Feast of Tantalus and Pindar's theory that Pelops was abducted by Poseidon amounts to little more than the presentation of the basic theme—erotized anxiety and passivity in the face of aggression—in oral, respectively in homosexual-Oedipal, terms. This suggests that a given theme has an inherent and specific latent significance, which no amount of voluntary or involuntary, or else conscious or unconscious, distortion can obliterate (*16*). In fact, such distortions only serve to highlight certain additional psychological implications of the basic theme. Thus in mythology, as in dream-work, one is constantly confronted with the fact that *plus ça change, plus c'est la même chose.* This finding has an important bearing not only upon the study of dreams, fantasies and mythology, but also upon such everyday matters as false perception (*17*), embellished and distorted rumours, deliberate lying, false evidence in courts of law, etc., all of which, though they are distortions of the manifest content, adhere rather closely to the latent content. Finally, this inference also has a bearing upon those clinical psychological tests in which the subject is expected to repeat a story told to him, as well as upon such partially structured projective tests as the Rorschach, the TAT and perhaps the Draw-a-Man Test.[23] Needless to say, these suppositions are fully compatible with classical psychoanalytic theory.

The one conclusion which one can offer with any degree of confidence is that, as long as there are human beings, the task of psychoanalytic research will never be finished.

NOTES

[1]Offhand, I can think only of one author who devoted considerable attention to the Jocasta complex, and that author was not a psychoanalyst but an anthropologist (*28*).

[2]This development led to a shift toward greater conservativeness in matters pertaining to the ethics of sexual acts, and also to the theory of the death-instinct, or primary self-aggression, which psychoanalytically well-informed theologians have sometimes compared to the doctrine of original sin.

[3]This outlook—represented, e.g., by such attitudes as "spare the rod and spoil the child", or "children should be seen and not heard"—had as its complement the conception of the "angelic" nature of children (*14*). Similar institutionalizations of ambivalence towards children also occur in primitive society (*6*).

[4]The audience hooted the cynical and hedonistic defence of incest, that whatever gives pleasure is good, in one of Euripides' plays (*Aeolus, fr.* 19) so violently that the line had to be changed to an admission that whatever is dishonourable *is* dishonourable, regardless of how pleasant it may be. Of course, in this instance, the incest was that of a brother and a sister, which was both psychologically and economically unacceptable to parents in the audience (*30*).

[5]These sources include some fragments of the epic *Oidipodeia*, of Praxilla, of a fragmentary play by Euripides and some other fragments (*26, 30*).

[6]Hera's anger is, in itself, a problem of some magnitude, which can only be partially understood in terms of her position as the custodian of family life and in terms of her own experiences with Zeus' various heterosexual and homosexual loves. Her choice of the Sphinx—whom Rank (*30*) views as a phallic woman—as the special instrument of her retribution is equally perplexing. Lack of space prevents me from discussing this interesting mythological problem.

[7]Some aspects of the problem of chastity in marriage were discussed in another essay (*10*), in connection with certain ancient Indian traditions regarding two kings, each of whom killed a father-figure at the very moment when the latter was engaging in marital relations.

[8]If the Sphinx was killed in a physical combat, then its death was, in a sense, similar to the death which Laius brought upon himself. If the Sphinx killed itself after Oedipus guessed its riddle, the suicide of the Sphinx resembles that of Jocasta. These seemingly divergent versions of the same plot-element therefore actually converge and further support the thesis that Jocasta, when mating with Oedipus, represented both herself and the castrated and feminized Laius.

[9]A Hungarian military joke specifically describes an incident in which adultery with the wife is at the same time represented as anal cohabitation with the woman's husband, thus further substantiating Freud's theory of paranoid jealousy (*18*, chap. 7).

[10]Only in those versions which attribute Laius' death to a quarrel over the right of way is there any mention of Oedipus' own proneness to violence, which is, of course, *similar to that of Laius*. In other words, even where impulsiveness is attributed also to Oedipus, this character-trait of the son is derived from, or correlated with, the father's character structure.

[11]In certain primitive societies the murderer is adopted as a replacement for the murdered kinsman (*7*).

[12]The providing of heirs was analyzed elsewhere (*10*).

[13]In many primitive societies cohabitation is prohibited during the long period of lactation. This situation, as it pertains, e.g., to the Sioux Indians, was discussed elsewhere (*12*).

[14]In this connection, too, Pelops' fate is similar to that of a personage in the Oedipus myth. Just as Laius had to protect his life against his son Oedipus, so Oenomaus stood in danger of death from his daughter's suitor Pelops (*15*).

[15]According to another version, Pelops' victory was due to the direct intervention of his erstwhile lover Poseidon who, at the crucial moment, caused the wheel of Oenomaus' chariot to become detached. That Myrtilus also represents Oenomaus is shown by the tradition that Oenomaus was *in love* with his daughter (*15*).

[16]A note on unconscious insight may not be out of place in this context. H.J. Rose, whose style is usually of exemplary clarity, at this particular point fails to make it clear whether the blood-guilt which Pelops had to shoulder was for the death of Oenomaus or for that of Myrtilus (*32*). Since Professor Rose was not an analyst, his slip is of special interest, in that it reveals his unconscious insight into the identity of Oenomaus and Myrtilus. Correctly stated, the blood-guilt fell upon Pelops as a result of the murder of Myrtilus.

[17]Compare here the story that Tantalus concealed a golden dog, sacred to Zeus, which had been stolen by a thief from Zeus' shrine.

[18]Among the Ba-Thonga a man setting out to hunt the hippopotamus first commits incest with his daughter, so that his terribleness shall match that of the hunted beast (24).

[19]Adkins' theory (1) of the psychological structure of early Greek society, in which hybris could run riot, fails to convince me: so brutal a society could not exist for many centuries.

[20]The psychological situation obtaining in Pueblo Indian society is in some respects the same. These tribes profess to follow a way of life which Ruth Benedict calls Apollonian (3). Yet, underneath this peaceful façade there bubbles a witch's cauldron of hate which finds expression in constant panicky preoccupation with witchcraft (34, 12). As regards the tendency to condemn with admiration those who violate the social form: in Central Australia incestuous men are condemned with admiration (31). The same attitude also prevails in at least one of the Moi tribes of South Vietnam (5).

[21]The problems of the cultural and psychological formulation of the criteria of literary plausibility are discussed elsewhere (8).

[22]It is of considerable interest that Laius' character-structure, i.e., his proneness to thoughtless violence, is put in relief more strikingly in the bowdlerized versions than in those unexpurgated versions of this incident in which the grosser instinctual elements are more prominent. This is not surprising, since character-formation results from attempts to cope with the instincts and with unmanageable external stimulation.

[23]These considerations seem to provide a theoretical basis for an interesting idea advanced by Linton in a private conversation (27). He suggested that divergent versions of primitive tales may represent a kind of cultural Thematic Apperception Test, in which the basic plot—corresponding to a TAT picture—is subjectively elaborated by various tellers of tales. It also sheds light on Lévi-Strauss' theory (25) of the structural invariants of all versions of a myth.

BIBLIOGRAPHY

1. ADKINS, A.W.H.: *Merit and Responsibility*, Oxford, Clarendon Press, 1960.

2. BALINT, Alice: "Liebe zur Mutter und Mutterliebe," *Internationale Zeitschrift für Psychoanalyse und Imago*, 24:33–48, 1939.

3. BENEDICT, Ruth: *Patterns of Culture*, London, Routledge, 1934.

4. BUNKER, H.A.: "The Feast of Tantalus," *Psychoanalytic Quarterly*, 21: 355–372, 1952.

5. DEVEREUX, George: *My Field Notes* (MS).

6. Id.: "Mohave Beliefs concerning Twins," *American Anthropologist*, n.s., 43: 573–592, 1941.

7. Id.: "Social Structure and the Economy of affective Bonds," *Psychoanalytic Review*, 29:303–304, 1942.

8. Id.: "Mohave Coyote Tales," *Journal of American Folklore*, 61:233–255, 1948.

9. Id.: "Status, Socialization and Interpersonal Relations of Mohave Children," *Psychiatry*, 13:489–502, 1950.

10. Id.: "The Oedipal Situation and its Consequences in the Epics of Ancient India," *Samiksa, Journal of the Indian Psycho-Analytical Society*, 5:5–13, 1951.

11. Id.: "Cultural and Characterological Traits of the Mohave Related to the Anal Stage of Psychosexual Development," *Psychoanalytic Quarterly*, 20:398–422, 1951.

12. Id.: *Reality and Dream: The Psychotherapy of a Plains Indian*, New York, International Universities Press, 1951.

13. Id.: "The Technique of Analyzing Occult Occurrences in Analysis," (in) Devereux, George (ed.): *Psychoanalysis and the Occult*, New York, International Universities Press, 1953.

14. Id.: *Therapeutic Education*, New York, Harper, 1956.

15. Id.: "The Abduction of Hippodameia," *Studi e Materiali di Storia delle Religioni*, 36:3–25 (= *Femme et Mythe*, Paris, Flammarion, 1982), 1965.

16. Id.: "The Exploitation of Ambiguity in Pindaros *O*. 3.27," *Rheinisches Museum für Philologie*, 109:289–298 (see note 17), 1966.

17. Id.: *From Anxiety to Method*, Mouton & Co, Paris, The Hague, 1967.

18. Id.: *Ethnopsychoanalysis*, Berkeley, California, University of California Press, (chapter 7), 1978.

19. Id.: *Basic Problems of Ethnopsychiatry*, Chicago, University of Chicago Press, 1980.

20. FERENCZI, Sandor: "Confusion of Tongues between the Adult and the Child," *International Journal of Psychoanalysis*, 30:225–230, 1949.

21. FRAZER, Sir J.G.: "The Succession to the Kingdom of Ancient Latium," (in) *The Magic Art, The Golden Bough*, London, Macmillan, 1951.

22. FREUD, Sigmund: "Repression," *Standard Edition*, vol. XIV, 1915.

23. GRUPPE, Otto: *Griechische Mythologie und Religionsgeschichte*, München, Beck, 1897–1906, 2 vols.

24. JUNOD, H.A.: *The Life of a South African Tribe*, 2nd ed., London, Macmillan, 1927.

25. LÉVI-STRAUSS, Claude: *Anthropologie Structurale*, Paris, Plon, 1958.

26. LICHT, Hans: *Sexual Life in Ancient Greece*, London, Routledge, 1932.

27. LINTON, Ralph: Personal Communication.

28. RAGLAN, Lord: *Jocasta's Crime*, London, Methuen, 1933.

29. RANK, Otto: *Das Inzestmotiv in Dichtung und Sage*, Leipzig, Deuticke, 1912.

30. ROBERT, C.: *Oidipus*, Berlin, Weidman, 2 vols. 1915.

31. ROHEIM, Géza: "Psycho-Analysis of Primitive Cultural Types", *International Journal of Psycho-Analysis*, 13:1–224, 1932.

32. ROSE, H.J.: *A Handbook of Greek Mythology*, London, Methuen, 1928.

33. ROTTER, L.K.: "A Nöi Genitalitas Pszichologiajarol," (in) *Lélekelemzesi Tanulmanyok* (Ferenczi Memorial Volume), Budapest, Somlo, 1933.

34. SIMMONS, L.W. (ed.): *Sun Chief*, New Haven, Yale University Press, 1942.

The Indian Oedipus

A.K. Ramanujan

*To conclude the volume, we have chosen an exciting essay by
A.K. Ramanujan, Professor of Dravidian Studies and Linguistics at
the University of Chicago. This paper is a thoroughly revised and
expanded version of an earlier (1972) study by the same title, and
was written especially for this casebook. In this investigation,
Professor Ramanujan brings together the most complete set of
Indian Oedipus texts to date. On the basis of this corpus, he is able
to demonstrate a remarkable difference between the Indian and the
western traditions within a basic shared structure. As Devereux
ingeniously looked at Oedipus from the father's point of view,
Ramanujan considers the mother's perspective. Besides all this, he
also presents the texts in a cultural context with valuable ethnographic glosses.*

*Among the fascinating details in a version which Professor
Ramanujan collected himself in 1963, we find a lullaby, the lyrics of
which constitute an incest riddle. This is a striking parallel to the
incest riddle lullaby in the Albanian text with which this casebook
began. So the Indian Oedipus shows similarities with European
stories, but at the same time, it has its own distinctive characteristics.
We may generalize from this that potential universals like the
Oedipus story should ideally be examined in culturally relative
contexts.*

Introduction

Searching for stories of the Oedipus type (Tale Type 931) some years ago in the myth and folklore of the Indic area (i.e., India, Pakistan, Bangladesh, Ceylon), I found very little that looked like the Sophocles play, where a young man kills his father and marries his mother. The very few instances I found were of the following kind: (a) A Tamil folk-anecdote about Gaṇeśa. Once Pārvatī asked him whom he would like to marry; he replied, "Someone exactly like you, Mother," and Mother got outraged by such an open incestuous wish and cursed him with everlasting celibacy; that's why he is still a bachelor. (b) An averted "Oedipus" from Tamilnad, Ceylon (etc.), Indic Type 674. A son grows up without knowing who his true mother is. When full-grown, he sees his mother, falls in love with her (N 365.1.1) and goes to her at night hoping to become her lover. On the way he overhears animals talking (N 451) and learns the truth. (c) In certain versions of the *Rāmāyaṇa,* Sītā is Rāvaṇa's daughter, born with a curse on her head that she would bring death to her father. Rāvaṇa tries to get rid of her, and she ends up in a strange Northern land where she marries Rāma, gets abducted by unsuspecting Rāvaṇa, and Rāma of course kills him. Son-in-law Rāma can be seen as a substitute son. The father-daughter relations suggested in this story call for further discussion. (d) In the *Mahābhārata* and a popular Kannaḍa *Yakṣagāna* play based on it, Arjuna fights with his own son Babhruvāhana who slays his father in battle, but Arjuna is later revived. (e) In the Bengali *Rāmāyaṇa,* Rāma's sons Lava and Kuśa kill Rāma in battle. (f) And there are instances in the *Ṛgveda*: "Who, O Indra, made thy mother a widow? What god was present in the fray when thou did slay thy father, seizing him by the foot?" (Rg. IV. 18.12).

But all these instances seemed to me rather marginal, generally not known or preserved in the most influential versions of the *Rāmāyaṇa,* the *Mahābhārata* or the popular lore. I found nothing as explicit as the Greek myth. Others had searched before me (e.g. Spratt, 1966) and concluded that Indian narrative has no Oedipal tales, and therefore, of course, Indians have no Oedipus complex. According to one writer, at least, the unfortunate lack of an Oedipus complex had prevented Indians from developing a form like the novel or from overthrowing the Mughals or the British by a bloody upheaval, etc., etc.

In the present paper I wish to report on a few Oedipus-like patterns in Indian myth and folklore and suggest an interpretation.[1]

The Oedipus Type (AT 931)

For the purpose of our search, we may briefly look at the familiar European pattern, as in the classical play of Sophocles' *Oedipus Rex*. A young man, fated to kill his father and marry his mother, tries to escape the curse of fate, but ironically, unwittingly, fulfills it. The Electra-story displays the same relational pattern with the sexes reversed: Electra-figures love their fathers and hate their mothers. For our purposes, all four types of dyadic relations, father/son, mother/son, father/daughter, mother/daughter, will be considered "Oedipal." In the Greek myths of Oedipus and Electra,

1. Son kills father.
2. Son marries mother.
3. Daughter loves father, wishes to avenge his death, etc.
4. Daughter hates mother, wants her killed, etc.

If we call "love, pursue, desire to marry, or wish to do any or all of these" + *Relations*, and "hate, castrate, kill, or wish to do any or all of these" − *Relations,* we get the following patterns:

If we extend father, son, mother, daughter to other figures who have similar functions, and on whom these parent-child relations are projected, we have a whole body of narratives which exemplify the pattern of whom Hamlet and Oedipus are only two instances. The signal Indian instance is Krṣṇa, fated to kill Kaṁsa, his uncle. But no tragic fate befalls Krṣṇa, as it befalls Oedipus.

Indian Examples

Relations of Mother and Son

In 1963, an illiterate, half-blind old woman in a North Karnatak village startled me with the following tale:

> A girl is born with a curse on her head that she would marry her own son and beget a son by him. As soon as she hears of the curse, she wilfully vows she'd try and escape it: she secludes herself in a dense forest, eating only fruit, forswearing all male company. But when she attains puberty, as fate would have it, she eats a mango from a tree under which a passing king has urinated. The mango impregnates her; bewildered, she gives birth to a male child; she wraps him in a piece of her sari and throws him in a nearby stream. The child is picked up by the king of the next kingdom, and he grows up to be a handsome young adventurous prince. He comes hunting in the self-same jungle, and the cursed woman falls in love with the stranger, telling herself she is not in danger any more as she has no son alive. She marries him and bears him a child. According to custom, the father's swaddling clothes are preserved and brought out for the newborn son. The woman recognizes at once the piece of sari with which she had swaddled her first son, now her husband, and understands that her fate had really caught up with her. She waits till everyone is asleep, and sings a lullaby to her newborn baby:
>
> > Sleep
> > O son
> > O grandson
> > O brother to my husband
> > sleep O sleep
> > sleep well
>
> and hangs herself by the rafter with her sari twisted to a rope.

Since 1963, I have found several variants of this tale from other districts; I also found Marathi versions collected in neighboring Maharāṣṭra, and variants in some old Jaina texts. In the next few pages we shall examine these variants, discuss the variations episode by episode, comparing parallels in texts and oral traditions, and suggest the significance of each episode.

The tale is strikingly exact in its parallels to the Greek Oedipus, but the narrative point of view is entirely different. It is the mother, the Jocasta-figure, who is accursed, tries to escape her fate, and when finally trammelled in it, it is she who makes the discovery and punishes herself with death. The son is merely a passive actor, a part of his mother's fate—unlike the Greek Oedipus. Such reversals of narrative point of view are yet to be studied in comparative and structural mythology. The Greek and Kannada Oedipus-tales provide a very neat example of a pair of tales in which a *structure* is the same, but the narrative *point of view* is exactly in reverse. Parallels were hard to find earlier because I began with the Greek pattern; the search was too literal-minded, and I did not see that in a different cultural context a familiar pattern may appear standing on its head—the great Indian image of the cosmic tree is the tree with its branches in the earth and the roots in the air.

The Variants

In the eight variants (three from my fieldnotes, five from the following: Karve, 1950, Dhavaḷaśrī, 1968, Paramaśivayya, 1970ₐ and 1970ᵦ, Lingayya, 1971) I shall consider; variations occur at the following points in the sequence.

1. The Prophecy

Instead of a curse, an astrologer's prophecy initiates the action in one. In others there is a divine parent: we have Vidhiyamma (Mother Fate) or Seṭivitāyi, who writes the fates of newborn babies on their foreheads. When Fate's daughter is twelve years old, she discovers her mother's "profession" one night when the latter returns from a nocturnal visit to a newborn baby, accosts her, and insists on knowing what she wrote on her own daughter's forehead. When she hears that Mother Fate had written that she (the daughter) would marry her own son, she flies into a rage and proceeds to defy her "lifescript."[2] It is significant that the daughter is twelve years old, an age when Indian girls enter puberty.

2. How She Gets Pregnant

In none of the variants does the girl get pregnant by actual sexual intercourse. Only in one variant, semen is mentioned: a king sits on her sari spread out to dry in the sun, is excited by it, leaves his seed on it. She wears the sari later and gets big with child. In several she gets pregnant by eating a mango from a tree, or a patch of greens, watered by a king's urine. In one, she drinks from a pool where a bull has urinated. In another, she gets pregnant by drinking water from a pool in which a king has rinsed his mouth. Either way, his body fluids (saliva and urine are two of the polluting body fluids mentioned by the ancient law-giver, Manu—sweat, blood, semen, tears and mother's milk being the others) are treated as capable of impregnating the woman. In other folk tales, and in myths, "blood, sweat, and tears" are all seen as capable of making babies. In this worldview, no body fluid is non-sexual, at least non-procreative. Another interesting aspect here is the confusion of the procreative and alimentary channels, noted by Freud as characteristic of the child's view of reproduction.[3]

3. The Lullaby

Only two variants contain the lullaby at the end which describes the "unnatural" confusion of kinship relations.[4] Mother marrying son and begetting another son by him collapses generational differences: By this act, son and grandson become one. It conflates the difference between kin by birth and kin by marriage: son and husband become one, so do mother-in-law and mother; and so on. The most fantastic of these kin-confusions is in Jaina tales (my examples here are all literary). In one, a courtesan has twins whom she abandons;

they grow up separately, meet and marry, but recognize their kinship by the rings they wear; the son travels far, becomes his mother's lover and begets a son; his spouse and sister, who renounces the world, acquires magical vision, comes to warn her mother and brother, sees their son, and addresses him thus:

> O child! you are my brother, brother-in-law, grandson, son of my co-wife, nephew, uncle. Your father is my brother, husband, father, grandfather, father-in-law, and son. Your mother is my mother, mother-in-law, co-wife, my brother's wife, grandmother, and wife.

(Jain, 1977, Appendix I. 566; for other examples see Karve, 1950). It is clear that in the Jaina examples, the point of the tale is not Fate, nor Oedipal patterns of mother/son relations, but the destruction of the kinship diagram. Such a confusion of clear-cut kinship relations (son/husband, mother/mother-in-law, etc.) would be devastating to a child, would make a shambles of his ordered family world. That seems to be part of the terror of the incest taboo and the poignancy of some of the folktales. (The Jaina literary tale defuses the charge of the tale by its clever elaboration and overdoing the list of paradoxical relations.) The characteristic response to such a disorienting sin in these tales is suicide (of the mother, the heroine) or a renouncing of the world by the hero. Such a renunciation, a withdrawal from all relations, in Indian terms, is a kind of social suicide—one becomes a *sanyasi* by performing a funeral rite on oneself.

4. The End

The end of the tale is interestingly different in three of my variants. Instead of the heroine killing herself or renouncing the world, she recognizes that her fate has been fulfilled or she prays to a goddess who counsels her to accept her fate; she doesn't tell anyone about her incestuous marriage, lives happily with her husband, "blessed by her aged parents-in-law to whom she was always kind and dutiful." When anthropologist Karve asked the illiterate Maratha woman (who told the story to her daughter) what she thought of it, she replied, "But what else could she do? You know, madam, it was written so." Not only that; Karve says, "At the end of the tale my little daughter and the narrator were both laughing at the queerness of the happening." (Karve, 1950)

As Karve remarks, many of the incest-tales (like the Jaina one above) are told as illustrations of the sinfulness of all wordly relations or as conundrums and guessing games—not as deeply tragic tales. In a variant from Salsette, the girl is foretold that she would marry a lowcaste man and later marry her own son. When the prophecies come true, she is disgusted by the former but accepts the latter as her fate (D'Penha, 45). How different in ethos from the Greek Oedipus!

It should be noted here that this story is told invariably by women and to girls. The protagonists of the story are women; the men are pawns in the story of women's fate. Karve's Maratha woman heard it from her old sister-in-law when she was about fifteen and told it to Karve's daughter. All my Kannada variants were collected from older motherly women.

We may now summarize the variations in the form of an archetype or composite tale. As this type of Oedipus tale has not been clearly identified so far, we may suggest a number like 931B (Ind.?).

I. *The prophecy.* An astrologer or a divine parent (Brahmā, Vidhiyamma/Mother Fate, or Śeṭivi tāyi) prophesies that a girl will marry her own son and beget a son by him. When the girl learns of it (usually at puberty), she flees home and (a) secludes herself in a forest, or (b) magically enters a tree, coming out only for food.

II. *The prophecy fulfilled.* (a) She eats (a_1) a mango from a tree, or (a_2) greens from a patch, where a king has urinated; or (b) drinks water from a pool where (b_1) a king has rinsed his mouth or (b_2) a bull has urinated; or (c) wears a sari on which (c_1) a king has sat or (c_2) spilled his seed. (d) She gets pregnant, and when she gives birth to a son, she (d_1) pounds the child's head with a rock and/or (d_2) leaves him on the hillside, or (d_3) sets him afloat in the river after wrapping him in a piece of her sari. (e) The boy is rescued by (e_1) fishermen or (e_2) shepherds, and grows up. (f) Years later, unwittingly, (f_1) she goes to her son's house, or (f_2) the son comes hunting. Or (g) the king's men try to cut down the tree in which she lives, and discover her. (h) Mother and son meet, marry, and she gives birth to a son.

III. (a) *The discovery* takes place (a_1) when she is delousing her husband (son) and sees scars, or (a_2) when she discovers her sari-piece, in which she had wrapped her first son and which is brought out (according to custom) for her newborn's naming ritual.

IV. *The consequence.* (a) She sings a lullaby about the incestuous confusion of kin-relations (e.g., son is also grandson and husband's brother), and hangs herself. Or (b) she accepts her fate and lives happily with her son/husband and offspring, (b_1) after being advised by a goddess.

Chief motifs

A	463.1	The Fates
M	301	The prophets (astrologers)
M	344	Mother-son incest prophecy
M	370	Vain attempts to escape fulfillment of prophecy
M	371	Exposure of child to avoid fulfillment of prophecy
S	331	Exposure of child in boat (floating chest)
S	141	Abandonment in forest
R	131.3.1	Shepherd rescues abandoned child
T	412	Mother-son incest
N	101	Inexorable fate
H	51	Recognition by scar

In an earlier paper (1972), I compared the Greek Oedipus myth with the Kannada Oedipus tale. A glance at the motifs is enough to show how close yet how different the two are. The Greek myth is central to that culture; it is the object of much literary elaboration and psychological discussion. In it the killing of the father, Laius, is as important as the son marrying the mother. The story is told entirely from the viewpoint of the young male, the son: He is the cursed one, he is the one who tries to escape fate and fulfills it, he is the one who discovers the truth about himself. The Kannada tale, told by village women, is not the source of tragic intensity nor the object of great literary elaboration. There is no Laius-figure, and therefore no patricide, in any of the tales. The tale, in its episodic sequence, is exactly the same as the Greek one but told entirely from the woman's, the mother's, point of view.

To structural analysis, we need to add *point of view*, before we can interpret a tale. One may ultimately decide that such reversals (male to female, son fated to marry mother instead of mother being fated to marry son, etc.) as structurally or psychoanalytically reducible to a single pattern. But the presence of such differences in point of view should be interpreted in the light of other parts of the cultures.

The great importance of sons to mothers in the politics of the Indian family (Kakar, 1978:57), the prolonged period of breast-feeding, the practice in many families of sons sleeping next to mothers almost until they are adolescent does make the mother-marries-son tale significant. It expresses a mother's desire and real temptation to cling to her son. Furthermore, Hindus believe that fathers are reborn as sons.[5] The rivalry between fathers and sons for the mother is because the mother loves her son and the father is left out. We shall see other aspects of this father-son rivalry in the next section. Here are a few more supporting examples of the closeness of mother and son, with the father left out.

There is a recurrent motif in folktales in South India and elsewhere (Motif J 21.2): A father returns from a long exile or journey and enters his bedroom to find a strange young man sleeping next to his wife. He draws his sword to kill them both, when either his waking wife or a remembered precept ("Don't act when angry") stays his hand. The young man is really his son grown to manhood during his long absence but still sleeping innocently in the same bed as his dear mother.

A rare example of mother-son relations in mythology is the Bengali legend about the goddess Durgā, whose intercourse with her son is watched and noisily interrupted by peacocks. Durgā gets angry with the peacock for being a peeping Tom and curses the peacock with impotence and an ugly squeal for a voice. She relents later and allows peacocks to have offspring by means of their tears. One could also add the Potiphar's Wife motif (K 2111.1), of which we have many examples in India; e.g., the Tamil story of Kuṇālan (Type 706). A stepmother desires her stepson who rejects her advances. She accuses him of making improper advances to her and his father punishes him by blinding his eyes. (Blinding, here or in Oedipus, is a well-recognized symbol for castration.)

Relations of Father and Son

The most striking difference between the Kannada tale and the Greek myth is the absence of the father and hence of patricide. There are very, very few stories of actual patricide in Hindu myth, literature, and folklore. A few marginal instances were listed at the beginning of this essay: Arjuna killed by his son, Rāma killed by his sons, both in battle, both revived later. The most explicit instance I know is in the 16th-century Tamil next *Tiruvilaiyāṭalpurāṇam* (13th c.?), cited by Hart 1980: A brāhman sleeps with his willing mother again and again. Once his father interrupts him in the act, so he axes his father. From then on, his father's shadow-form sticks to him, interrupts with its cries all his daily activities and gives him no rest. His sin is expiated by the grace of Śiva and by the penance of rolling round the corridors of Śiva's temple. But such stories are rare or little known. Even here, as Goldman (1978:370) points out,

> [the] expiation involves the reconstruction of the lost family, the original oedipal triangle, which occurs through the sinner's being adopted by Śiva and his wife. The wretch is saved only when he can accept the status of a submissive and devoted son to his divine parents.

But another pattern is very common: the aggression of the father towards the son. In all these stories the son willingly gives up (often transfers) his political and sexual potency. In the epic *Mahābhārata*, Bhīṣma, the first son of Śantanu, renounces both kingdom and his reproductive sexual life so that his father may marry a fishergirl and continue his (father's) sexual/reproductive life. Bhīṣma, lifelong celibate, lives on to become the most revered old man of the epic, warrior and wise man.

Yayāti, a king cursed by a sage to suffer senility, wishes to prolong his life of pleasure and asks his five sons to transfer their youth to him. The elder sons refuse and earn his curses. The youngest son exchanges his youth for Yayāti's age for a thousand years. For this sacrifice, the son receives great honor, and inherits the whole kingdom later.

A more explicit instance of a father's aggressive rivalry towards a son is the following: The sage Bṛhaspatī desires his elder brother's wife, Mamatā. She protests that she is pregnant, and that the embryo in her womb, which already knows the Vedas, will not allow his seed to grow in her womb; he should therefore wait till she has delivered. Nevertheless he insists, but the embryo cries out and prevents him from fulfilling his desire. Bṛhaspatī therefore curses the embryo with blindness. The child is called Dīrghatamas, deep darkness.

This story opens with the positive Oedipal pattern: a younger man desires an older woman (an elder brother's wife is equal to a mother), and the embryo in the womb resists the father-figure. But it ends with the latter striking the embryo with blindness.

It is significant that the Dīrghatamas story is told by Bhīṣma, and in the *Rāmāyaṇa* the Yayātī story is told by Rāma when he is exiled by his aged father. Such replication and reminiscence, such evocations of precedent at a crucially parallel moment by a character participating in the very patterns set by the precedent—these are part of literary technique as well as evidence for a major cultural "imprinting" of themes.

Many more instances may be cited of the father-son conflict with the father as victorious aggressor. I shall add only one more: the story of Gaṇeśa, the elephant-headed god. Pārvatī went to bathe, and stationed Gaṇeśa, her son, at the door, telling him to let nobody in. (In the *Śiva Purāṇa*, the scene is set in the bedchamber.) Her husband Śiva wanted to enter; and when Gaṇeśa tried to stop him, Śiva cut off his head, which was later replaced by an elephant head. In some legends, Gaṇeśa already had an elephant head, and Śiva broke off one tusk (as seen in the iconography). The Freudian implications of the father beheading or breaking off the son's tusk are obvious.

Goldman (1978), in the paper cited earlier, takes issue with my point regarding the "reverse Oedipus" in India. He enlarges on some of my examples (and adds several more) with great erudition, makes several acceptable corrections (which I have incorporated here), and points to an important displacement of the "positive" Oedipal

theme: the rivalry between brahmans and kṣatriya kings. The most
famous of these conflicts is that of Sage Vasiṣṭha and king Viśvāmitra, over the former's all-nurturing cow ("India's eternal mother
symbol," Goldman 1978:353). The triangle is: aged brahman
(father), covetous king (son), and cow (mother). Helped by the
cow's magical powers which create whole outcaste armies, Vasiṣṭha
destroys Viśvāmitra's forces and his hundred sons. Viśvāmitra,
dejected by defeat, acquires terrible weapons by penance, and
returns to destory Vasiṣṭha's hermitage. Vasiṣṭha's staff absorbs all
of Viśvāmitra's weapons. In a final show of rage, Vasiṣṭha "assumes
a dreadful form with flames shooting from the pores of his body, a
veritable nightmare fantasy of paternal rage." Fearful of the destruction of the whole world, the hosts of sages, a sort of chorus
representing collectively the voice of the paternal conscience or
superego, begs Vasiṣṭha to calm himself. The sage is appeased.
Viśvāmitra "realizes the incomparable potency of the paternal phallus as symbolized by the upraised staff of the aged brahman. He
resolves to acquire this same potency himself . . . [through painful
austerities] he attains the status of a brahman in one lifetime . . .
Vasiṣṭha relents and befriends his old rival, according him the
paternal blessing [by addressing him as a brahman sage]." In the end
Viśvāmitra does homage to Vasiṣṭha (Goldman, 1978:351–354).

The Kannada temple legend of Piriyāpaṭṭana (Rajashekhara
1980:527) also expresses the Brahman/King Oedipal conflict in
symbolic ways too obvious to need comment:

> A brahman gives a king a sacred pot for safekeeping. The
> king's servants discover that the water in the pot turns iron into
> gold. The king covets the pot, kills the brahman when he
> returns. But the betrayed brahman becomes a demon and
> torments him by attaching himself to him. The brahman
> demon leaves him only when he enters a Śiva temple but
> swoops on him again when he comes out of it. The mother
> goddess (Urimasaṇi) at the Vaidyeśvara temple saves him by
> letting the king through one of the temple's three doors and
> letting him out unexpectedly through another.

Note the meaningful motifs of coveting the father-figure's pot, the
tormenting guilt that follows him everywhere, and release through a
mother-figure (with three doors to the temple) in a fatherly god's
abode.

The Oedipal conflict is most explicit in such brahman-king relations as well as in guru-disciple relations. For a fuller exposition, see Goldman, 1978.

Though there is no clear word for "incest" in Indian languages, as Nicholas (1978:14–15) points out, there are a series of words for the crime of "sexual intercourse in the bed of the guru" (*gurutalpābhigamana*). This offense is included in their codes by Manu (IX.235) and by other *Dharmasāstra* writers among "great sins," (*mahāpataka*) along with brahminicide. The foremost meaning of *guru*, however, is "father" in Manu (II.142); also "preceptor," any senior or "weighty" person. Thus one sees that the Hindu writers are quite aware of transferences and generalizations of an "object-cathexis." To their definition of this incestuous sin of intercourse with a *guru*'s wife, they add a list of other sins "of the same form" (*tādrūpya*) or "equal" (*sāmya*). Nicholas (1978:16) continues and cites the longest of such enumerations from the *Nāradasmṛti*.

> If a man has sexual intercourse with any of these women viz. mother, mother's sister, mother-in-law, a wife of a paternal uncle or a friend or a pupil, a sister, a sister's friend, daughter-in-law, the wife of one's Vedic teacher, a woman of the same gotra (clan), one who has come for protection, a queen, an ascetic woman, one's wet-nurse, a woman performing a *vrata* (vow) and a *brāhmaṇa* woman, he becomes guilty of the sin of the violator of the guru's bed (i.e., incest). For that crime no other punishment is laid down except that of cutting of the penis.

In all these cases, we must note that the son never wins, almost never kills the father-figure. Where a younger man kills the older, as when Arjuna kills Bhīṣma, it is clear that it is the latter who teaches him a way of doing so. The power of the father-figure is never overthrown.

The only instance, and it is a very important one, is that of Kṛṣṇa killing Kamsa, his demonic uncle who has tried to destroy him in many ways ever since he was born. Kṛṣṇa also incites Arjuna to kill in war all his father-figures, especially Bhīṣma. Here too, one must note that Kṛṣṇa is a god, supreme in power, and invulnerable—unlike all the son-figures.

As Goldman concedes, the pattern of the aggressive father and submissive son (who by submission becomes a hero, and attains power and honor in later life, as Bhīṣma does) is "without doubt representative of an Oedipal type that the culture strongly favors"; such figures as Bhīṣma and Rāma, ideal sons, "do constitute the ego-ideal for Hindu men." (Goldman, 1978:364).

Relations of Father and Daughter

The most ancient myths bear witness to a father's desire for his daughter. We shall cite here only two: *The Sathapatha Brāhmana* 1.7.41-4 has the following: Prajāpatī, the father of the gods, the creator, cast his eyes upon his own daughter, desiring "May I pair with her." So saying, he had intercourse with her. This was a crime in the eyes of the gods, who said, "He is guilty who acts thus to his own daughter, our sister: pierce him through." Rudra aimed at him and pierced him. Half of his seed fell to the ground.

In later times Prajāpatī is called Brahma, the Grandfather. A new version of the above, "positive Oedipus" story appears in the *Matsya Purāṇa* III, 30–34:

When Brahma began his work of creation, the goddess Gāyatrī appeared in the form of a girl from one half of Brahma's body, who mistakenly took her for his daughter. Seeing that form of exquisite beauty, he was fired with love . . . The sons of Brahma, taking Gāyatrī for their sister, expressed indignation and contempt . . . Gāyatrī began to circumambulate him in reverence . . . he felt shy of turning his head in her direction, as his sons were close by. He therefore created four heads, each facing one of the directions, so that he might see her undisturbed. Seeing Brahma in this state, Gāyatrī went to heaven, and as she journeyed upward, Brahma put a fifth head on top . . . After this Brahma lost the powers that he had acquired by asceticism. For more instances, see O'Flaherty (1975: 26, 29–31, 34–35, 117–31) and the Bengali examples in Nicholas (1978).

In the Kannada *Vaḍḍhārādhane* (a Jaina work ca. 9th century), a king falls in love with his youngest daughter, and asks his wives and counsellors, "If there is a lovely thing born in my kingdoms, to whom does it belong?" They say, "Of course, the best horses, elephants, pearls, precious stones and the loveliest women in a kingdom belong to the king." Then he asks the sages the same question, who (being sages) answer, "You'll have to tell us what particular thing you are thinking of. Then we can tell you what belongs to whom and what doesn't." The king gets angry and drives them out for dissenting and asking inconvenient questions. Then he marries his youngest daughter. She bears him children. Her son Kārtīka goes for some sort of boys' picnic in the woods where all the rest of the boys get (apparently according to custom) food, flowers and clothes from their families, especially from grandparents. When Kārtīka doesn't receive anything from his grandparents, he comes home and asks his mother, "Mother, where is your father, my grandfather? Do I have one or not?" She tells him in grief, "What shall I tell you, my son? Your father is also my father." As soon as he hears it, Kārtīka is shocked, finds it reason enough to renounce the world and become a wandering ascetic.

Note here, as in the Oedipus stories, the emphasis placed on the resulting confusion of normal kin-relations, especially the conflation of generations (grandfather-father-son-brother) resulting from incestuous relations—and the son's horror at such a discovery.

A Tamil tale has a similar father-daughter pattern, but here the father doesn't get the daughters. A king has no children. He prays to Śiva, who appears to him and tells him, "You have a choice. You can either choose one ordinary son or four beautiful talented daughters." The king chooses the daughters (note the preference!). They do grow up to be four talented, divinely beautiful young women. One day the daughters are watching from the balcony while a clumsy tone-deaf masseur is patting oil into the king's body with all the wrong rhythms. The daughters are disgusted with the unmusical performance, come down from the balcony, dismiss the lout, and proceed to give the delighted father an oil-bath, all four of them massaging and patting oil into his limbs in pleasing rhythms, conducting a very orchestra of touch. After the bath, which sends the king into an ecstasy of pleasure, he is filled with desire for them and goes into the dark room specially reserved in ancient Indian palaces for doldrums, tantrums and sulks. When the family and the counsellors gather to ask him why he is sullen and unhappy, he asks a question similar to the one in the Kannada Jaina legend: "If I have something precious, should I enjoy it myself or give it away?" The unsuspecting ministers tell him, "Go ahead. Enjoy what you have." Delighted, he answers, "I'm in love with my daughters. I want to

marry them right away. Make the necessary arrangements." The
ministers think he is mad, but humor him by saying that they would
take care of it. Then they rush to the daughters with the bad news;
the resourceful daughters pray to the goddess Pārvatī who trans-
ports them into a sealed lacquer palace in the heart of a jungle—a
seven-storied palace, with living quarters on the first, and food and
clothing of every kind stored up in the six upper stories to last
several years. The palace has no doors or windows: a good image for
virginity, indeed. Several years later, a prince strays into the jungle
and hears strange *viṇa* (lute) music which lures him to the sealed
palace, and it opens miraculously to let him in. He falls in love with
all four of them and marries them. The young women's virginity was
offered only to the rightful young man, after being denied to the
incestuous father (Sastri, 1968).

In a Kannada folk-*Rāmāyaṇa* (Rāgau, et al. 1973:150 ff), we see
one more transformation of the Oedipus pattern:

> Rāvaṇa brings his barren wife a magic mango, a boon from
> Śiva. On his back, he is hungry and so eats the fruit and
> becomes pregnant himself. His nine days are equal to nine
> months and he sneezes nine times, and a daughter is born. He
> casts the child as inauspicious in the Ganges. Later he is
> infatuated with her, tries to marry her, and fails in the marriage-
> test. Rāma wins and marries her. Later Rāvaṇa abducts her.
> Rāma kills him with the help of Rāvaṇa's wife, and rescues Sītā.

The interesting features of this pregnant-father motif (found
elsewhere in India, too) are (a) the envy of female fertility/potency,
or womb-envy, (b) the way the father bypasses a mother to beget a
daughter so that there is no father/mother/daughter triangle, (c) the
way he tries to marry his daughter, thereby trying to be his own son-
in-law.

These tales clearly express a common Indian folktale theme, the
sexual assault of the young woman by older non-marriageable kin—
here a father, in many tales an elder brother—and non-kin (e.g., a
lecherous ascetic or guru). Dozens of tales open with the flight of the
daughter from the lecherous father-figure. The young woman's
character and chastity are tested by such incestuous and adulterous
assaults (e.g., the Kannada tale of Hanci, in Ramanujan 1982); she
withstands them till she meets her legitimate husband. As noted

earlier, father, elder brother and guru are equivalent. As we well know, and as the Oedipus tales point out, kinship organization and the social order based on it depend on the distinction between sisters (or mothers) and wives, fathers (or brothers) and husbands.

The famous epic instances of Sītā's abduction, and Draupadī's disrobing in a public place by her older in-laws, the many tales where ascetic father-figures or elder brothers desire the young woman, are all instances of this basic pattern. Such and other chastity-ordeals for the young woman parallel the long exile, symbolic castration or heroic ordeals of the young male heir, usually required by the father. In the *Rāmāyaṇa*, the elder two sons Rāma and Lakṣmaṇa go to the forest for fourteen years to fulfil their father's promise to his youngest wife. They divest themselves of all royal powers and privileges and don ascetic bark-garments. In the forest Rāma's wife, Sītā, is abducted by Rāvaṇa who arrives in the guise of a venerable sage.

Relations of Mother and Daughter

I have not yet found striking and explicit tales of a mother's rivalry with her own daughter, but one could cite numerous tales of stepmothers tormenting or exiling their stepdaughters, and cruel mothers-in-law trying to kill or harm daughters-in-law. Demonic mother-goddesses, ogresses, stepmothers and mothers-in-law are mother-figures specializing in the terrible aspects of mothers toward daughters; the evidence in the tales is not as neat as in the above three dyads (father-son, mother-son, father-daughter): these cruel mother-figures never win in the folk tales. In Tamil, in-law tales are told from both the younger and the older woman's point of view. There are two kinds of mother-in-law tales: (a) The cruel mother-in-law, and (b) The mother-in-law as victim. Certainly the conflict between mother- and daughter-figures is very much in evidence in these tales. Mother-in-law tales, like all Oedipal tales, exhibit a rivalry and conflict over a loved one; here the rivalry is between an older and a younger woman vying for the support and attention of the same man (who is, here, both son to the mother and husband to the daughter-in-law). It is significant that in all these mother-in-law tales, the father is rarely in evidence.

Dead Father   Mother

△   =   ○

+ |

△   =   ○

Son   +R   Wife

The rivalry between the barren elder queen-mothers and the youngest queen who becomes pregnant is blatantly for sexual success with the king (Type 707, found plentifully all over India). It also approximates a mother-daughter rivalry, with the older mother-figure vilifying and exiling the younger woman who is finally vindicated.

Generalization

If we consider the above four relationships, we see that the Indian and the Greek tales, where they differ, do not differ in the basic pattern: (a) like sexes repel, (b) unlike sexes attract, across generations. But they do differ in the *direction* of aggression or desire. Instead of sons desiring mothers and overcoming fathers (e.g., Oedipus) and daughters loving fathers and hating mothers (e.g., Electra), most often we have fathers (or father-figures) suppressing sons and desiring daughters, and mothers desiring sons and ill-treating or exiling daughters or daughter-figures.

The structure or matrix of relations and actors is the same, but the *direction* is in reverse:

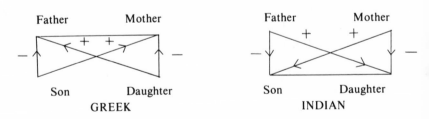

Furthermore, if the Greek (western) son wishes to (or actually does) supplant the father, we find in many tales that the Indian father wishes to supplant his son-in-law by marrying his own daughter. Similarly the mother wishes to supplant her daughter-in-law by marrying her own son; the western Electras wish to get rid of mothers and take their place. There are no Laius-figures killed in the Indian tales where mother marries son. There are no fathers in the mother-in-law tales either, where the mother competes with the son's wife; and no mother in the father-daughter tales. The prize sought is not the older cross-sex member of the triangle but the younger.

Speculations

I have a few observations and some questions.

The Indian Oedipus pattern, especially in the father-daughter stories, is closer to "screen memories," "seduction memories" that Freud describes in his Letter 69 to Fliess, in 1897. "In my analyses, I find it's the closest relatives, fathers or brothers, who are guilty men," he says on April 28, 1897. Within a few months he changed his mind: "I no longer believe in my neurotica," or seduction theory. In every case, "the blame was laid on perverse acts by the father" (September 21, 1897). Though he was torn over this theory, by 1905, when the Dora case was published, he had decided that such stories were projections of a daughter's sexual drive towards the father. A memory of a parental seduction is only a defensive reversal of the child's own wish to possess the parent. There has been much heated debate on the reasons for Freud's changes of mind—the debate even made newspaper headlines (*The New York Times,* Tuesday, August 25, 1981). For an earlier scholarly discussion of this important matter, see Ricoeur, 1972:188–9 and elsewhere.

Why do the Indian tales cited here present the reverse, defensive, "negative" Oedipus-type? And the Greek Oedipus the "positive" (son-marries-mother, etc.) type? Is there a correlation to other aspects of the two cultures? Even if we think of the two types as transformations of each other, we still need an explanation (cultural, psychological, or other) for the predominance of one sub-type or another.

The problem of psychoanalytic universals is a difficult and important one. Is the Oedipus complex universal? Does it take the same form regardless of culture? People in all cultures have fathers, mothers, sons and daughters. But the relations between them are not culture-free. Kinship patterns, property laws, the dominance of male or female in power, lineage or residence, attitudes to old age or childhood, and more, are all influential in deciding psychological patterns. While intergenerational competition (Kluckhohn's phrase, 1959) seems universal, the direction of aggression and desire, and the outcome, seem different in different cultures. We may explain away the Indian pattern as only a projection, a reversal, a transformation of the Greek one; or that Indian tales manifest a cultural repression (if one may speak of such) so deep that the killing of the father is entirely absent; or that the child projects its own desires (to rival, exile or kill the father, and to marry his own mother) on to his or her father or mother, as Freud found in his patients' "screen-memories." If that is the case, we still need to ask why it is that Indian tales are more like "screen-memories" and the Greek one is so straightforward. Does this kind of pattern affect or reflect patterns of neurosis, repression, child-rearing, patterns of emotional development, social institutions? There is, for instance, less repression of "the wish to be female" (Sinha, 1966:430) than in Western literature and religion: Indian poetry and Indian saints' lives are full of female identifications, transvestite imagery, etc. (Ramanujan, 1976). One is often struck by the impression that Indian males repress their "independence" as American males repress their "dependence." So, the predominant kinds of neuroses may be quite different in the two cultures and may need different emphases in therapy.

Indian conceptions of heroes and heroism are also quite different from the Greek or other European notions. Freud says, "A hero is someone who has had the courage to rebel against his father and has in the end victoriously overcome him" (Freud, 1937:12). The modern Western quest is individuation, achieved through an overthrow of the father, whereas the Indian hero's quest is to fulfill his father, his family. Recent psychoanalysts (Roland, 1980) have spoken of a Familial Self in the Indian personality. This medieval Kannada poem (Ramanujan, 1973:70) says it well:

> Don't make me hear all day
>   "Whose man, whose man, whose man is this?"
> Let me hear, "This man is mine, mine,
>   this man is mine."
> O lord of the meeting rivers,
>   make me feel I'm a son of the house.

Furthermore, *both patterns exist in both cultures,* but different cultures emphasize different patterns through their *favorite* tales and psychologies. A traditional culture needs to use and absorb the vitality of the young, as Santanu had to use Bhīṣma's, Yayāti his son's. An innovative culture needs to overthrow its parents. If Indian family patterns change in their basic ways, its Oedipus tales may acquire new endings.

It is also clear both from the examples in this paper, and from a second look at Oedipus and Hamlet, that both kinds of Oedipal patterns—e.g., son overthrowing or killing father and father taking son's powers or life—are present often in the same stories. Bhīṣma willingly sacrifices his political and sexual potency to his father; but he also fights his guru Paraśurāma, and is later killed by his grandnephew Arjuna (as Goldman points out). But what the Hindus remember, idealize, and retell over and over is the story of Bhīṣma's sacrifice (and other such stories).

In the Greek myth the father Laius is not innocent. He tries to mutilate and destroy infant Oedipus; he also assaults a younger man, Chrysippus, homosexually, and was therefore cursed to beget a son who would kill him and marry his own mother. But the celebrated story (especially seen through Sophocles' eyes earlier, and through Freud's later) is only that of Oedipus killing his father and marrying his mother. "Laius and Oedipus both have an Oedipus complex," wrote Géza Róheim (Friedman and Jones, 1963:72). After writing the above, I discovered George Devereux' "Why Oedipus killed Laius, a note on the complementary Oedipus complex in Greek drama" (1953). He speaks of the general neglect in psychoanalytic theory of the Laius complex and the Jocasta complex—two patterns that are greatly highlighted by the Indian tales. Such complementary patterns, Devereux suggests, are "scotomized" because the adult (at this time) needs to "place all responsibility for the Oedipus complex upon the child and to ignore, whenever possible, certain parental attitudes which actually stimulate the infant's oedipal tendencies" (Devereux 1953:132):

> The concept of the Laius and Jocasta complexes was even more egosyntonic and culturally objectionable than was the theory of the Oedipus complex, which, in a sense, merely confirmed the nineteenth-century adult's low opinion of children in general.

I refer the reader to his excellent discussion of Laius the father. As for father-daughter relations, the Indian pattern is also clearly seen in the Lear-story (Dundes, 1980). Though others (e.g., Ferenczi in 1932) in the western tradition have recognized it earlier, it is only in this decade that psychoanalysts are openly admitting to it:

> Seventy-five percent of the girls we accept at the Villages have been molested in tender childhood by an adult. And that's today in Kansas! I don't think Vienna in 1900 was any less sophisticated,

says Dr. Karl Menninger (quoted in *N.Y. Times*, August 25, 1981). Witness also the recent interest in incest studies with titles like *Father's Days* (Brady 1979). *Books in Print 1981–82* lists 14 such titles. The mythology of a culture contains many patterns; the culture of a time and place chooses only some for literary, even psychoanalytic, elaboration.

Conclusion

Patterns similar to the favored Indian one appear elsewhere in world mythology and folklore. In the intergenerational competition of parent and child, the outcome depends of course on family and other cultural patterns. In the Irish Cuchulain myth and in the Iranian epic about Sohrab and Rustum, fathers kill sons. (For several Iranian examples, see Baraheni, 1977:64–70) Italian courtship practices and father-daughter relations as reported by Anne Parsons also show a partial "Indian"-like pattern.

Other cultural patterns in India seem to corroborate the mythic and folk materials. A common Indian scandal-type (n.b. a new genre for folklorists) is that of the father getting his idiot or near-idiot son married to a young woman who becomes the old man's mistress. Nicholas, 1979, reports similar stories from Bengali gossip. In the long history of India, there have been Hindu and Muslim dynasties. In Hindu history no major instance (to my lay mind) seems to be recorded where a son overthrows or assassinates his father and usurps the throne. (Is this unconscious taboo so great that Hindu historians have repressed any such instances?) But in Muslim (Moghul and pre-Mughal) history, fathers or elder brothers are regularly imprisoned or assassinated by son or brother—it is almost a *rite de passage*, a ritual of succession. Some writers point to the rule of the elders in India, the general pattern of political gerontocracy, and even the long tolerance of foreign rule (noted by Spratt) as patterns that are too tempting to pass by. There are no Prometheus or Cronos figures overthrowing or defying the elder gods in Indian mythology. Would these patterns change and other patterns emerge (or be recognized) with changes in Indian family, child-rearing, economy and politics? I have no clear answer.

Furthermore, it is significant that Freud (with his overwhelming emphasis on the Greek "positive" Oedipus-pattern) has received little attention or recognition till recently in Indian psychological circles which probably did not recognize his type of Oedipus-pattern as theirs at all.

Lastly the patterns persist and resonate through the modern Dravidian literatures I know. I shall give only two examples. In a long allegoric poem with "modernity" itself for its theme, a Kannada poet C. Kambār adapts a folktale of his region. A village chief, the hero's father, is killed by a tiger-demon who returns to the village in the shape of the chief himself. The demon-father impregnates the hero's mother and, speaking from her womb, sends the hero out for impossible quests like tiger's milk, etc., to satisfy her pregnancy longings, till finally she asks him (or he, through her) for his five senses. At the end of the poem, the young heir is blind, deaf, and mute, unable to reach out for the elixir that would make him whole. Shankara Kurup's moving celebrated Malayālam poem, "The Master Carpenter" (Perundaccan), speaks of the bitter rivalry of a father and the young talented son; the poem ends with the father killing the son by "accidentally" dropping a chisel on him from above, while the son is working below him on the same pavilion (George, 1968). The ancient Yayāti story, where the father borrows the youth of his son, is a favorite among modern dramatists in Kannada. The persistent popularity of such themes in movie, novel, play and poem adds further weight to the dominant pattern presented here.

The next thing to do is to talk to a psychoanalyst who knows the Indic area, armed with a (Buddhist) passage like the following:

> Finally, as the time of the human being's death approaches he sees a bright light, and being unaccustomed to it at the time of his death he is perplexed and confused. He sees all sorts of things such as are seen in dreams, because his mind is confused. He sees his (future) father and mother making love, and seeing them a thought arises in him. If he is going to be reborn as a man he sees himself making love with his mother and being hindered by his father; or if he is going to be reborn as a woman, he sees himself hindered by his mother. It is at that moment that the Intermediate Existence is destroyed and life and consciousness arise and causality begins once more to work. It is like the imprint made by a die; the die is destroyed, but the pattern has been imprinted. (Conze, 1954:283)

NOTES

[1]This paper is a revised and enlarged version of an earlier paper (1972). I have retained most of the examples, added counter-instances, and expanded the discussion further in the light of others' responses (e.g., Goldman, 1978) and significant earlier papers (e.g. Devereux, 1953) I discovered since 1972. The tale-types and motif-numbers are from the well-known indexes by Stith Thompson and his colleagues.

[2]The notion of a child's "life-script" written by a mother should be interesting to psychotherapists, especially of the Bernean persuasion. Resistance to a parent's injunction or suggestion and fulfilling it willy-nilly, as if under hypnosis, follows well-known patterns of compulsive behavior. There are also tales of "outwitting Fate," about finding creative solutions by wisely using the very conditions laid down by Fate. For instance, it is written that a girl is fated to earn her living each night by selling her sexual favors. She is advised by a clever friend to ask for a bushel of pearls as payment for each night, so that no one but a divine being (Brahma Himself, who wrote her destiny) can be her lover; she is also advised to give it all away in charity the

next day so that she ensures both her own *punya* (cumulative merit) and the certainty of the nightly visit by her divine lover (Śāstri, 1968, also found in Kannada: Type 936).

In contrast to the stories where a parent writes an adverse fate for his child, one should also examine the many stories of a father or guru giving his son three or more precepts in Type 910. The precepts will be useful to him in crisis situations like his wedding night or when he is lost in strange places or chosen to be king or in the hour of danger. For instance, Type 910H-J Never Travel Without a Companion, Stay Awake, Never Plant a Moon Tree, seem to be special to India. Many of the parental precepts save the hero's life, especially on his wedding night. In these stories the bride has poisonous snakes which issue from her nostrils; in one, his companion, a crab, kills them; in another, he remembers and follows his father's precept to stay awake and so is able to kill the snakes and make his bride safe to live with. The Freudian gloss on the dangers of the "first night" is obvious.

³Folklore, here and elsewhere, uses common, uncensored, childhood beliefs. [The child] "first supposes that children are made by mixing some special thing with the food taken; nor does he know that only women can have children. Later he learns of this limitation and gives up the idea of children being made by food, though it is retained in fairy-tales," Freud, 1920:279.

For the confusion of sexual and alimentary channels, consider the American hospital joke about the nurse who swallowed a razor blade, and three doctors were circumcised as a result.

⁴For Western examples of the incest-riddle lullaby, see Brewster, 1972.

⁵All these complex attitudes are explicit in this passage from the *Yogattatva Upanishad* (q. by Kakar, 1978:95):

> That breast from which one sucked before he now presses and obtains pleasures. He enjoys the same genital organs from which he was born before. She was once his mother, will now be his wife, and she who is now wife, mother. He who is now father will be again son, and he who is now son will be again father.

REFERENCES

Baraheni, Reza, *The Crowned Cannibals,* New York: Vintage Books, 1977.

Brady, Katherine, *Father's Days: A True Story of Incest,* New York: Dell, 1979.

Brewster, Paul G., *The Incest Theme in Folksong,* FFC 212, Helsinki, 1972.

Carstairs, G. Morris, *The Twice-Born: A Study of a Community of High-Caste Hindus,* London: The Hogarth Press, 1957.

Conze, E. (ed), *Buddhist Texts Through the Ages,* New York: Harper and Row, 1964 (first edition, 1954).

Devereux, George, "The Oedipal Situation and Its Consequences in Epics of Ancient India," *Samīkṣa,* Vol. 5, No. 1, 1951.

Devereux, George, "Why Oedipus Killed Laius, A Note on the Complementary Oedipus Complex in Greek Drama," *International Journal of Psycho-Analysis* 34.2, 1953.

Dhavalasri (ed.), *Janapada Kathāmṛta-2*, Doddabele: Padmasri Prakāsana, 1968.

D'Penha, George, "Folklore of the Salsette," *Indian Antiquary* XXI.

Dundes, Alan (ed.), *The Study of Folklore*, Englewood Cliffs: Prentice-Hall, 1965.

Dundes, Alan, "To Love My Father All: A Psychoanalytic Study of the Folktale Source of *King Lear*," in *Interpreting Folklore*, Bloomington and London: Indiana University Press, 1980.

Freud, Sigmund, *Moses and Monotheism*, in the Standard Edition, Vol. XXIII, London: Hogarth Press and the Institute of Psychoanalysis, 1937-39.

Freud, Sigmund, *A General Introduction to Psychoanalysis*, New York: Garden City Publishing Company (1943 ed.). First edition, 1920.

Freud, Sigmund, "Dora," in *Collected Papers*, Vol. III *Case Histories*, London: Hogarth Press and the Institute of Psychoanalysis, 1925-50.

Friedman, Niel and Richard M. Jones, "On the Mutuality of the Oedipus Complex. Notes on the Hamlet Case," *The American Imago*, Vol. 20, Summer, No. 2, 1963.

George, K.M., *A Survey of Malayalam Literature*, Bombay: Asia Publishing House, 1968.

Goldman, R.P., "Fathers, Sons and Gurus: Oedipal Confict in the Sanskrit Epics," *Journal of Indian Philosophy* 6, 1978.

Grey, Allen, "Oedipus in Hindu Dreams, Gandhi's Life and Erikson's Concepts," *Contemporary Psychoanalysis*, Vol. 9, 1973.

Hart, George L., "The Theory of Reincarnation among the Tamils," in Wendy D. O'Flaherty (ed.), *Karma and Rebirth in Classical Indian Traditions*, Berkeley: University of California Press, 1980.

Jain, Jagdish Chandra, trans. *Vasudera Hindi*, Ahmedabad: L.D. Institute of Indology, 1977.

Jones, Ernest, *Hamlet and Oedipus*, New York: Doubleday and Company, 1949.

Kakar, Sudhir, "Aggression in Indian Society: An Analysis of Folk-tales," *Indian Journal of Psychology*, 49.2, 1974.

Kakar, Sudhir, *The Inner World, A Psycho-Analytic Study of Childhood and Society in India*, New Delhi: Oxford University Press, 1978.

Karve, Irawati, "A Marathi Version of the Oedipus Story," *Man*, No. 99, June 1950.

Kluckhohn, Clyde, "Recurrent Themes in Myths and Mythmaking," in Dundes, 1965.

Lessa, William A., "On the Symbolism of Oedipus," in Dundes, 1965.

Lingayya, D. (ed.), *Padineraḷu*, Siḍlaghatṭa: Kannada Kalā Sangha, 1971.

Masson, J.L. Moussaieff, *The Oceanic Feeling*, Dordrecht: Reidel, 1980.

Narain, Dhirendra, *Hindu Character (A Few Glimpses)*, University of Bombay Publications, Sociology Series No. 8, Bombay: University of Bombay Press, 1957.

Nicholas, Ralph, "On the (Non-existent) Incest Taboo in India with Particular Reference to Bengal," typescript, 1979.

O'Flaherty, Wendy Doniger, *Hindu Myths*, Harmondsworth: Penguin Books, 1975.

Paramasivayya, J.S. (ed.), *Āyda Janapada Kathegalu,* Mysore: Kannada Adhyayana Samsthe, 1970a.

Paramasivayya, J.S. (ed.), *Kannada Janapada Kathegalu,* Mysore: Kannada Addyayana Samsthe, 1970b.

Parsons, Anne, "Is the Oedipus Complex Universal?" in *Belief, Magic and Anomie: Essays in Psychological Anthropology,* New York: Free Press, 1969.

Ragau, P.K. Rajashekhara, and S. Basavayya (eds.), *Janapada Ramayana,* Mysore, 1973.

Raglan, Lord, "The Hero of Tradition," in Dundes, 1965.

Rajashekhara, P.K. *Dakṣina Karnātakada Janapada Purānagalu,* Ph.D. dissertation, University of Mysore, 1980.

Ramanujan, A.K., "The Indian Oedipus," in *Indian Literature:* Proceedings of a Seminar, ed. by A. Poddar, Simla: Indian Institute of Advanced Study, 1972.

Ramanujan, A.K., *Speaking of Siva,* Harmondsworth: Penguin Books, 1973.

Ramanujan, A.K., "Men, Women, and Saints," lecture, Harvard University, 1976.

Ramanujan, A.K., "A Kannada Cinderella," in A. Dundes' *Cinderella: A Folklore Casebook,* New York: Garland, 1982.

Ricoeur, Paul, *Freud and Philosophy: an essay in interpretation,* trans. Denis Savage, New Haven: Yale University Press, 1972.

Roland, Alan, "The Indian Familial Self in Its Social and Cultural Contexts," unpublished typescript, 1980.

Roy, Manisha, "The Oedipus Complex and the Bengali Family in India (A Study of Father-Daughter Relations in Bengal)," in *Psychological Anthropology,* ed. by Thomas R. Williams, The Hague: Mouton, 1975.

Sastri, S.M. Natesa, *Tirāviṭa Nāṭṭu-k-kataikal,* 2nd ed. Madras, 1968. (Original edition, 1884?)

Sastri, S.M. Natesa, *Folklore in Southern India,* Bombay, 1884–88.

Sinha, Tarun C., "The Ego Factor in Psychoanalysis," *Samīksa,* 1967. Vol. 21, pp. 67–80.

Sivakumar, K.Y. (ed.), *Eppattondu Janapada Kathegalu,* Krishnarajanagara: Aruna Prakāsana, 1971.

Spratt, P., *Hindu Culture and Personality: A Psycho-Analytic Study,* Bombay, Manaktala, 1966.

Turner, T., "Oedipus: Time and Structures in Narrative Form," in *Forms of Symbolic Action,* edited by Robert F. Spencer, Seattle: University of Washington Press, 1969.

Reference Material

Suggestions for Further Reading
on Oedipus: A Selected Bibliography

Bachofen, J.J.
1926 *Der Mythus von Orient und Occident: Eine Metaphysik der alten Welt,* ed. Manfred Schroeter. Munich. Pp. 259–271. Bachofen saw a three-stage evolution in the marriage laws of human society: the tellurian ("wilde, ehelose Geschlechtsverbindung"), the lunar, i.e., matriarchal, and the solar, i.e., patriarchal. The Oedipus legend represents progress into the second stage and, through the association of the legend with the Delphic Oracle, even into the third.

Baum, P.F.
1916 "The Medieval Legend of Judas Iscariot." *Publications of the Modern Language Association of America,* 31 = NS 24:481–632. The standard article on the subject.

Berkowitz, Luci, and Theodore F. Brunner, eds.
1970 *Oedipus Tyrannus.* New York. This Norton critical edition includes a new translation of Sophocles' play accompanied by passages from Homer, Thucydides, and Euripides plus more than two dozen commentaries mostly by modern literary critics.

Binder, Gerhard
1964 *Die Aussetzung des Königskindes: Kyros und Romulus.* Beiträge zur klassischen Philologie 10. Meisenheim am Glan. Part I: Various cult and ritual practices in relation to the Cyrus legend in particular and exposure stories in general; the Romulus legend and the Lupercalia festival. Part II: Summaries, with references to primary and secondary sources, of 121 exposure stories. Cf. Redford.

Bréal, Michel
1863 *Le Mythe d'Oedipe.* Paris. The main statement of the solar-lunar interpretation of the Oedipus legend.

Comparetti, Domenico
>   1867　*Edipo e la Mitologia Comparata.* Pisa. Opposes Bréal; argues that the Oedipus legend is composed of common folklore elements.

Constans, Léopold
>   1881　*La Légende d'Oedipe.* Paris. The first part deals with Oedipus in antiquity; the second and by far the longest part deals with Oedipus in the Middle Ages, especially the *Roman de Thèbes*; and the third with literary treatments of the Oedipus legend from the Renaissance up to Constans' time.

Daly, L.W.
>   1937　"Oedipus," in *Real Encyclopaedie der classischen Altertumswissenschaft,* eds. A. Pauly, G. Wissowa, et al. (1893-). 34th half vol. Cols. 2103-2117. A complete survey of the ancient evidence for the Oedipus legend. This article is continued and concluded in op. cit., suppl. vol. 7 (1940), cols. 769-786. Cf. Höfer for the other standard survey.

Delcourt, Marie
>   1944　*Oedipe ou la légende du conquérant.* Liège. A myth-ritual interpretation of the legend. Scapegoat rituals, *rites de passage*, and fertility rituals, with copious references to Frazer, Harrison, and Cook, are invoked to explain various elements of the legend.

Dundes, Alan
>   1962　"The Father, the Son, and the Holy Grail." *Literature and Psychology,* 12:101-112. An application of the Raglan hero pattern to Arthurian material with a psychoanalytic interpretation of this Oedipal configuration.
>   1980　"The Hero Pattern and the Life of Jesus." In Alan Dundes, *Interpreting Folklore.* Bloomington. Pp. 223-261. The Raglan pattern is applied to the biography of Jesus and the pattern analyzed from a psychoanalytic perspective.

Edmunds, Lowell
>   1976　"Oedipus in the Middle Ages." *Antike und Abendland,* 25:140-155. Surveys the various ways in which Oedipus was known to the Middle Ages, including the "Planctus Oedipi." Emphasizes the lost preface to the medieval commentary on Statius' *Thebaid* as an important source for the Middle Ages' knowledge of Oedipus.

Fischer, John L.
>   1966　"A Ponapean Oedipus Tale: Structural and Sociopsychological Analysis," *Journal of American Folklore,* 79:109-129. Breakdown of a Ponapean text into 121 linguistic-semantic segments followed by ethnographic and psychological glosses on the tale's Oedipal content.

Höfer, O.
>   1908　"Oidipus," in *Ausführliches Lexikon der griechischen und römischen Mythologie,* ed. W.H. Roscher, vol. 3, cols. 700-746. A complete survey of the ancient evidence for the Oedipus legend. Cf. Daly for the other standard survey.

Kallich, Martin, Andrew MacLeish, and Gertrude Schoenbohm, eds.
>   1968　*Oedipus: Myth and Drama.* Indianapolis. Translations of Oedipus dramas by Sophocles, Dryden and Lee, and Hofmannsthal, with a wide range of

selections from literary critical, anthropological and psychological writings on these dramas.

Karve, Irawati
1950 "A Marathi Version of the Oedipus Story." *Man*, 50:71–72. Publishes a possible Indian cognate of the Oedipus-type tale. Discussed by Ramanujan in this casebook.

de Kock, E.L.
1961 "The Sophoklean Oidipus and Its Antecedents." *Acta Classica*, 4:7–28. The most thorough survey in English of the pre-Sophoclean evidence for the Oedipus legend.

Köhler, Reinhold
1870 "Zur Legende von Gregorius auf dem Steine." *Germania,* 15 = NR3: 284–291. Repr. in *Kleinere Schriften zur erzählende Dichtung des Mittelalters,* vol. 2 (Berlin 1900), pp. 173–184. The Gregory legend in Swedish, in 17th-century Spanish drama (Juan de Matos Fragoso), and in relation to the legend of Paul of Caesarea (on which see also Seelisch).

Lehman, Paul
1930 "Judas Iscariot in der lateinischer Legenden-Überlieferung des Mittelalters." *Studi Medievali,* NS 3:289–346. Repr. in *Erforschung des Mittelalters,* vol. 2 (Stuttgart 1959), pp. 229–285. Important supplement to Baum's study.

Luria, S.
1927 "*Ton sou huion phrixon* (Die Oidipussage und Verwandtes)," in *Raccolta di Scritti in Onore di Felice Ramorino*. Pubblicazioni della Università Cattolica del Sacro Cuore, 4th series; Scienze Filologiche, vol. 7. Pp. 289–314. Milan. Studies a large group of Greek myths and legends concerning kingship and establishes a typical pattern. Parricide, intentional or unintentional, and murder of uncle, step-father or father-in-law are the key element. On the basis of the pattern, attempts to establish the original form of the Oedipus story.

Mitchell, Roger E.
1968 "The Oedipus Myth and Complex in Oceania with Special Reference to Truk." *Asian Folklore Studies,* 27:131–145. A review of the universalist and cultural relativist positions with respect to Oedipus is followed by a critique of Lessa's contention that Oceanic Oedipus stories diffused from somewhere between Europe and South Asia. A Trukese text is interpreted in terms of intergenerational rivalry.

Nilsson, M.P.
1922 "Der Oidipusmythos." *Göttingische Gelehrte Anzeigen,* 184:36–46. Repr. in *Opuscula Selecta,* vol. 1 (Lund 1951), pp. 335–348. Review of Robert's *Oidipus*. On the basis of a folkloristic analysis, criticizes Robert's theory of a cult origin of the legend.

Nilsson, M.P.
1932 (repr. 1972) *The Mycenaean Origin of Greek Mythology*. Berkeley. Pp. 100–112. As in the review of Robert, argues that Oedipus was

originally a *Märchen*-hero. The legend dates from the Mycenaean age. The war of the Seven against Thebes is an historical reminiscence.

O'Brien, Michael J., ed.

1968   *Twentieth Century Interpretations of Oedipus Rex.* Englewood Cliffs. Nine literary interpretations of the play are followed by seventeen short passages consisting of brief selections from a range of authors from Plutarch and Voltaire to Erich Fromm and Marshall McLuhan.

Pasolini, Pier Paolo

1971   *Oedipus Rex,* trans. John Mathews. New York. The screenplay, with illustrations and an introduction by Pasolini.

Prat Carós, Joan

1979–   "Mito e Interpretación: El Caso de Edipo." *Universitas Tarraconensis,*
1980   3:151–188. A useful overview of modern analyses of Oedipus.

Redford, Donald B.

1967   "The Literary Motif of the Exposed Child." *Numen,* 14:209–228. Discusses thirty-two examples of this motif; observes variations within the motif; argues historical-geographical diffusion. Cf. Binder.

Robert, Carl

1915   *Oidipus: Geschichte eines poetischen Stoffs im grieschischen Altertum.* 2 vols. Berlin. Argues that the legend originated in a cult of Oedipus at Eteonos in Boeotia and that the Sphinx episode is the kernel of the legend. Extensive study of the handling of the legend by ancient epic poets and tragedians and in the ancient mythographical tradition.

Rose, H.J.

1930   *Modern Methods in Classical Mythology.* St. Andrews. Pp. 24–30. Argues historical origin of the Oedipus legend. Cf. Schachter.

Sanderson, James L., and Everett Zimmerman, eds.

1968   *Oedipus: Myth and Dramatic Form.* Boston. Translations of Oedipus dramas by Sophocles, Seneca, Voltaire, Gide, and Cocteau, with selections of critical commentary by various authors.

Schachter, A.

1976   "The Theban Wars." *Phoenix,* 21:1–10. Useful assessment of the question of the historicity of Theban legends. Cf. Rose.

Seelisch, Adolf

1887   "Die Gregoriuslegende." *Zeitschrift für deutsche Philologie,* 19:385–421. Problem of the relation of the Gregory to the Oedipus legend; the eleventh-century legal and ecclesiastical controversies over incest as background to the Gregory legend; the various medieval narrative traditions of the legend and related traditions.

Vernant, Jean-Pierre

1978   "Ambiguity and Reversal: On the Enigmatic Structure of *Oedipus Rex.*" Trans. Page duBois. *New Literary History,* 9:475–501. Studies the structure of the tragedy as analogous to a scapegoat ritual observed at the Athenian festival of Thargelia. The ambiguity of Oedipus embraces the extremes of divine king and scapegoat.

Zuntz, Günther

    1954   "Oedipus und Gregorius." *Antike und Abendland,* 4:191–203. Repr. in
            Hartmann von Aue, edd. Hugo Kuhn and Christoph Cormeau (Darms-
            stadt, 1973: Wege der Forschung, 359), pp. 87–107 and in *Sophokles,* ed.
            Hans Diller (Darmstadt, 1967: Wege der Forschung, 95), pp. 348–369. On
            the parallel between Sophocles' *Oedipus the King* and the version of the
            Gregory legend in Hartmann von Aue.

Bibliographical Addendum

Oedipus has continued to intrigue scholars from a variety of disciplines. Since the original publication of this casebook in 1983, a number of interesting essays have appeared. In this addendum, we shall not attempt to review literary studies of the Sophoclean dramaturgical version of Oedipus. Nor will we review the ongoing discussions of the so-called Oedipus Complex per se. Our emphasis in the addendum—as in the casebook itself—will concern orally transmitted traditional narratives containing the Oedipus plot. Reference to the psychoanalytic interpretations of the Oedipus narrative will be kept to a minimum, first because they tend to restrict their scope exclusively to the Sophocles tragedy, ignoring the many other texts available in print, and, second, because the numerous articles appearing without surcease in medical and psychoanalytic journals can now be easily accessed in Medline, the on-line database of which the print counterpart is the *Index Medicus*.

We wish to remind the reader of the critical distinction between the tale of Oedipus proper, which conforms to Aarne-Thompson tale type 931, Oedipus—with its set sequence of specific motifs including M343 Parricide prophecy, M344 Mother-incest prophecy, N323 Parricide prophecy unwittingly fulfilled, and T412 Mother-son incest—and any traditional tale with possible Oedipal content. In theory, any story with a father-son conflict could be construed as an Oedipal tale, but such a tale would not necessarily be an example of A-T 931. Indeed, the son's rival need not even be his biological father in order for the tale to carry Oedipal overtones.

The distinction is important because Oedipal tales, that is, tales with Oedipal content, may be universal even if the Aarne-Thompson tale type is clearly not found among all peoples past and present. Let us give an example of a tale with possible Oedipal content. Social anthropologist Raymond Firth, in a chapter entitled "Sociology of Sex" in his classic ethnography *We, the Tikopia* (London, 1936), includes a tale in which a married woman, by singing an erotic song, is able to induce her lover's penis to separate from his body and to approach her whenever she wishes. One day after using it, "she made it fall out and lie in the pool while she went and fished. But her son came along and saw it lying there, took it for a sea-slug and shot it" (pp. 500–501). The tale, and, for that matter, the entire chapter were unfortunately omitted by the author in the later 1963 paperback edition. Firth was a dedicated student of Bronislaw Malinowski who wrongly believed that he had proven that Oedipal tales could not exist in Oceania, even though Malinowski's own field data included tales which were unequivocally Oedipal in content (cf. John Ingham, "Malinowski: Epistemology and Oedipus," *Papers of the Kroeber Anthropological Society* 29 [1963], 1–14; Murray L. Wax, "Malinowski, Freud and Oedipus," *International Review of Psycho-Analysis* 17 [1990], 47–60; and the new edition of Melford E. Spiro's *Oedipus in the Trobriands* [New Brunswick, 1992]). Curiously enough, Malinowski in his controversial diary, written in Polish while he was in the field, repeatedly reports his erotic fantasies about women in his life, fantasies which more often than not ended with his thinking about his own mother. See *A Diary in the Strict Sense of the Term* (New York, 1967), pp. 15–16, 28, 52, 229, and 241. The free association was sometimes so obvious that Malinowski himself could not forbear commenting upon it: "All day long very strong feelings for E.R.M. In the evening I longed for her. Thought . . . about the happiness of being with her again, *intimement* . . . Same thoughts when I went to bed, and awakening at night. Identity of this feeling with feelings of child for mother (*vide* Freud's theory)" (p. 245). So Malinowski, who devoted so much effort and energy to debating Ernest Jones in an attempt to refute the claim of universality for the Oedipus Complex, may well have had personal reasons for the vehemence of his argument.

In 1985, Lowell Edmunds published a scholarly anthology of virtually every Oedipus tale in print. This compilation, *Oedipus: The Ancient Legend and Its Later Analogues* (Baltimore), contains no fewer than seventy-six Oedipus texts. It opens with an introduction which gives a detailed survey of the ancient evidence for the Oedipus story, and also provides useful bibliographies covering ancient, medieval, and modern analogues and far-flung sources of the texts included in his compendium. Another comprehensive anthology should appear in 1996: Douglas Price-Williams, Allen Johnson, and Robert Desjarlais, *Oedipus Ubiquitous: The Family Romance in World Mythology* (Stanford).

In the field of the classics, research continues on the pre-fifth-century, or pre-tragic, form(s) of the Oedipus myth. Passing references in Homer and Hesiod and fragments of Theban epic indicate considerable differences from the canonical Sophoclean version. The passage in the *Iliad* on the death of Oedipus has been reinterpreted in Ettore Cingano, "The Death of Oedipus in the Epic Tradition" (*Phoenix* 46.1 [1992], 1–11). A considerable papyrus fragment (about thirty fully readable lines) was found in the wrappings of a mummy in Lille in the 1970s. Attributed to the lyric poet Stesichorus (7th–6th c. B.C.E.), the fragment treats of the division of the estate of Oedipus between his sons. It was published in 1976, and a French translation, with full discussion, can be found in Jan Bollack, Pierre Judet de la Combe, and Heinz Wismann, *La réplique de Jocaste: Sur les fragments d'un poème lyrique découverts à Lille (Papyrus Lille 76a, b et c)* (Lille, 1977). An English translation, without commentary, can be found in the Loeb Library: David A. Campbell, *Greek Lyric,* vol. III (Stesichorus, Ibycus, Simonides, and Others) (Cambridge, Mass., and London, 1991), pp. 137–143. The book by Marie Delcourt cited in the Suggestions for Further Reading above was reprinted in 1981 (Paris), with an introductory essay, "Oedipe-Roi selon Freud," by Conrad Stein.

Another consideration of Oedipus from the classicist's perspective is Jan Bremmer's stimulating essay "Oedipus and the Greek Oedipus Complex," in Jan Bremmer, ed., *Interpretations of Greek Mythology* (Totowa, 1986), pp. 41–59. Bremmer, after considering and rejecting a myth-ritual interpretation involving initiation, claims that "the myth of Oedipus is concerned with the succession to the throne," albeit a *perverted* succession. In his words, "Oedipus is a model of how not to succeed to the throne."

Perhaps the most important publication in classics studies within the time-frame of this addendum is Jean-Marc Moret's magisterial *Oedipe, la Sphinx, et les Thébains* (Geneva, 1984). Moret's book reeducates us in the iconography of Oedipus and the Sphinx. He shows that the two scenes to which the vase-painters limited themselves (Oedipus and the

Sphinx; the Thebans and the Sphinx) do not speak from an assumed narrative but from an autonomous iconographical tradition going back to Near Eastern ancestors. For Moret, iconography and narrative belong to two separate, incommensurable orders of mythical representation. The Oedipus myth is expressed in these two scenes, yes, but not as a single episode selected from a narrative. The scenes must be regarded as depicting a *Grundsituation*. The fidelity of the Greek eye to this "fundamental situation" is shown by the astonishing fact that there are only two vase-paintings illustrating other episodes in the life of Oedipus.

Two conferences on Oedipus were held in Italy in the early 1980s (Urbino, 1982; Turin, 1983), and the papers were published: Bruno Gentili and Roberto Pretagostini, eds., *Edipo: Il teatro Greco e la cultura Europea: Atti del convegno internazionale* (Urbino 15-19 November 1982, published in Rome, 1986); Renato Uglione, ed., *Atti delle giornale di studio su Edipo* (Turin 11-13 April 1983, published in Turin, 1984). Both of these collections contain some papers on the Greek myth of Oedipus as distinguished from the Oedipus tragedies. The Turin collection has two comparative papers: Mario Piantelli, "Alcuni paralleli indiani ai mitologemi collegati alla figura di Edipo," pp. 157-167, which complements the contribution of Ramanujan to this casebook; and Maria Costanza De Luca, "Edipo in Giappone," pp. 147-156, which has a few pages of observations on the existence or non-existence of the Oedipus motifs in Japanese myth. The Urbino collection contains a study of the mythical conception of the body of Oedipus based on psychoanalytic and comparative-mythological approaches: Lowell Edmunds, "Il corpo di Edipo: Struttura psico-mitologica," pp. 237-253; trans. and revised as "The Body of Oedipus," *The Psychoanalytic Review* 75 (1988), 51-66. Edmunds brings together myth and psychoanalysis again in "Freud and the Father: Oedipus Complex and Oedipus Myth," *Psychoanalysis and Contemporary Thought* 8 (1985), 87-102.

Edmunds' study of the Burmese story of Pauk Tyaing (cf. the articles of R. Grant Brown and Melvin E. Spiro in this casebook, each of which provides a version of the story) also has psychoanalytic implications, confirming, on the basis of a comparison between the Burmese and the ancient Greek story-patterns, the idea that Jocasta and the Sphinx represent a decomposition of the mother into two figures: "La sphinx thébaine et Pauk Tyaing, l'Oedipe birman," in Claude Calame, ed., *Métamorphoses du mythe en Grèce antique* (Geneva, 1988), pp. 129-138, trans. and revision, "Oedipus in Burma," in *Classical World* 88 (1995).

After the famous essay of 1955 on the Oedipus myth (cf. the introduction to the article by John Peradotto in this casebook), Claude Lévi-Strauss was to offer two further structuralist interpretations of this myth. In *Anthropologie structurale deux* (Paris, 1973), pp. 31-35, (trans. Monique Layton, *Structural Anthropology,* vol. 2 [Chicago, 1976], pp. 21-24), he compares the Oedipus myth with an Algonquin tale in order to show that the one can be understood as, not the cognate, not the adaptation, but the logical transformation of the other. Although the Sphinx is apparently absent from the Algonquin tale, the owl plays a role, and in this bird Lévi-Strauss discovers the Sphinx. The owl, he says, is the American Sphinx (1976:22), and his demonstration of the connection between the two narratives is as follows. The role of the owl in the Algonquin tale is to denounce the hero's incestuous marriage. In addition, in other Algonquin lore, owls pose neck-riddles (Halsrätseln). Thus the Algonquin owl does two things: it poses riddles and it denounces incest. Now, riddles are extremely rare amongst the North American Indians. Besides the Algonquin riddles, the only other example is the one posed by the ceremonial clowns of the Zuñi. These clowns, as it turns out, are believed to be the offspring of incestuous unions. Thus, riddles in both contexts "present a double Oedipal character: by way of incest, on the one hand; on the other, by way of the owl" (1973:33). Lévi-Strauss goes on to propose a relation of homology between incest and riddle. "Like the solved riddle, incest brings together terms destined to remain separate: the son is united to the mother, the brother to the sister just as the answer [to the riddle] does in succeeding, contrary to all expectations, in reuniting itself with its question" (1973:34). (The affinity of the Oedipus folktale for riddles [see Edmunds' introduction to the 1985 collection, p. 35] corroborates Lévi-Strauss's suggestion. Cf. also the anonymous *Historia Apollonii regis Tyri*, in which a king poses a neck-riddle to his daughter's suitors. The subject of the riddle is the king's incestuous relationship with his daughter.) In *La potière jalouse* (Paris, 1985), trans. Bénédicte Chorier, *The Jealous Potter* (Chicago, 1988), Lévi-Strauss offers an interpretation of an Oedipal creation myth of the Jivaro Indians of Ecuador and Peru. In the final chapter of this book ("A Jivaro Version of *Totem and Taboo*"), he continues the critique of Freudian myth interpretation begun in the 1955 essay, and offers a new interpretation, based on a detailed comparison with a nineteenth-century comedy by Eugène Labiche of Sophocles' *Oedipus Rex*. The main points of the critique of Freud are that the sexual content of the Oedipus myth, or any other, is not its meaning but is rather a code that conveys some other meaning; and that the sexual code is just one amongst others and is not obligatorily employed. In Lévi-Strauss's view, Freud is himself a mythical thinker, one who has created the most recent version of the Oedipus myth.

The entire issue of *L' écrit du temps* 12 (Autumn 1986) was devoted to Oedipus. It contains a discussion by René Major ("La honte d'Oedipe," pp. 55–65) of Lévi-Strauss's *The Jealous Potter*.

The cross-cultural debate about Oedipus continues, fueled by a steady stream of anthropological and folkloristic contributions. Representative are the following: discussions of the Finnish tradition by two psychoanalysts, Tor-Björn Hägglund and Vilja Hägglund, "On the Message of the Oedipus Myth in Modern Times," *Psychiatria Fennica* (1979), 43–50, and "The Boy Who Killed His Father and Wed His Mother: The Oedipus Theme in Finnish Folklore," *The International Review of Psycho-Analysis* 8 (1981), 53–62; a report from Central Africa, Hermann Hochegger, "Oedipus Rex in Zentralafrika: Zwei Varianten des Oedipusmythos aus dem Erzählgut der Mbuun (Zaire)," in Inge Hofmann, ed., *Festschrift zum 60. Geburtstag von P. Anton Vorbichter,* Part 2 (Vienna, 1981), pp. 67–84; several ancient Chinese and Japanese Buddhist texts, Victor A. Mair, "An Asian Story of the Oedipus Type," *Asian Folklore Studies* 45 (1986), 19–32; and a discussion of folktales of the Yafar people in Papua, New Guinea, Bernard Juillerat, *Oedipe chasseur: une mythologie du sujet en Nouvelle-Guinée* (Paris, 1991).

Finally, for Oedipus in literature and the arts, see Lowell Edmunds, "Oedipus in the Twentieth Century: Principal Dates," *Classical and Modern Literature* 11 (1991), 317–324, and Debra A. Moddelmog, *Readers and Mythic Signs: The Oedipus Myth in Twentieth-Century Fiction* (Carbondale and Edwardsville, 1993). Moddelmog distinguishes twenty-three mythemes in the Sophoclean Oedipus myth; proposes a theory of how myth functions in literature; and explores the Oedipal mythemes in several twentieth-century novels.

Judging from the past richness of sources devoted to Oedipus, we have no reason whatsoever to doubt that this remarkable plot will continue to disturb and stimulate scholars and students for centuries to come. It is our sincere hope that this casebook will facilitate future discussion and debate about one of the world's most celebrated stories.